The Creation of the Common Law

THE MEDIEVAL YEAR BOOKS DECIPHERED

The Creation of the Common Law

THE MEDIEVAL YEAR BOOKS DECIPHERED

Thomas Lund
University of Utah

TALBOT
PUBLISHING
Clark, New Jersey

ISBN 978-1-61619-504-5

TALBOT PUBLISHING

AN IMPRINT OF

THE LAWBOOK EXCHANGE, LTD.

33 Terminal Avenue

Clark, New Jersey 07066-1321

Please see our website for a selection of our other publications and fine facsimile reprints of classic works of legal history:
www.lawbookexchange.com

Library of Congress Cataloging-in-Publication Data

Lund, Thomas Alan, 1942- author.
The creation of the common law : the medieval year books deciphered / by Thomas Lund.
pages cm
Includes bibliographical references and index.
ISBN 978-1-61619-504-5 (hardcover : alk. paper)
1. Law--England--History--To 1500--Sources. 2. Law reports, digests, etc.--England. I. Title.
KD606.L86 2015
340.5'7--dc23

201404725

For

Anna Lund

Table of Contents

FOREWORD

In Praise of the English Year Books:

The Modern Relevance of Mediaeval Documents

IT IS A REGRETTABLE FACT that the study of early English legal history is now in a general state of decline in American law schools. The modern legal universe is populated with large statutory schemes whose administration is entrusted to a complex network of agencies—one never seems to be enough these days—that deal with a bewildering array of substantive and procedural issues in pursuit of a wide range of substantive ends. In the midst of the massive expansion of the administrative state, too many people hastily conclude that early English legal history is rightly relegated to the back burner—a field to be studied by the resolute and curious few, but not one that should be regarded as an essential component of the toolkit of the modern American lawyer.

Taking this view is a serious mistake. It is always worth inquiring into the sources of the political stability and the long-term social and economic success of countries that developed within the common law tradition. Any answer to that question will surely point to a multitude of factors. But one such factor that looms large is the dedication and intelligence of the English judges who disposed of various cases long before the emergence of the modern state. These judges, and the corps of lawyers who appeared before them, performed an extraordinary public service in setting the law on a path from which it has not deviated. Understanding the origins of our legal tradition gives us ample reason to respect the rules and practices it generates. But for most people, it is hard to break into this early body of law. Modern lawyers and laypeople are often daunted by the inaccessibility of the early sources, often written in either Latin or law French in ways that add to their air of weary strangeness. It is for just this reason that this masterful compilation and commentary by Professor Thomas Lund offers such a great contribution to the study of the history and evolution of our legal culture.

The progenitor in chief of this volume, William Bereford, may not be a household name today, but his not inconsiderable intellect and pointed wit made him a great judge. Bereford served from 1290 until his death in 1326. He was appointed to the bench by Edward I, and elevated to Chief Justice by Edward's son Edward II. His influence on legal developments was enormous. The great challenge some 700 years after he served is how best to work ourselves back into his life and times. I do not think that there is any easy entrée into this world. In my view, the best way to understand this period is to stress the close connection between the early and modern texts.

Thomas Lund has reduced the cost of entry into this intellectual market. His text is organized by subject matter, and it contains an ongoing narrative that links together these medieval cases both with each other and with the range of modern issues that either derive from, or are analogous to, the problems that challenged Bereford and his contemporaries. In one sense, the more the differences, the more things repeat themselves. Many social issues speak of conflict and cooperation; they talk about matters of birth, marriage and death. They address the relationship between business and commerce on the one hand and religious and charitable obligations on the other. They speak about the need to have, side-by-side, regimes of common and private property. The various categories seem clear at the outset, but often blend in practice. Litigation tends to bring to the surface difficulties that were either ignored or avoided in statutory language or in decided cases. One reason why the Roman and mediaeval scholars attached so much weight to natural law was that they had a healthy appreciation for the common elements of all legal systems, which in turn had to be meshed with distinctive local institutions. These early materials are not only fascinating in themselves, but they speak to future generations by offering us a set of rich examples from which it is easy to draw analogies to current problems. Today's lawyer should be enriched by looking through another window on the modern world.

I make this general claim not only as an abstract matter, but because it was ever so true in my own life. In retrospect, the most distinctive feature of my intellectual growth was that I departed from the ordinary path and began my legal education in Oxford, where Thomas Lund also studied. I went there with an eye to becoming an American academic and was fortunate to study Roman Law (with Alan Watson and David Daube), legal history (with J.M. Kaye) and property with A.W.B. Simpson. Their influence and those of my other tutors (Donald Harris, Bernard Rudden, John Eekelaar) had much a more enduring influence on my world view than I had imagined The single most important lesson that I derived from a close study of this early history is the incredible sophistication of the lawyers and legal writers who put these materials together. As a discipline, law ages well.

In many areas of science, for example, the lack of suitable tools of analysis makes early speculations about such simple matters as evolution and human reproduction seem laughable to anyone with access to a microscope or computer. That is, however, decidedly not the case with legal materials. The fundamental relations between ordinary people today are not all that different from those that existed thousands of years ago. People have to marry and raise children, they have to enter into contracts for services and the transfer of property and they have to deal with the potential fallout of aggression by one person against another. The early speculations of the natural law, while much derided today, represented an attempt to build a legal system whose individual components dealt with all these issues. The propositions that are originally announced often take on high levels of generality about the importance of these fundamental arrangements. But there is a vast gap between the articulation of some general principle and its use in the crucible of disputes that make their way into a legal system.

It is here where the Year Books hold so much fascination. The brevity of the exchanges between lawyers and judges should be treated as a sign of the subject matter mastery by judges and lawyers alike, which is evidenced by their great ability to compress complex arguments into a small space, without losing track of the nuances. What Thomas Lund has achieved in this volume is to organize with running commentary the cases that came before the Court of Common Pleas, which starts at the end of the great statutory reforms of Edward I, and continues into the reign of his successor. Historical investigation invariably demonstrates, once again, that the law always lives in interesting times, given the perennial challenges of integrated new legislation and new social challenges with an established body of legal doctrine that is itself always in need of renourishment and repair.

True to form, the period during which Bereford sat was a time of great legal imagination, largely because of the force of his person and intellect, which shines through on all of these pages. It is all too often thought that there is little that modern judges, lawyers and academics, can learn from historical authors who are thought to have led some blinkered intellectual life because of the narrowness of the historical circumstances in which they wrote. If there is one myth that these materials should dispel, it is the notion that modernity can learn nothing from the past. On topic after topic, reading the colloquies at the bench, we can see all the players jockeying for rhetorical advantage. The lawyers spar with each other; they are goaded on by the judges. Then suddenly a resolution appears that more often than not sheds light on the entertaining dialog that it has just concluded. We should read these materials with the hope of learning insights that have been forgotten, and not as some complacent commentator who thinks little of these peculiarities.

One of the great joys of Lund's writing is that he casts these materials as part of a complex narrative, organized by topic. Beautifully encapsulated in paraphrase, the cases preserve the urgency and spontaneity of the arguments. They also show that many attitudes that are often thought of as modern have their origins in earlier times. One of the most common issues of modern dispute is the endless topic of statutory construction, where all too often the so-called originalist position has been derided as a form of narrow textualism that loses sight of how a given law is situated within some larger tapestry. But reading these materials show just how much the judges care about reading statutes in light of their larger social context.

This particular issue was not just a matter of judicial innovation. It was also a matter of statutory authorization, for in 1285 Parliament passed a statute that authorized the Chancery to issue writs "to help litigants whose cases do not fall within the letter of the law." The issue here is just how far beyond the letter the Chancery can go when it departs from the letter of the law, without becoming inconsistent with its spirit. (Lund 100) That is no easy task to solve, and it gives rise to the great lawyer's challenge of trying to reason by analogy from a baseline that is made secure by prior legislation. In working through this task, it is critical to take small but confident steps.

Let me start with one example among many. If it turns out that a parson can purchase a writ to protect his grazing rights, consistent with the law so too can his successor in title. Figuring out why this is the case requires some neat appreciation of the role that assignments play in the overall operation of any legal system. A rule that protects the assignor, but that does not protect the assignee, is a rule that makes it impossible to sell rights without impairing their content. The rule of analogy is not just some idle philosophical chatter, but a way to prop up critical social institutions against their destruction. Just this problem arises in modern cases of land use regulation where it is often, but incorrectly claimed, that someone who purchases property from its current owner cannot raise challenges to the government action that were available to its prior owners. This theme is central to modern constitutional litigation under the Takings Clause of the United States Constitution: "Nor shall private property be taken for public use without just compensation." Anyone who got the case of the parson right would be less likely to make the mistake in modern times.

The 1285 statute did not only have a substantive dimension, it also cast an interesting light on the processes for how legal rules are interpreted. The English statutory framework provides that in cases of disagreement, of which many are sure to arise, the clerks "should ask Parliament for help." It takes little imagination to see that this simple injunction raises at least as many questions as it answers. How do clerks ask for help? Separately or as part of a team? Once they seek the help of Parliament can they disregard its recommendations? If so, do they have to show cause? And can their decision then be questioned by a court if an improper writ is issued? Is the same process available when a writ is denied? If so, what mechanism allows the judges to hear the case? The statutory provision here is short and to the point, but anyone who thinks through the issues can see that it offers modern lawyers a tutorial on the complex interactions of the various branches of government, as the Parliament, the Chancery and the courts each play a key role in sorting out the issues, which were as pressing in their time as environmental permitting or drug licenses are in ours.

Yet there are limits to the flexibility that should be allowed in the creation of new writs. One of the permanent features of land law is that the permanence of land requires security in the conveyance of property from one hand to another. In dealing with this issue, flexibility on the adoption of new forms and new writs presents a threat to the stability of title. As Lund notes, Bereford was sensitive to the difference in the context of the creation of writs. (At 60-62) He instances a claim for the transfer of land based on the alleged claim that Adam conveyed to Bogo and his son, but if Bogo died childless then to Cosmo. Bogo indeed died childless, but the original conveyance was not as Cosmo said, for the land was to revert back to the grantor for life before going to Cosmo. Cosmo then complained that the Chancery did not sell a writ that covered this situation, so that, as a last resort, he used the standard form because the transaction itself was neither contrary to law nor offensive to public policy.

In this setting, Bereford refused to celebrate the spirit of the law relative as against its letter. Instead Bereford adheres to the traditional rule that holds once land returns to a grantor on a single deed it cannot be transferred again to another person without a fresh deed. The debate here offers an instructive view of the tension between freedom of conveyance and the need for certainty between deeds. This tension is reflected in the modern debates over the *numerus clausus*, i.e. the doctrine that the class of estates that the law permits is closed to certain kinds of grant. The hard question is whether there is any institutional change from Bereford's time to ours that should alter the outcome. In some instances, a limitation on the form of deed is needed to protect innocent third parties, at least in the absence of a system of recordation. Cosmo's case shows no trace of this risk. One can disagree or defend Bereford's outcome, but there is little reason to chalk up the difference to some change in overall social practices or legal institutions. Indeed, it is the timeless nature of the debate that helps explain the relevance of these Year Books to modern discourse.

I will close with one other example of the same sort of tension, only now the interests of third parties intrude, again in a case of land. One such illustration involves the law of dower, which gives the widow a one-third life estate in the lands of her deceased husband. Everyone knows of course what land is—until they don't. To a lawyer land is often not land. Sometimes it is a set of interlocking interests in land and so the question arises whether dower attaches to those interests that are carved out of land. (299-302) And sure enough the old cases bring this point to a head. Under early English law, a renter did not have a property interest in land. By analogy to the earlier Roman law of hire, there was only a contract right against the rented land. Does this contract right support dower? Can the same be said of grazing rights that attach to, or are appurtenant to land? On this question, the issue arose whether the adoption of a new statutory remedy to enforce grazing rights could defeat the widow's claim that was protected under earlier statute. Bereford refused to let the change in remedies alter the substantive law. The entire discussion offers a nice counterweight to the nineteenth century reforms of English pleading law, where the issue was whether the abolition of the forms of action altered the balance between strict liability and negligence, or whether the old substantive views survived the changes. Clearly there is room on matters of this sort for divided opinions.

And so the beat goes on. In topic after topic, Lund begins with a lucid introduction that eases us into the life and times of Bereford, by taking us through these topics: Bereford Takes Charge; The King, Parliament, and King's Bench; Chancery; pleading; proof; The Thing's Been Decided (or res judicata); private courts, the Church, women, serfs. The progression is elegant. We start with the general setting, understand the distribution of power between the various key actors within the system, then follow routine litigation through its various stages, and consider various institutions and individuals with special status. Only the hardy will try to read this book straight through from cover to cover. But much of the great fun of looking at this old text is that there is no need to march down that path. Treat the book as a series of connected episodes that can be read in large or small chunks. Open up to any page or section, read for amusement and enlightenment, and then return to the larger text on some future day. These materials are rich, and they will richly reward those who are willing to work their way through them.

Richard Epstein
New York University School of Law

ACKNOWLEDGMENTS

THIRTY YEARS AGO I READ a few medieval cases in Prof. John Dawson's mimeograph teaching materials. One spoke about a fellow who "broke into the pigeon house and took some pigeons." The report made no sense until I realized the man wasn't a thief. He wanted to show he possessed the land by taking its fruits. I was hooked—a walk in the dark followed by a burst of light. That's the kind of thrill I like. My romance with the Year Books began.

Reality set in when I learned the cryptic reports went on for thousands of pages. Because I had just published *American Wildlife Law,* Dean Walter Oberer said I could look at the materials for a few years before Utah would expect me to write anything. Scholars ask why the complete history of English law hasn't been written. The answer is no mystery to me. Publish or perish. Most intruders in the jungle of medieval reports will perish before they can publish. I devised a career plan. I thought I could almost understand a few cases. I would write an article about them. The process would educate me so that I could then find other interesting cases and write more articles. I had fun for twenty-five years.

Five years ago I decided to write this book. The historian Holdsworth complained—apparently with a straight face—that England hadn't supported "the most deserving of the poor" (his phrase!), those who studied legal history. I've got no complaints. The University of Utah and the S. J. Quinney College of Law have given me a sabbatical and many faculty development grants.

Many people have supported me during the journey.

My family most of all. My darling wife Janet, my wonderful daughter Anna, my brother Daniel and my sister Nancy Lund Gould.

Friends have held my hand: Lawrence Ross and Hope Forer, Roberto Bissone, David Leinsdorf, Paul Neuthaler, Tara Anderson.

I am in debt to some very kind law teachers. The legendary Victor Tunkel of the Selden Society, Benedict Kingsbury of Utah and NYU, Richard Alderman (Houston), John Tehranian (Southwestern), Ofer Raban (Oregon).

My editor Valerie Horowitz has been splendid. The support provided by Greg Talbot, Talbot Publishing/The Lawbook Exchange not only to this work but also to legal history in general is greatly appreciated.

Finally—Richard Epstein. We were born within six months of each other in New York City, and I have enjoyed reading his work for decades. But I never dreamed he would comment on my work, let alone write a preface. What a treat. I can't think of anyone who could have made me happier by introducing my book. Richard, you're the cat's meow!

Thomas Lund
November, 2014

CHAPTER 1
Introduction

MEDIEVAL ENGLAND INVENTED a new way to portray a legal system.[1] In Europe scholars described the codes that kings or legislatures created. In England, however, the legal system—"the common law"—derived in part from court decisions that relied on reason and custom. Since English law cannot be understood without reference to court decisions, some lawyers decided to describe their legal system not by writing texts, but by reporting arguments that judges and lawyers made in court. Unlike modern court reports, these medieval reports were created for instructional purposes.[2] Modern litigants refer to court reports to establish their rights; no one referred to the medieval reports to establish rights.[3] They were designed to teach

---

[1] "[W]e see something that is very new, new in England, new in the world: the vernacular report of an oral debate." 17 Selden Society xi (1903) (introduction by F.W. Maitland).

[2] "Various forms, like the *Brevia Placitata* and the *Casus*, were used to disseminate knowledge of the common law, and the practice of taking notes in court to be used in teaching law became a fruitful custom. This custom was, perhaps, what inspired the men in the 1270's to make that 'verbatim report of an oral debate'—the very foundation of the Year Books." 69 Selden Society xl–xli (William Dunham) (1952) citing Percy Winfield, "Early Attempts at Reporting Cases, 40 *Law Quarterly Review* 316 (1924).

[3] In contrast to the unofficial Year Book reports, the court kept its own official records, the "plea rolls." In an unusual case a litigant supported his legal argument with a reference to a plea roll entry. Bereford disagreed with the case and told an official "that he should

the techniques of legal argument. These reports are now known as the "Year Books."[4]

The reporters' novel decision to report concrete cases in a series of reports was not inevitable. The reporters could have extracted the legal rules the cases adopted, and put them into a text.[5] In fact English scholars have produced such texts from the twelfth century through the present.[6] In comparison with seemingly stenographic accounts of courtroom arguments[7] these summaries are a more efficient way to explain existing law.

Since a great text summarizing English law, Bracton's *On the Laws and Customs of England*,[8] was widely disseminated before the reporters began their work,[9] the reporters must have pursued a different goal.

---

write upon it Error. And this he did." 26 Selden Society 114 (1310–11). Year Book reports infrequently refer to precedents. In an unusual case a reporter asserts Bereford's opinion contradicts his own earlier ruling. 43 Selden Society 11, 12 (1313).

[4] "The medieval law reports are called 'year books' not because they were produced according to some coherent scheme … but simply because (being anonymous) they have to be cited by year." J. H. Baker, *Why the History of English Law has not been Finished* 18 (1999).

[5] "I, Henry de Bracton, to instruct lesser judges, if no one else, have turned my mind to the ancient judgments of just men… and have collected whatever I found therein worthy of note into a *summa*, putting it in the form of titles and paragraphs, without prejudice to any better system, by the aid of writing to be preserved to posterity forever." 2 Bracton 19 (Samuel Thorne edition). Hereinafter Bracton.

[6] Glanvill started the process.

[7] Although the reports appear stenographic, their concise nature exceeds anyone's ability to speak extemporaneously. They summarize rather than portray word for word the arguments.

[8] Henry de Bracton, *On the Laws and Customs of England*, Samuel E. Thorne translation. (circa 1235).

[9] Regarding the precise date for Bracton's work, *see* T. F. T. Plucknett, *A Concise History of the Common Law* 259 (5th ed. 1956). In recent years under the title The Earliest English Law Reports, Paul Brand has collected and translated law reports from shortly before 1284. *See* Selden Society volumes 111, 112, 122, 123.

The decision-making process they observed explains their strategy. The continental legal systems adopt the theory that judges reach their decisions by interpreting a code. In contrast the common law system that emerged in the thirteenth century allowed judges to alter general rules to achieve justice in a particular case. Although a text can summarize existing law, a text cannot explain the process by which judges reform the law.

No one has ever figured out the reporters' identities. But their work shows their methods and goals. The reports are so comprehensive; the reporters must have been in court.[10] The reports are so coherent; they must have been legally sophisticated. The reports are so arcane they must have been written to educate lawyers.[11] A thousand years of English legal writing has created nothing as mysterious.[12] Nonetheless two kinds of modern readers might be interested in them: those interested in history, and those interested in law. Neither group has shown much interest.

Historians interested in the development of the institutions of government could find the reports valuable. The cases created a novel legal system, a system interesting in itself, and also worth study in context as a modification of its antecedents and a source of subsequent doctrine. But historians prefer medieval treatises. A treatise provides a coherent summary, a summary that may even reflect the modern historian's approach. The medieval text writer Henry de Bracton explained English law in the context of Roman legal

---

[10] That is, their original authors. Scribes may have altered the reports they reproduced.

[11] Including the reporter himself. Some reports were probably written as aide-memoires.

[12] Paul Brand addresses the beginning of English law reporting at 123 Selden Society xi–xxi (2007).

thought;[13] Frederic William Maitland, the modern master of medieval English law, did the same.[14]

The reports present daunting problems. Unlike the text writer, the reporter takes a chronological rather than thematic approach.[15] Unlike the text writer, the reporter assumes his reader understands the conventions of law practice and the minutia of legal doctrine. Unlike the text writer, the reporter omits information he assumes his reader knows. To the reporters' non-lawyer contemporaries the reports would have been incomprehensible. Seven centuries have made them more mysterious.

Although these impediments deter historians, the cases include information not only about law, but also about life. Litigation touches everything, and the cases describe the way life was actually lived. "It will some day seem a wonderful thing," Maitland wrote, "that men once thought they could write the history of medieval England without using the {case reports of the era, the}[16] Year Books."[17] The cases, he said, "should be {England's} glory, for no other country has anything like them; they are our disgrace, for no other country would have so neglected them."[18] As a remedy Maitland founded the

---

[13] Bracton "is Roman in conception and partly in content." S. F. C. Milsom, *Historical Foundations of the Common Law* 41–42 (2d ed. 1981).

[14] "If Maitland set his watch by any one source, it was by Bracton." 1 P&M lxxii. (introduction by S.F.C. Milsom).

[15] Sometimes the reports present clusters of cases on a similar theme. *See, e.g.*, 36 Selden Society 110–122 (jurisdiction); 27 Selden Society 126–136 (efforts to cheat women).

[16] In the subsequent quotations from the Year Books, the modern reporters' additions are identified by brackets. To prevent confusion the author's interpolations will be set off in curly braces.

[17] 17 Selden Society xx (F.W. Maitland introduction).

[18] 1 F. Pollock and F. W. Maitland, *The History of English Law* (2d ed. 1968). Hereinafter P&M.

Selden Society to advance the study of early English law.[19] Since then a tiny coterie of brilliant scholars has located the medieval manuscripts, expanded their short hand into their full language (Anglo-Norman),[20] and published about eight thousand pages of translations. Every major law library has the books. Historians still ignore them. The challenges presented by medieval jargon, medieval legal doctrine, medieval legal argument, and medieval law reporting mean only a few specialists can make sense of them.

In contrast to historians, those predominantly interested in law bring a different perspective to the old common law cases. Historians and American lawyers use the phrase "the common law" differently. By "the common law" historians mean the general doctrines that have long characterized English law.[21] By the phrase "the common law" American lawyers mean judge-made law. Common law judges create law. They do not hide behind the smokescreen that they are interpreting the will of the executive or the legislature. They openly declare they are improving existing law. This book, title and all, adopts the American lawyer's definition of the common law. The phrase refers to judge-made law.

By discussing the way the judges exercised their power, the medieval reporters produced something still valuable to lawyers. Texts teach doctrine. Since the medieval rules are dead, the texts are valuable only to historians. The reports do not teach doctrine. They teach

---

[19] Before Maitland created the society the British government published the Rolls Series, an important collection of redacted and translated Year Book manuscripts.

[20] The language of England's ruling class when the reports were written.

[21] *See* Paul Brand, *The Making of the Common Law* (1992). The phrase "the common law" contrasts country-wide rules with local customary law.

the way to persuade a judge to change the law. Today's lawyers need that skill.

The medieval reporter knew his reader did not need another text. His reader knew everything the text said. He needed more. His client had a tough problem, a problem the texts did not solve. He needed to know how other lawyers with similar problems had done. If their experience was encouraging, he needed to know how to argue once he got into court. The reports told him about comparable controversies. The reports told him about arguments that won.[22]

The reporters pursued their novel pedagogical approach because late in the thirteenth century Sir William Bereford took control[23] of the Court of Common Pleas.[24] He cut himself loose from settled law whenever his sense of justice told him to change the law.[25] As he freed himself from the past, he created a system that needed to be described as a process rather than a set of rules. Rather than learning the letter of the law, lawyers had to learn the spirit of the law.

Late in the nineteenth century an American law teacher, Christopher Columbus Langdell of the Harvard

---

[22] The ancient Greek concept of "mimesis" probably captures the reporters' educational philosophy.

[23] Bereford appears as a lawyer in a majority of reported cases from 1285. He becomes a Common Pleas judge in 1292, chief justice in 1309, and dies in office in 1326. Paul Brand describes his career in 112 Selden Society at viii–xxi (1996). Bereford's colleagues deferred to his knowledge and wisdom. Justice Stanton, for example, describes a difficult question, and then says "Therefore wait until Sir William of Bereford comes." 26 Selden Society 149 (1311).

[24] Reporters had used the technique at an earlier time. *See* Paul Brand, Earliest English Law Reports, Selden Society volumes 111, 112, 122, 123. The technique flourished during Bereford's tenure.

[25] His revisions were based upon his belief that "the law is founded on reason...." 20 Selden Society 78, 80 (1310) (Chief Justice Bereford).

Law School, adopted the same approach.[26] He changed American legal education from a text-based system into a case-based system. He is still celebrated for creating the "case method" form of legal instruction, a method that continues to be the way American law schools teach legal analysis and argument.[27] Because they teach in a country that has a federal legal system—a collection of many states' different laws—American law teachers cannot teach law from a single text. But they can teach students to think like lawyers by discussing cases decided by any common law court. The doctrines may vary but the techniques remain the same.

The remarkable success of lawyers within American society owes a debt to Langdell's system. The lawyer's skills are valuable everywhere. Not just in a law office or courtroom, but also in negotiations, the corporate boardroom, political debate. The case method prepares a student for all the arenas where analysis and persuasion count. The case method, however, requires a partnership between teacher and student. A casebook is an educator's tool, not a stand-alone instructional manual. A modern court judgment is a lawyer's argument in favor of an outcome—the lawyer is the judge, and the outcome is her choice between different arguments. Often she hides the losing argument behind her judgment's authoritative tone. A law teacher helps students see the rejected

---

[26] The cases in the thirteenth century *Casus Placitorum* "belong to the long tradition of legal education which lies behind the modern 'case method' of instruction in the law." 69 Selden Society xxxi–xxxii (William Dunham) (1952).

[27] The teaching of legal analysis once dominated American legal education. Analysis remains important, but law school classes now pay more attention to law reform, the description of complex systems (such as commercial codes), and the skills law practice requires.

arguments. The teacher uses the casebook to teach students analysis and argument.

In contrast to the modern report's judgment, the medieval reports show the debate itself. They track the dialogue between the opposing lawyers. One lawyer makes an argument; his opponent answers. If the answer is effective, the first lawyer creates a new argument. Rather than providing a version of a modern court judgment, the medieval reports present a version of an American law school class. The arguments, however, are not made by novices. They are made by outstanding lawyers. The medieval report helps the modern reader learn what she really wants to know. She wants to learn how lawyers think because she sees the power lawyers have. If she learns law from a text, she will not learn how lawyers think. She will just learn a bunch of rules. She does not want a text. She wants to see the way lawyers argue.

No lay person has ever looked at the reports. No one but a specialist can read them. This book will change the cases into a form that anyone can read. William of Occam, an English scholar who lived when the cases were decided, said the best explanation is the simplest one that can account for all the relevant phenomena.[28] This book turns "Occam's razor" into an editorial tool.[29] Complicated facts and language are distilled into their modern essence.

Here is a three part demonstration. The first presents a scholar's expansion of the report's shorthand; the second, his translation for specialists; the third, this book's version for modern readers.

---

[28] He lived from approximately 1285 to 1349.

[29] The medieval reporters occasionally do the same. Compare Version II with I, 33 Selden Society 214 (1312); versions III with II and I, 27 Selden Society 126 (1313–1314).

a.[30]

Un Alice porta bref de dower ver B. —*B*. Sire, ele ne deit dowere aver; pas la resone ke ele deguerpi son baron, e demora od cely ke ore la ad espose, en adulterie; prest &c.—*Tiltone.* Sire, nus vus diom ke son baron la enchasa de ly: e ke ele ne osa pas demorer od ly; par quey il covendreit ke ele alat; e demandom jugement &c.—*Kynge.* Ke ele demora od ly, prest &c.—*Tiltone.* Ke yl la enchasa de ly, prest &c. —*Tiltone.* Key yl la enhasa de ly, prest &c.—Yl convendreit ke *Kenge* deit le revers, ke yl ne la enchasa nent, prest &c., mes ala de sa bone volunte, e demora et cetera, prest &c.—Ideo &c.

b.

One Alice brought a writ of Dower against B.—B. Sir, she ought not to have dower; for the reason that she abandoned her husband and lived in adultery with him who has now married her, ready &c.—*Tiltone.* Sir, we tell you that her husband drove her out; and that she was afraid to remain with him; so need was that she must go; and we pray judgment &c.—*Kynge* She lived with him; ready &c.—*Kynge* ought to have said the contrary, viz. that he did not drive her out, ready &c., but that she went off at her own free will and lived &c., ready &c.—Therefore &c.

1. (1292)

[1] Anna sued[31] her stepson[32] Bogo for her widow's share of her late husband's land.

---

[30] 1 31a Rolls Series 182. "a" is Alfred J. Horwood's transcription of the manuscript; "b" is Horwood's translation; "1" is the author's version for lay readers.

[31] Writ of dower.

> [2] Bogo: You left my father to live with the boyfriend you've now married. You don't deserve a widow's share.[33]
>
> [3] Anna: Your abusive father made it impossible for me to stay home. {The statute[34] says a wife who "willingly" leaves her husband and lives with another man forfeits her widow's portion. I didn't have a choice.}[35]
>
> [4] *The Reporter:* The court said Anna would get her widow's share if her husband drove her out of the house.

Writing for an audience of lawyers, the reporter does not explain background laws or law reporting conventions. Writing for an audience of specialists, the modern editor adds value to the manuscript. As a paleographer—an expert in reading ancient manuscripts—he has located it, deciphered its handwriting and shorthand, and provided a translation that tracks the original. Working to provide access to a source, the editor does not interpret the case. That is not his business. His business is to provide other scholars an accurate version of the report.[36]

---

[32] The defendant's identify has been fabricated to facilitate the reader's understanding of the case. The defendant's actual identity is irrelevant to the legal question the case concerns.

[33] For elopement as a bar to dower, *see* 19 Selden Society 145 (1309).

[34] Statute of Westminster II, c.34 (1285) English Historical Documents 1189–1327 pg. 448. (Harry Rothwell, editor. 1975) (volume 3) (hereinafter EHD).

[35] Every medieval reader of the report would have known the case focused upon whether (as the statute said) the widow had "willingly" left. The author's version makes the implicit explicit. Because the modern translators identify their interpolations by brackets—"[]"—the author's additions are identified by curly braces—"{}".

[36] The Rolls Series were "edited in such a manner as to represent with all possible correctness the text of each writer, derived from a

Archaic language puts a dusty window between now and then. By using an American law teacher's voice the lay version wipes the window clean. The reporter taught law. He digressed into irrelevant but interesting asides. He embraced profanity, vulgarity, and direct speech.[37] He would not have wanted jargon to suck the air out of his courtroom. The text stays faithful to his legal principles but gets rid of his language.[38]

This book's case selection aims at a variety of goals. The theme of judge-made law provides a thread throughout the text, but the text also presents a survey of the topics medieval law addressed. Many remain relevant in modern law. The text also provides instruction for medievalists who want access to eight thousand pages of translated manuscripts. By comparing the text's modern language with the footnotes that quote the primary source

---

collation of the best MSS., and that no notes should be added, except such as were illustrative of the various readings." 1 31a Rolls Series 4. The influence of the Rolls approach appears in the format of the Selden Society volumes. Some Selden Society volumes were produced by editors who disclaimed full knowledge of the legal issues the cases raised. Some recent volumes "have had to be prepared by philologists who cannot claim to be versed in the legal technicalities which at every turn the Year Books present." 81 Selden Society xi (1964) (John Collas, editor).

[37] *See* 17 Selden Society xv–xvi (introduction by F. W. Maitland). As a Victorian scholar noted "As might have been expected, where men of high education were speaking, it usually appears that the rules of courtesy were observed among them. They lived, however, in a comparatively rude age, and in the midst of rough surroundings. Thus we find sometimes a directness of expression which would hardly occur in modern times." O. Pike, An Action at Law in the Reign of Edward III: The Report and the Record, 7 Harv. L. Rev. 266, 278 (1893).

[38] Scholars can critique the author's case interpretations by comparing the text with the footnotes. For the most part they keep the translators' original language. However, the names within the translations are changed to help facilitate comparisons.

translations a reader can learn to read the primary sources. They have been hiding in plain sight for more than a century. This book provides the only instructional manual ever written.[39]

Since most past scholarship has dismissed the Bereford era reports as a jumble of incomprehensible debates about pleading rules, few secondary sources investigate the Bereford cases. No one has identified the "leading cases" of the era. Even if a reader stumbles upon an important case, the case provides no access to other allied cases—medieval cases typically do not refer to other decisions.[40] Lacking modern research tools, the medieval lawyer had to rely upon his memory or a private index to exploit the lessons of the Year Books; the American scholar David Seipp has created a data base that provides modern readers better access.[41]

---

[39] In his translations Maitland occasionally expanded the Year Book reporters' headnotes so that a case was easier to understand. For example he rendered "*Dower porte del assent cely vers qy le bref fust porte, ou il dit qe ceo fust d'altri dreit et demanunda jugement etc. Quere.*" as "On marriage Son endows Wife with assent of Father out of land held by Father and Mother. After Son's death Wife has no action for dower against Father and Mother, but perhaps can sue Father alone and obtain dower for his life." 20 Selden Society 68. (1310). Subsequent Selden Society editors provide some modern commentary in volume indices. Paul Brand, a recent editor of the Selden Society reports, provides particularly helpful indices. *See, e.g.*, 112 Selden Society 365–391 (1996).

[40] Even if a lawyer or judge makes an unusual reference to a decision, the reference consists of a personal memory. Formal citation of cases had not yet developed. *E.g.*, "And on the other hand, Alice de Stirkely had no aid in the like case in the summer of last year." 3 31a Rolls Series 388 (1303), and "Justice Brumpton. Do you not remember, O King, the Quo Warranto which was brought against me in the Cambridge Eyre, in a like case?" 3 31a Rolls Series 220 (1302).

[41] Legal History Database, Index and Paraphrase of Printed Year Book Reports, 1268–1535 (2009) http://www.bu.edu/phpbin/lawyearbooks/search.php.

Sir John Baker, a successor to Maitland as Downing Professor of English Law at Cambridge, recently said

> Trying to glean law from the year books is like trying to learn the rules of chess or cricket merely by watching video-recorded highlights of matches. The reader soon senses that contemporaries must have known something he does not, some common understanding to enable them to appreciate the moves. There must have been a body of presuppositions and ground rules which do not appear in the books themselves, except in oblique glimpses.[42]

This book contends that a century and a half of scholarship has produced enough "video tape" so that the "presuppositions and ground rules" can now be deciphered.

The text aspires to be readable. A collection of many cases taxes the reader with the effort to remember the names of litigants, a pointless task. Litigants' names are replaced with fictional names designed to make the cases easier to follow. Plaintiffs typically will be given a name beginning with A; defendants a name beginning with B. To make the connection between characters easier to understand the first letter of a name will also provide a hint as to the relationship of characters: Adam,[43] for

---

While the database creates a tool to research specific topics (such as particular writs) the database provides no insight into the legal analysis within the cases, the subject of this book.

[42] Baker 26, *supra*. He continues "If only a tiny percentage of students could be diverted from those other branches of history, or literary studies, where staple topics seem to be revisted with dreary frequency, the gains might yet be substantial. Once the fear of technicality can be overcome, few other fields apart from archaeology can offer as much opportunity to delve into unbroken ground and recover lost worlds." *Ibid* at 32.

[43] The medieval reporters typically ignore the actual litigants' names as they appear in the case record. They frequently use the name "Adam" to refer to the plaintiff.

example, might be Anna's father, son, or husband; while Bogo[44] could be Babs' father, son, or husband. In an elaborate case Cosmo may at times show his face.

The structure of this book starts with an explanation of Bereford's techniques for taking power to create new law. Then the book examines the institutional framework: the relationship between the Court of Common Pleas and other branches of government. The book then investigates three topics that are peculiarly the concern of courts rather than society in general: pleading, proof, and the binding effect of past judgments. After an excursion into the court's relationship with two entities that tried to escape royal supervision—private courts and the church—the book concludes with a focus on the law that applied to women and serfs. The United States Supreme Court has speculated that politically powerless groups deserve special protection.[45] Bereford's policy provides early support for a common law court's intervention to protect the disadvantaged. While the claim that a fourteenth century judge implemented a "modern" judicial philosophy might at first blush appear incredible, concern for the powerless is hardly "modern"—it reflects the philosophy of virtually all religious teaching, and perhaps humanity's genetic code.[46] Finally the book closes with a description of past scholarship's denigration of the Bereford era and a brief appreciation of Bereford's spectacular contribution in creating a legal system in which common law judges consider not just rules but also the need to do justice.

---

[44] A masculine medieval name. *See* 42 Selden Society 52 (1311).
[45] United States *v.* Carolene Products Company, 304 U.S. 144 (1936) footnote 4.
[46] *See* L. Arnhart, *Darwinian Natural Right* 147 (1998).

A SAMPLE CASE

Subsequent chapters group cases together into common themes. This chapter concludes by investigating the virtues of a single report.

Serfs were peasant farm workers attached by law to the land where they were born. They could escape. A medieval text says

> If a serf escapes to a royal town for a year[47] his owner can't bring an "ownership" claim against him. The king profits from immigration to his towns.[48] However, a man can't complain about being treated as a serf if his owner has recently "possessed" him.[49]

The text does not solve the following controversy.

---

[47] In order to fend off some of the tedium of legal writing the text sometimes speaks in lay generalities. For example medieval statutes of limitation are often for "a year and a day." Rather than repeatedly inflict the full phrase the text says "a year."

[48] Interpreting "Villains may also recover their freedom by the negligence of their lords, as if any lord suffer his villain to … abide within our demesne without challenge for a year and a day,—a privilege which was heretofore granted to us by common allowance for our profit and for the improvement of our towns." 1 Britton 200 (Francis Nichols translation 1865). [Hereinafter Britton].

[49] Interpreting "The exception of villenage shall only hold good between the lord and his villain, and that only when the lord has been in recent possession of him and of his suit, or at least has been seised of him as his villain within a year and a day." 1 Britton 199.

2. (1308)[50]

[1] Simon of Paris sued[51] Sir Robert Tony for falsely imprisoning him.

[2] Robert: You were born on my land. When I discovered you had come back to my manor I told you to get to work as my serf manager.[52] You refused. Since I possessed you,[53] I had the right to punish you by locking you up.[54]

[3] Simon: You say I'm a serf but I'm not. I became free by living in London. I'm a prominent citizen there. I've represented the king as his sheriff, his chief envoy to the city.[55] I'm still a London alderman.

[4] Robert: I don't care what happened in London—that has nothing to do with your status here. My family

---

[50] 17 Selden Society 11. The actual defendant was Robert's agent, his bailiff. Although Selden Society reports identify medieval cases by the names of litigants, this book adopts the medieval reporters' and Rolls Series practice of presenting cases without a title. Since the book's versions are all derived from the Selden Society and Rolls Reports translations, the book drops the convention of referring to early published versions of the Year Books.

[51] Writ of trespass. Since a serf can sue in royal court for a violation of the peace, Robert doesn't ask the court to dismiss Simon's complaint. Instead he denies he violated the peace. He says he used only the force necessary to implement his privilege to discipline a serf he possessed. An owner in possession can use reasonable force to detain a recalcitrant serf. *See* 33 Selden Society 231 (1312). Atypically the text uses the litigants' actual names because of the significance of their identities.

[52] Interpreting "Office of reeve." Case at 11.

[53] Interpreting the implications of Robert's reference to the nest.

[54] Interpreting "He avowed the arrest." Case at 11. An "avowry" is a justification for an act claimed to be wrongful.

[55] "Este vicounte le Roi" Case at 12.

has always owned [56] you and your family. My grandfather and my grandfather's grandfather owned your granddam and your granddam's granddam. My ancestors have always treated your ancestors as serfs.[57] We took what we wanted from them, and we forced them to pay when their daughters got married.[58] Your brothers are still serfs on my manor.

[5] Simon: So what? The jury will still say you didn't possess me as a serf.[59]

[6] Justice Bereford: I remember a story about a fellow who was safe at home but he just had to visit a brothel. He wound up getting hanged. You had it all, Simon. Why did you ever leave the city?[60]

[7] Simon: Robert didn't get possession of me just because he found me on some land where all my ancestors were serfs. That's not enough.[61]

[8] Robert: My possession started when you were born and resumed when you came back.[62]

---

[56] "He is the villein of Robert." Case at 12.
[57] Interpreting "Robert's ancestors were seized of the villein services of Simon's ancestors." Case at 12.
[58] Interpreting "Ransom of flesh and blood, marriage of their daughters, tallaging them high and low…" Case at 12. *See* 1 Britton 196.
[59] Interpreting "They were not seised of him as of their villein." The theoretician Maitland insists on the distinction between "seisin" and "possession." The Bereford era decisions pay little attention to theory, and "possession" provides a coherent synonym for the lay reader.
[60] Interpreting "I have heard tell that a man was taken in a brothel and hanged, and if he had stayed home no ill would have befallen him. So here. If he was a free citizen, why did not he remain in the city?" Case at 12.
[61] Interpreting "*Toudeby* held to the assertion 'not seised of him as of his villein nor of his villein services.'" Case at 12.
[62] Interpreting "So our seisin is continued." Case at 12.

> [9] Justice Bereford: Simon talks about possession, but Robert you keep on talking about ownership. This case can't go to the jury unless you both agree to disagree about the same thing.[63]
>
> [10] Robert: What do you mean? I've been talking about possession.
>
> [11] Justice Bereford: No you haven't.[64] You've got to agree to ask the jury if Simon did serf work after his return.[65]
>
> [12] *The Reporter:* Robert capitulated, and said he had forced Simon to do serf work. The jury was asked whether Simon did serf work for him.

The treatise says Robert could not sue to prove he owned Simon after his year in London. But the treatise

---

[63] Interpreting "One side pleads on the seisin, and the other side pleads on the right; in that way you will never have an issue." Case at 12. "Seisin" means "possession;" "right" means "ownership;" "issue" means a question for the jury.

[64] Interpreting "The court will not receive such a traverse." A "traverse" is a proposed question for the jury.

[65] Perhaps Bereford is rejecting earlier precedent. About fifteen years before this controversy Justice Mettingham claimed the return to the nest itself provided the owner possession. "If my serf has a child on my land, and the child escapes from my manor but returns to that manor six or seven or more years later, and I find him in his nest, I can treat him as my serf because once he returns to my manor, he has returned to the legal status he had when he left." 2 31a Rolls Series 446,448 (1294) As the owner's lawyer quips "He fell into the pit which he hath digged." *Ibid.* The case ends inconclusively. Elsewhere in dicta delivered only two years before this case Bereford apparently agreed. "[I]f while {an owner's writ of naifty} was pending, {the owner} found you in your nest, for what purpose should he sue out his writ?" 5 31a Rolls Series 202–204 (1306). Bereford implies the owner would have acquired possession the moment the serf returns.

also says Robert can treat Simon as a serf if he has taken possession of him as a serf.

The study of law is not an exercise in rote memory. The study of law develops the techniques of legal reasoning. Bereford insists "ownership" and "possession" are different. Law teachers often use hypothetical facts to explain legal principles. You leave your umbrella at a sushi bar; later you see a stranger sheltered under the object. You own it; he possesses it. But a serf presents a more difficult problem. Physical custody of an umbrella proves possession, but physical custody cannot always prove possession of a person as a serf. Not all prisoners are serfs. The legal criteria to prove possession—the "elements" of possession, as lawyers put it—must require more than naked custody.

Robert suggests another criterion: past status as a manor's serf. Since his ancestors owned Simon's ancestors, Robert says he acquired possession when Simon came home. Bereford says their ownership has nothing to do with Robert's possession. Bereford says Robert has to show a different criterion. He has to show Simon worked as a serf after his return. The sentence provides (in lawyers' language) the "holding" of the case, the essential point behind the judge's decision. Robert cannot show possession by proving he has captured Simon, by proving Simon is present on the manor where he was born, by proving Simon has a blood relationship with his manor's serfs. Robert must prove that Simon worked for him as a serf after he returned to the manor.

The reader might like to see the jury's verdict but the reporter is not interested. He has provided a report about two lawyers and a judge arguing about possession. From his perspective the actual outcome is just gossip.[66]

---

[66] Robert's opening statement suggests the jury's verdict will go against him. He said he locked up Simon because he refused to work as serf manager. The jury does find for Simon. The Selden Society

Other Perspectives

Unlike a treatise a report presents a three dimensional picture.

Modern Legal Analysis

Law teachers use case reports as a starting point for creative thinking. If Robert's lawyer could show an exception to the axiom that possession requires work, he would have leverage to convince a judge to take his side. He does have an exception. He says Robert took possession the moment Simon was born. A newborn performs no labor. This point creates a "hook" on which a judge could hang a decision for Robert.

A modern lawyer would devise some policy reason to encourage use of the hook. Policy arguments do not focus on legal theory; they focus on social consequences. A lawyer who convinced Bereford his decision was bad policy might persuade him to rule differently. The king has given serfs freedom because they contribute to a vibrant urban culture. He wants ambitious peasants.[67] Bereford's definition of possession contradicts that goal. His definition encourages a brain drain. After a year in the city a fugitive can return to his family and friends as a free man. The court should use the "hook" of birth to tell urban peasants they cannot go home.

Apart from mastering doctrine and policy, however, lawyers must be realists. A lawyer's maxim says "hard cases make bad law." When the facts demand an

---

editor located another account of the case. Case record at 17 Selden Society 13.

[67] Cf. the engraved language on the American Statue of Liberty: "'Give me your tired, your poor/Your huddled masses yearning to breathe free,/ The wretched refuse of your teeming shore." The New Colossus, Emma Lazarus.

outcome, judges usually reach that outcome regardless of precedent or theory. Robert's lawyer may have hoped he would win with a judge who had a visceral contempt for puffed-up serfs. His hope was unrealistic. Robert had insulted the king. Could the king's court possibly let Robert say "See that fellow over there mucking out my pigpen—he used to be the king's envoy to London"? Common Pleas was going to rule for Simon; the only question was how.

Medieval History

The language and facts of the case illuminate medieval social life. The language shows that free people thought serfs occupied a niche between humans and animals. A serf's grandmother is described in the language of animal husbandry as a "granddam." At the other extreme, the report chronicles an instance of spectacular mobility. An escaped serf becomes the king's chief representative to London. Born into a family that spoke Middle English, Simon had to become fluent in Anglo-Norman, the language of the ruling class. After childhood few can acquire a perfect accent. Simon probably adopted his phony surname "of Paris" as a cover for his suspect accent.

Historians can sometimes create a three dimensional picture of an event captured within a single court proceeding. Controversies in the country's high courts typically concern litigants important enough to appear in other records.[68] Perhaps the case has left tracks in the

---

[68] Throughout volume 38 of the Selden Society reports Vinogradoff and Ehrlich connect litigants to other records. Among more modern editors Paul Brand has been spectacularly successful in this enterprise.

manorial records. The official report of the case[69] says the jury awarded Simon two hundred pounds. If Robert could not pay, maybe Simon took possession of the manor. The case may have ended like those fables in which the slave becomes the master.

Literature

Teachers have to present their materials in an engaging way. A monotonous drumbeat of doctrine puts everyone to sleep. The medieval law teacher makes his dramatis personae come to life. The reporter gives a sense of Bereford's personality, his easy command over the court room, the theater in which he takes up his role as star. "I remember a story about a fellow who was safe at home but he just had to visit a brothel. He wound up getting hanged. You had it all, Simon. Why did you ever leave the city?" Bereford's dominant personality comes through as he interrupts the case to make an irrelevant off-color quip. By including the chit-chat the reporter treats his hero with the respect Boswell gave Dr. Johnson. Reportage is literature.

Literature creates a world with more depth than a legal code. Like literature the medieval reports spur speculation. Why did Simon go home? Graced with ambition and talent, he became rich and powerful. He would not have gone back on a whim. Maybe his agents set up a deal so that he could buy his siblings. Maybe Robert found out his secret and demanded hush money. A novel could be written about Simon's squalid birth, his shining ascent, his imprisonment and triumph.

---

[69] The plea rolls or "record."

CHAPTER 2
Bereford takes Charge

THIS BOOK EXPLORES the way Bereford's court, the Court of Common Pleas, created new law. Judicial law-making contradicts the stereotype of three part governments. Their law is supposed to be created by the legislature, applied by the courts, and enforced by the executive. Bereford took his court into the law-making business. Common law courts still exploit that power. Bereford's background and dominant personality explain how he pulled off the coup. He was the first practicing lawyer to become a high court judge.[1] Typically his successors have had glorious careers as lawyers before they put on their gowns. They made their marks by focusing on results. Theory said they could not create law, but they looked at barriers as targets of opportunity.

In common with many great men Bereford had the good luck to live in a time of transition. Once the dominant force in English law, the clergy had just dropped out of secular law. A church council told them to stop appearing in cases that did not concern the church.[2] Many clerics gave up judicial appointments because they could not swear to prefer secular over ecclesiastical doctrine.[3] Their departure frayed the court's connection

---

[1] T.F. T. Plucknett, *Studies in English Legal History* xix, at 332 (1983).
[2] The Lateran Council of 1279. *See* 22 Selden Society xvi.
[3] *See* William Blackstone, *An Analysis of the Laws of England* xliv (5th ed. 1762).

to Roman law, the great legal system that still underpins European justice. The clergy took their language with them. As Anglo-Norman replaced Latin, lawyers jettisoned the past.

The Institutional Context

William the Conqueror and his successors let other court systems complement royal justice.[4] Access to Bereford's court was restricted to those who bought a "writ" from the king's Chancery.[5] On its face the writ defined both the extent of royal jurisdiction and the content of royal law. The writ defined the extent because Common Pleas would hear only cases brought by writ.[6]

---

[4] Among them church, landowner, and merchant courts.

[5] Although claims in King's Bench were typically brought by writ, Bereford asserted King's Bench, unlike Common Pleas, could proceed without a writ. "I do not think {Common Pleas} would have power to try this plea without the King's writ in which [that power] is witnessed. [But] why should not {the king} himself in lieu of a writ warrant the holding of a plea {in King's Bench}?" 22 Selden Society 115, 122 (1310).

[6] "No one can sue without a writ, since the party is not bound to answer without a writ unless he wishes to…." Bracton, 413b, 414b. The text ignores as inconsequential such procedures as cases brought by bill. Two parties agreed a dispute about the use of land "should be addressed by an award of the neighborhood without plea.… Stanton, J. The natural issue of this action is recovery of the freehold, and that cannot be by the award of any without the King's writ. So plead over." 20 Selden Society 182, 183 (1310). Once the court acquired jurisdiction by a writ, the court could itself issue orders in conjunction with the litigation. *See, e.g.*, "If a man brings his writ of right of advowson and recovers {he} may, whenever the church is void, either bring his *quare impedit* or sue the {judicial} writ of *scire facias* … even though he has presented since his recovery." 81 Selden Society 39 (1310). Bereford rejected a litigant's attempt to sidestep the writ process through manipulation of the authority Common Pleas retained to issue a *scire facias* or *quid jurisclamat.*

The writ defined the content because the writ said what the plaintiff had to prove.

Here is a royal writ:[7]

> The king to the sheriff, greeting. Anna says her husband sold her farm to Bogo. She couldn't object then because a wife has no access to court; but her husband is now dead. If Bogo refuses to give the farm back, tell him to appear in royal court to explain why.[8]

Suppose a woman had inherited a farm, but her husband sold it. She could not complain because a married woman had no access to court. At his death she became free to do whatever she wanted. But she still could not get into royal court without a writ. This writ tells Common Pleas to hear her case. What will she have to prove? The writ defines the elements of her case. She has to show she owned the land; her husband sold it to the defendant; her husband is dead.

Theory

Today a widow would look at legislation and court decisions to find out her rights. Before Bereford took charge she would just look at the writs that Chancery sold.[9] Her rights were defined there. By writing the writs Chancery seemed to control the creation of the common law. If Chancery's authority had been supreme, English law would not have been created by the king, or Parliament, or the courts. Chancery would have created

---

"Judicial writs (*e.g.*, *scire facias* and *quid iuris clamat*) must not be used as substitutes for original writs." 19 Selden Society 43, 45 (1308–1309) (Maitland's version of the medieval headnote).

[7] A *cui in vita*.

[8] Paraphrasing Early Registers of Writs, 87 Selden Society 292 (#793).

[9] Chancery kept a list called The Register of Writs. Bracton gave Chancery some power to create new writs.

the common law by writing writs. The thirteenth century scholar Bracton put restrictions on Chancery. He said Chancery's authority to write writs derived from a delegation of power by the king and his advisors.[10] Bracton told the courts to strike down writs that exceeded the limits of the delegation.[11]

In Bracton's analysis the king and Parliament were in the law-making business. Both could announce new laws. Both delegated some authority to Chancery to create law. The courts, as Bracton saw it, did not have a creative role. They had a watchdog's role. They kept Chancery in its place.[12] Bracton described a legal system. But he did not describe what American lawyers call a "common law" legal system. American lawyers define a common law system as a system in which judges create law.

In order to capture law-making power Bereford had to exploit some strategy Bracton had not anticipated. As a

---

[10] "If a writ is brought without warrant of the law, it shall be sustained as long as it is consonant with reason and not contrary to the law, provided it has been granted by the king and approved by his council. Such a writ must be personal and must be granted only as a special favor, and it does not matter that the magnates have not given their assent expressly so long as they have not expressly dissented and not sufficient reason is shown why it should not be valid; for it pertains to the king to provide a competent remedy for the suppression of every wrong." Bracton 414b. Bracton said writs with a long history necessarily satisfied the limits. "There are some formed writs (*brevia formata*) in certain cases which are de cursu and which are granted and approved by the common counsel of the realm and cannot be changed in any way without their will and consent…." Bracton 414b.

[11] "A writ will abate if it has been brought against the law and custom of the realm, especially against the charter of liberties {*i.e.*, the Magna Carta}." Bracton 413b, 414b. Bracton expected the court to abate the writ.

[12] As an American scholar might have put it, he viewed the courts as "the least dangerous branch." Alexander Bickel, *The Least Dangerous Branch* (1986).

righteous cleric Bracton expected a judge to behave honorably. He thought a judge would say a plaintiff lost if she could not prove what her writ said.[13] Bereford did not behave honorably. Bereford said the writ's language meant what he said it meant. If the writ said "black," he might say "proof of 'white' constitutes proof of 'black.'" When he wanted to change the law he let a plaintiff prove something different from what her writ required.[14]

The plaintiff's bar provided Bereford a wide vista for skullduggery. In buying a writ the plaintiff was in control. She could lie, and the Chancery clerks could not test her veracity. They were salesmen, not investigators. The defendant could not complain either. He did not learn about the writ until the sheriff served it on him. The plaintiff's story was immune from attack until she got to court. Then she was in trouble. The defendant could ask for a jury verdict on any allegation within her writ.[15] He would choose her lie. She would lose. Or the defendant could wait until the plaintiff told the court what she

---

[13] He said the court would "abate {a writ} if it has been brought against the law and custom of the realm…" Bracton 413b, 414b. Perhaps by that statement Bracton implied a court should dismiss a writ that the plaintiff tried to distort into a vehicle to change the law. Perhaps Bracton said nothing about the strategy Bereford took. His failure to condemn the strategy does not imply that he approved. He would not condemn a technique he had not anticipated.

[14] A reporter described the freedom he invoked as "astonishing." A plaintiff relied upon a deed to prove the defendant's indebtedness of forty pounds. "Chief Justice Bereford awarded that he should recover his debt and his damages of sixty pounds more than he had counted—which was astonishing; but it was thought that this was because of the delay {by the defendant} after the plea was pleaded etc." 81 Selden Society 45 (1319).

[15] The defendant could plead "ready," that is, ready for a jury on anything her writ said. He might plead "ready" about some criterion within her writ the moment he appeared in court.

actually intended to prove.[16] Then the defendant would tell the court to dismiss her case. She had contradicted what her writ said. She would lose.[17]

The court could create new law when the defendant asked for a jury verdict. The court might say: Defendant, you want a jury verdict because you say the plaintiff cannot prove one of the allegations within her writ. We think the writ's allegations misstate the common law rule. We will ask the jury not the writ's question, but rather the question the correct common law rule requires.

The court could also create new law when the defendant asked the court to rule for him because the plaintiff's in-court statement contradicted what her writ said. The court might say: Defendant you think the plaintiff has contradicted her writ. But we have the power to say what her writ really means. The writ means something different from what you think it says. The plaintiff has not contradicted her writ.

As a phrase from contemporary American political debate would describe it, an "activist court" had changed the law.[18]

---

[16] If she kept to her lie, the defendant could ask for a jury verdict then also.

[17] Her in-court statement was called the "count," that is, her account of the facts she intended to prove. The defendant would tell the court to render "judgment" on the writ because the plaintiff's in-court statement either omitted or contradicted a criterion within her writ. "Judgment of the writ."

[18] American political turmoil typically arises in a context that does not apply to the medieval era. American judges are chiefly condemned as "activists" when they interpret the United States Constitution. These decisions can be repudiated only by a supermajority of Americans amending the Constitution. Any Common Pleas decision could be repudiated by the king or Parliament.

Practice

A case puts this abstract discussion into a concrete context. A widow buys a Chancery writ that says her husband sold her land, and she could not complain. But he is dead now. She wants it back.

1. (1310).[19]

> [1] Anna sued[20] Bogo. Her writ said her dead husband had sold her farm to him.
>
> [2] Bogo: A jury will say your husband never sold the farm to me.[21]
>
> [3] Anna: My writ says "sold" but the court should ask the jury if my husband let you take possession. It doesn't matter whether he got paid or not. Either way I lose my farm.[22]

---

[19] 20 Selden Society 118.
[20] Writ of *cui in vita*.
[21] Interpreting "In a *cui in vita* the tenant said that [the husband] never demised the tenements to him. Ready etc." Case at 119.
[22] Interpreting "Then you ought to say [by] whom [you had entry], for [your] plea is tantamount to 'We did not enter by your husband,' and so you traverse the whole." Anna is arguing the court should interpret Bogo's assertion her husband did not "sell" him the land as an assertion her husband did not let him enter. Piece by piece her statement means the following. "Then you ought to say [by] whom [you had entry]" means unless Bogo says a third person let him enter, the court should say he has conceded Anna's husband let him enter. "[your] plea is tantamount to "We did not enter by your husband'" means her husband's toleration of Bogo's entry hurts Anna as much as her husband's sale, and therefore the court should tell the jury a tolerated entry is the same as a sale. "So you traverse the whole" means that although Bogo says he is just denying a sale, the court should consider his denial to include a denial the husband let him enter. Therefore the court should say he has consented to a jury verdict about whether Anna's husband let him enter.

> [4] The Justice: {Despite your argument, Anna, this court will insist you prove exactly what your writ says. We'll ask the jury if your husband sold the land to Bogo.}[23]

In the language of American lawyers, the judge is a "strict constructionist." He refuses to engage in "judicial activism." He thinks his chief responsibility is to apply language literally. If Anna's late husband managed to conceal any payment Bogo made for the land Anna will live the rest of her life without the farm she probably inherited from her father.[24]

The Writ of Trespass

In contrast the Simon of Paris case shows a judge ignoring the plain meaning of a writ. Simon bought a writ of trespass:

---

[23] The reporter omits the judge's comments rejecting Anna's argument. But the reporter's analysis shows the judge did. The reporter says "So note in a writ of entry one can traverse the entry without giving a good writ." Case at 119. The reporter means the defendant can deny he entered pursuant to the husband's "sale" even though the widow claims the writ should mean any transfer by the husband, not just a transfer for payment. Her contention is embodied in her plea "you ought to give us a good writ." She means the court should consider the gratuitous transfer as tantamount to a sale unless the defendant can show some other writ that she could have used to get her land back. The "give us a good writ" gambit is discussed below in this chapter.

[24] The jury will not find out about the fraud. Although the wife could still sue to recover her ownership—her loss in the *cui in vita* would not prevent her from bringing the "higher" writ of right—the *cui in vita* statute itself said "it was hard that the wife after the death of her husband had no recovery other than by a writ of Right …." Statute of Westminster II, c.3 (1285) (3 EHD 430–431). The writ of ownership was virtually no remedy at all.

> The King to the Sheriff, greeting. If {Simon} shall have given you security for prosecuting his claim, then require {Robert} … to show why he insulted {Simon} with force and arms, and beat, wounded and ill-treated him so that his life was despaired of, and inflicted other outrages upon him, to {his} heavy damage and against our peace.[25]

Simon did not make out the criteria. His life was never "despaired of"—he was just locked up for a little while. By the time Simon sued, Common Pleas had changed the common law. The court said the plaintiff did not have to prove a deadly wound. The court no longer enforced the criterion. As lawyers put it, the criterion had become a "fiction."

2. (1304)[26]

> [1] Adam's writ of trespass said Bogo "beat, wounded, and imprisoned him."
>
> [2] Bogo: I'm not guilty.
>
> [3] The Jury: He didn't beat or wound Adam, but he did lock him up.
>
> [4] Justice Bereford: Adam wins. Because Adam has brought a trespass writ we'll have Bogo arrested if he doesn't pay Adam immediately.[27]

---

[25] *See* Early Registers of Writs, 87 Selden Society 177 (#299) (1318–1320).

[26] 4 31a Rolls Series 258. In a trespass case from the same year the jury said the defendant had taken the plaintiff's lumber without the use of force. Applying the same rule Bereford sustained the plaintiff's writ. 4 31a Rolls Series 258 (1304) (trespass, following case).

[27] Interpreting "He should recover his damages etc., and that they (the defendants) should be taken." Case at 258.

[5] *The Reporter*: Even though Adam didn't prove beating, wounding and mortal peril, Bereford said he didn't have to pay the penalty imposed upon a plaintiff who didn't prove his writ's criteria.[28] {He said trespass plaintiffs no longer had to prove deadly violence.}[29]

A lawyer representing a man who had been cheated in a commercial transaction thought the case would help his client. Bereford threatened to send the defendant to jail. Lawyers understand that a victory in court is worthless unless it can be enforced. A judgment in a trespass writ is easy to enforce: the defendant goes to jail unless he pays. Since Bereford had apparently dropped the violence criterion the lawyer brought a trespass writ against the man who had duped his client.

3. (1313)[30]

[1] Adam sued[31] Bogo for selling him bad flax. His trespass writ said that Bogo had violated the peace by adulterating the flax with hemp.

[2] Bogo: The court should dismiss this case. The writ says I violated the peace but Adam's claim is just a conventional commercial dispute.[32]

[3] Adam: The important thing is my claim that he cheated. The language "against the peace" doesn't really matter.[33]

---

[28] Interpreting "The plaintiff in this case was not amerced, although the Inquest passed against him on a portion of his plaint etc." Case at 258.
[29] The text generalizes Bereford specific ruling.
[30] 39 Selden Society 14.
[31] Writ of trespass.
[32] Interpreting "Judgment of the writ, for the plaintiff hath counted of an agreement which was made etc., and hath counted *contra pacem*. Judgment etc." Case at 14.

> [4] Chief Justice Bereford: The threat of violence is the reason the trespass writ allows the imprisonment of a defendant.[34] Nothing here suggests that. We won't expand the writ to include situations without such a danger. You can bring a different writ if you wish, Adam, but we will dismiss the claim you have brought by this writ.[35]

Although Bereford saw the danger of violence as the heart of trespass, the common law grows, as the American jurist Oliver Wendell Holmes put it, according to the "felt necessities" of the times.[36] No judge can always predict the future. Despite Bereford's restrictive view[37] English judges eventually transformed trespass into a remedy that reached far beyond acts of violence. Trespass became the standard remedy for personal and property damage, for the enforcement of contracts, and for the recovery of land.[38] Twenty years earlier Common Pleas had already begun the process by which trespass became the most versatile of all writs.

---

[33] Interpreting "The writ saith 'other offenses and against the peace.'" Case at 14.

[34] Interpreting "Naught can be against the peace unless it be done by force, and for that imprisonment is awarded...." Case at 14.

[35] Interpreting "Therefore advise yourselves." Case at 14. The reporter says Adam took the advice.

[36] "The life of the law has not been logic: it has been experience. The felt necessities of the time, the prevalent moral and political theories, intuitions of public policy, avowed or unconscious, even the prejudices which judges share with their fellow-men, have had a good deal more to do than the syllogism in determining the rules by which men should be governed." O.W. Holmes, *The Common Law* 1 (1881).

[37] Perhaps Bereford suspected trespass had a glorious future. *See* 34 Selden Society 146 (1312–1313).

[38] Trover, assumpsit, and ejectment.

4. (1293)[39]

[1] *The Reporter*: Lawyers need to know that trespass can be used to settle land law questions.[40]

[2] Adam sued[41] Bogo for using force and arms to take twenty shillings worth of pike out of a pond.

[3] Bogo: I didn't violate the peace. {The court should dismiss Adam's claim.}[42]

[4] {The Justice: We'll let Adam use the trespass writ anyway.}[43]

---

[39] Note, Trespass, 2 31a Rolls Series 206. The text turns the report's epilogue into a preface.
[40] Interpreting "And so note that the seisin may be tried in a writ of trespass." Case at 206.
[41] Writ of trespass.
[42] Although the case says nothing about a motion for dismissal, the reporter's notation that Bogo denied that he acted against the peace implies he moved to dismiss.
[43] Although the reporter says nothing directly about the rejection of Adam's motion to dismiss, the justice necessarily made such a ruling because the case proceeds. The reporter saves his time and parchment. Brief reports that end with an argument typically mean that argument won. For example a note in its entirety reads: "A. has complained to us that B. has raised a certain covert to the nuisance etc. And tortiously for this that whereas the said A. has his land adjoining to B's land on the north, B. has planted in his soil trees so that by reason of shade etc. the corn of A. cannot ripen.—Toudeby. Any one can make a covert except for birds, judgment of the writ." 5 31a Rolls Series 258 (1306). Toudeby argues that except for a planting designed to attract birds (which would cause significant agricultural damage) the court should enter judgment that any landowner is free to plant trees at his border (even though the trees cast a shadow on land to the north). The reporter must have included the case because of the plaintiff's unprecedented argument that his neighbor's right to plant trees was restricted because of the shade they would cast. The claimed doctrine would severely impact landowner rights. The English common law has never embodied

[5] Bogo: Then I'll plead the jury will find I bought the mill from a man who had always enjoyed fishing rights. As the buyer I enjoy the rights my seller had.[44]

[6] Adam: The seller didn't have the rights. He may have caught some pike but I always objected.[45]

[7] Bogo: The jury will say you never complained.

The court lets a trespass writ serve as the vehicle to enforce a common law rule: if a seller of land has exercised fishing rights without complaint his buyer can fish too.

If desirable results derived from a liberal interpretation of a writ, the court would choose the liberal interpretation. At times, however, equally for policy reasons, the court would insist on a strict adherence to the writ's criteria.

5. (1302).[46]

[1] Adam and Bogo owned adjacent houses in a town. Adam sued[47] Bogo for trespass because he refused to

---

such a restriction. The report is a senseless waste of time and parchment unless the reporter intended to alert the reader to the plaintiffs' interesting but failed theory. The case stands for the proposition the plaintiff's argument lost.

[44] Interpreting the seller "enfeoffed Bogo of the mill and of the pool together with the fishery; and he has fished … in the same way as his feoffor did before him, with the peace and not against the peace." Case at 206.

[45] Interpreting "The seller was not seised of the fishery without dispute, ready etc." Case at 206.

[46] 3 31a Rolls Series 22. The architecture of the houses is not easily envisioned: "whereas their houses adjoin each other, the windows and doors are opened in the house of H., so that by the doors he can go into the house of the aforesaid John, and through the windows he can see his domestic affairs, whereby a nuisance etc." Case at 22. Therefore the text describes the claim for privacy in a vague way.

[47] A trespass writ of nuisance.

"stop up" his windows.[48] He said Bogo had invaded his privacy.

[2] Bogo: A trespass writ must say the defendant acted wrongfully.[49] Since your writ doesn't say I built the house, the court should dismiss your writ.

[3] Adam: I can't meet that criterion because both of us have bought existing structures. The court should let me use the writ anyway.[50]

[4] Justice Hengham: Since you don't say Bogo or his ancestors built the house, you haven't made out a criterion in your writ. You lose.[51]

Today Adam would probably lose because of a doctrine known as "coming to the nuisance."[52] Adam knew he was buying a house next to a "non-conforming use." He had no right to complain later. Common Pleas achieves the same result by insisting upon a criterion within the trespass writ.

Common Pleas exploited the trespass writ to create new law. But in Bereford's Court of Common Pleas

---

[48] The term used by the case, implying a complaint about architecture rather than exhibitionism. Another passage refers to architecture rather than temporary window coverings such as curtains—"by whom the windows and doors were made." Case at 22.
[49] Interpreting "This is a writ of trespass, and the writ ought to lay the tort in a particular person, as for instance, that they were made by us or by our ancestors…." Case at 22.
[50] The paragraph interprets "We cannot have any other writ in this case, for we are purchasers, and you also…." Case at 22.
[51] Interpreting "Nuisance cannot be committed except by a particular person; and because you have not specified the particular person by whom the nuisance was committed, therefore the court adjudges that you take nothing by your writ." Case at 22.
[52] *See generally* Spur Industries *v.* Del E. Webb Development Co, 494 P.2d 700 (AZ 1972).

trespass was not an important writ.[53] Maitland wrote "when Edward I is dead {in 1307}, statutes will do little for our ordinary private law. The subsequent development of {the writs} will consist almost entirely of modifications of a single {writ}, namely, Trespass..."[54] Maitland was wrong. Bereford didn't just modify a single writ. He revised the entire writ system.

Statutes

A good introduction to Bereford's style of policy-oriented statutory interpretation appears in a case in which his colleagues reject his advice.

6. (1313)[55]

> [1] Adam sued[56] Bogo for embezzlement. Adam asked the court to have Bogo arrested, a statutory remedy available against estate managers who were flight risks.[57]

---

[53] In contrast, trespass dominated King's Bench litigation during the era. *See* C. Fifoot, *History and Sources of the Common Law* 55 (1949).

[54] 2 P&M 564.

[55] 39 Selden Society 9. Bogo brought a writ of deceit against Adam because he asked for his arrest pursuant to the statute creating the monstravit writ. Bogo said that Adam's deceit consisted of his claim Bogo owned no land.

[56] Writ of *monstravit*. The text simplifies the case by focusing upon Adam's writ of *monstravit* rather than Bogo's subsequent writ of deceit, the vehicle by which the court in fact hears the controversy.

[57] "[I]f bailiffs who are bound to render accounts to their lords take themselves off and have no lands or tenements by which they can be distrained, then they shall be attached by their bodies ..." Statute of Marlborough, c. 23 (1267) (3 EHD 391).

[2] Bogo: The statute applies only to managers who aren't landowners. Since I own land, I'm not subject to arrest.

[3] Adam: You cheated me out of a thousand pounds. You can't be immune from arrest just because you own a few acres of wasteland.

[4] Chief Justice Bereford: The statute authorizes arrest "if the estate manager doesn't have land by which his appearance can be guaranteed."[58] "Land" should be interpreted as "sufficient land" to make him appear. A small plot provides no security for a big claim. If Adam's right about the size of Bogo's land, Bogo should be arrested.[59]

[5] Justice Scrope: No, that can't be done. The statute doesn't say "sufficient land." The statute says "land." If Bogo owns any land he can walk out the doors of this court.[60]

[6] Adam: Your view completely nullifies the statute.

[7] Justice Scrope: If you think the court will subscribe to the Chief Justice's erroneous view, you are free to

---

[58] Interpreting "If he have not land etc. by which he can be brought to county court to render etc." Case at 9.

[59] Interpreting "Chief Justice Bereford: Adam hath offered to aver that Bogo hath not sufficient land to render [an account] at the county court—which is contrary to what Adam's writ saith, namely, that you have sufficient—and you refuse that averment. Reporter: And afterwards Adam was forced by the Court to say whether Bogo had or had not land, without regard to its sufficiency." Case at 9.

[60] Interpreting "Scrope, J. You said that he had land, but not sufficient; but if he have any land by which he can be distrained, that is sufficient for him; and therefore you must say whether he hath land or no." Case at 10.

ask the court to render a judgment on the proper interpretation of the statute.[61]

[8] *The Reporter*: Adam didn't dare take up Scrope's challenge. He said the jury would find that Bogo didn't own even a square foot of ground.

About a half century before this case Parliament decided to protect estate owners against corrupt agents. Scrope's interpretation lets dishonest estate managers buy immunity from arrest for the price of a few worthless acres. The legislators said "no land" but they could not have intended to protect scoundrels with foresight. The genius of the common law lets judges adjust rules to solve unanticipated problems. Scrope prefers to apply language mechanically rather than engage in the policy-oriented analysis that characterizes modern common law decisions.[62]

The medieval context makes Scrope's opinion particularly damaging. Today "strict constructionists" say that if legislators have made a mistake, they should correct it, not the courts. The option—if it is realistic today—did not apply during Bereford's time. Parliament had lost interest in private rights. Legislation about private rights was not frequently enacted.

Had Scrope's views prevailed, Common Pleas would have read everything literally. Scholars have provided a justification for such rigidity. Maitland said

---

[61] Interpreting "If that be your opinion and it be as you have said, admit that he hath a messuage etc." Case at 12.

[62] Scrope's decision contradicts earlier rulings. Justice Hengham asserted arrest would be proper if "the lands are not sufficient for bringing him into court..." 3 31a Rolls Series 324,326 (1303). As did Justice Howard. 4 31a Rolls Series 114 (1304).

> As time goes by there is always a larger room for discretion in the law or procedure; but discretionary powers can only be safely entrusted to judges whose impartiality is above suspicion and whose every act is exposed to public and professional criticism. One of the best qualities of our medieval law was that in theory it left little or nothing, at all events within the sphere of procedure, to the discretion of justices. They themselves desired that this should be so and took care that it was or seemed to be so. They would be responsible for nothing beyond an application of iron rules.[63]

If Bereford's court just applied "iron rules" the decisions would focus upon grammar rather than policy. However Bereford's philosophy of doing justice, of exercising discretion in applying flexible rules, dominated the court during his tenure. Scrope is the outlier. In the following case Bereford portrays the center.

7. (1313)[64]

> [1] Adam leased Stone Farm for ten years to Bogo. When the ten years were up Adam discovered Bogo had violated Adam's rights by destroying some buildings. Adam's suit[65] relied on a statute that gave him triple damages and recovery of the "wasted" land.[66]

---

[63] 2 P&M 563. Cf. "The role of the {medieval) courts, like that of a chess referee or cricket umpire, was not to make or develop the rules but merely to see that they were followed." Baker 80, *supra.*

[64] 39 Selden Society 32. The text hypothesizes a lease for a term of years and a concrete example of "waste."

[65] Statutory writ of waste.

[66] Statute of Gloucester, c. 5 (1278) (3 EHD 417).

[2] Bogo: Landlords have always had the right to get actual damages.[67] But you're using the statute because you want triple damages. You don't qualify to invoke it—the statute tells the court to put a victorious claimant into possession. The court can't—you already have possession.

[3] Chief Justice Bereford: Maybe I would take your side Bogo if Adam had thrown you off the farm and then asked for triple damages.[68] But he didn't do that; he just took the farm back when the ten years were up. Why shouldn't he collect the penalty?

[4] Bogo: Because the special statute applies only if the court can give the victor possession.[69] Although Adam doesn't qualify under the statute's plain meaning, the regular rules compensate him for the damage he's actually suffered.[70]

[5] Adam: If you're right, a renter wouldn't pay a penalty if he sold off buildings for scrap on the last day of his lease.[71]

[6] Chief Justice Bereford: Adam's example shows why this court will force Bogo to pay triple damages if he has committed waste.[72]

---

[67] Interpreting "While at the common law he could recover damages only." Case at 34.
[68] Interpreting "If the plaintiff had entered during the term…" Case at 33.
[69] Interpreting "That judgment could not be executed because etc." Case at 33.
[70] Interpreting "He ought to sue at common law." Case at 34.
[71] Interpreting "It would enable any termor to commit waste on the last day of his term…." Case at 32.
[72] Interpreting "Would you lay down this fine law that the waste which you have committed to his disherison during the term is to remain unpunished? *intimating that that was not the law.*" Case at 32. The text infers Bereford means Adam discovered the waste only

Common Pleas frequently had to integrate new and old law. When medieval legislators created new remedies they typically also kept the old ones in place. The new writ, Maitland implied, would have no impact upon the law that applied to the old one. Each writ, he said, stood on its own.

> [I]n the middle ages one could say next to nothing about actions in general, while one could discourse at great length about the mode in which an action of this or that sort was to be pursued and defended.[73]

Bereford's court took a different approach. In the next case he revises an old writ by looking to the policy Parliament adopted when it created a new writ, a writ the plaintiff did not use.

Lords found it difficult to staff the private courts they held to solve local disputes. The king could force his subjects to serve on his courts;[74] private landowners could not. They solved the problem by selling land by deeds that forced buyers to serve. But many buyers would not sign. They did not want their lives disrupted every few weeks by court service. Even though they had not signed, many tenants capitulated to various forms of duress and served on their lords' courts despite the exemption within their deeds. According to medieval doctrine the landlord then "possessed" the tenant's court service. If the tenant refused to continue to serve the lord took his livestock. Tenants used the writ of "replevin" to get back wrongfully confiscated livestock. But the writ of replevin gave the lord a defense. If he could show he "possessed" the tenant's service the rules of replevin

---

after resuming possession. Otherwise Adam would have sued during the term to recover both the land and triple damages.

[73] 2 P&M 562.

[74] In their capacity as jurors.

allowed him to keep the livestock. The terms of the deed did not matter. The duress ploy became a scandal. Parliament finally protected tenants.[75]

> If the tenant's deed doesn't expressly force him to serve on his lord's court, the lord can't confiscate his livestock even though he can show the tenant has served on his court. Tenants can get their livestock back by using the wrongful duress writ this statute creates.[76]

The statute spoke only about the wrongful duress writ; the statute said nothing about "replevin." But Bereford thought the legislators' goal gave him a good reason to change the law of replevin.

8. (1310)[77]

> [1] After Bogo took his cow because he would not serve on his court, Adam sued[78] to get it back. His

---

[75] Statute of Marlborough c. 9 (1267) (3 EHD 388).

[76] Interpreting the writ as presented in the Early Registers of Writs, 87 Selden Society 68 (#118a). The statute should be read as creating a unique writ not only because Chancery created one, but also because of the language of the statute. "[O]n complaint of those tenants {the lords} shall be attached to appear ... and have but a single essoin..." 3 EHD at 388. The mandated writ is not a conventional replevin, a writ that allows more than one essoin.

[77] 22 Selden Society 56. Although the transaction was made by an earlier generation the text treats it as done by the parties. Bereford's law reform agenda appears in a comparison of this case and an earlier note in which the reporter says a wrongful confiscation of livestock in violation of a deed freeing the tenant from suit of court allows the tenant to "bring the Prohibition formed in the terms of the statute forbidding him to distrein contrary to the terms of the feoffment ... but this matter cannot be tried by the Replegiare {*i.e.*, replevin} after the lord has been (whether rightfully or wrongfully) seised of the services." 2 31a Rolls Series 396 (1294).

lawyer did not buy a wrongful duress writ; his lawyer bought a replevin writ.

[2] Adam: My deed says my only obligation is to pay you two shillings a year.

[3] Bogo: So what? Under the rules that apply to replevin, if you have served on my court once, I can take your cow if you stop serving.[79]

[4] Chief Justice Bereford: Bogo, if you were talking about some other service Adam had done, you would win. You could say you had "possession"—a valid defense to a replevin writ. But lords have offended justice for too long by forcing their poor tenants to serve on their courts.[80] I'm not going to let you rely upon your possession of his service.[81]

[5] Bogo: Certainly some landlords have misbehaved. But Parliament solved the problem by creating the wrongful duress writ. For his own reasons Adam chose replevin. He has to live by his choice. Here's an analogous case. Parliament bans taking oxen {because landlords take them at harvest time when tenants will do anything to get them back.} Parliament gave

---

[78] Writ of replevin. The case says nothing about why Adam chose to use replevin rather than wrongful duress. Perhaps his lawyer just used a writ he knew well; perhaps he had some strategic goal.

[79] Interpreting "This is a possessory writ, where statute {Statute of Westminster II, c.2 (1285) (3 EHD 430)} allows us to make avowry [at any time] since the limitation of the writ of novel disseisin." Case at 57. The "limitation" was many decades before this case.

[80] Of the suit of court statute, Bereford said "For twenty years past there has not come into England so good a law for poor people." 4 Selden Society 162 (1310).

[81] The paragraph interprets "He has avowed for suit arrear. It would be different if he avowed for any other service. So have a care about demurring." Case at 57.

tenants a special writ to recover oxen.[82] But suppose some tenant decides to skip the special writ in favor of replevin. The replevin rules would apply. This case is no different. He served; he stopped serving; he can't get his cow back.

[6] Chief Justice Bereford: Thank you, Bogo. (*The Reporter*—Meaning, you are wrong.)

Common Law Rules

Most Common Pleas cases did not apply writs anchored in a particular statute. Most "common law" rules had murky origins. They may have come from Roman law, [83] or ancient edicts and legislation, or custom.[84] The court ignored the academic question of the writ's origin and instead looked to pragmatic considerations in interpreting the writs.

A ferret helped the court refine the law of self-help.

9. (1308–1309)[85]

[1] Adam sued[86] Bogo to get his ferret back.

---

[82] The tenant got his plow beast back unless the landlord could show the tenant had removed every chattel except plow beasts from his land. *See* 4 31a Rolls Series 330 (1304).

[83] In an unusual statement Justice Inge referred to "imperial law upon which the law of the land is founded..." 36 Selden Society 68, 70 (1313).

[84] The court might find a custom either proper or improper. *See* 5 31a Rolls Series 204 (1306) (mining rights after land sale).

[85] 17 Selden Society 87. The defendant also confiscated the plaintiff's nets.

[86] Writ of replevin.

[2] Bogo: I'm the only one allowed to hunt rabbits in the woods where my gamekeepers found your men hunting.[87] They properly confiscated their ferret.

[3] Adam: They took it outside the woods.

[4] Bogo: Since they were in hot pursuit they did nothing wrong.[88]

[5] Justice Stanton: If cattle invade cropland a farmer can chase them away and then corral them as security for his damage. But your men, Bogo, challenged Adam's while they had the ferret in their possession. Do you really think the common law lets them chase people beyond the woods and then wrestle a ferret out of their hands? The farmer cases don't justify that at all.[89]

[6] *The Reporter*: I think Stanton had two reasons. Adam's men had the ferret in their hands {so violence could have erupted}. Besides Adam's monopoly gave him the right to collect a penalty so he didn't need self-help to be made whole.[90]

---

[87] Interpreting "We have warren in our freehold…." Case at 87.
[88] Interpreting "We found them doing damage, and they fled out of our warren, and we pursued them and took them, and thus we took them in our warren etc." Case at 87. Bogo interprets "in his warren" to include hot pursuit outside its physical boundaries. The hot pursuit privilege of confiscation of damage feasant livestock also appears in 2 31a Rolls Series 84 (1293).
[89] The paragraph interprets "If they took up their nets and their ferret and fled out of the warren into the common field, and you came in pursuit, think you that you could take these things out of their hands, as you might take a horse or ox or other beast which you saw going forth out of your growing corn? Certainly not. It behoves that the taking be made in your warren." Case at 87.
[90] Interpreting (and adding a rationale to) "Note that the reason of this may be double, either because the things were in their hands or because the lord might have sued for a forfeiture, etc." Case at 87. Maitland says "The forfeiture here mentioned may be the forfeiture

In another case the danger of fraud caused the court to revise the common law. A wise land buyer always had the seller guarantee his title. If a stranger later sued the buyer claiming a right to the land the buyer could enforce the guarantee. He would "vouch the seller to warranty." The seller would have to step into the buyer's shoes and defend his land sale. If he lost he would have to give the buyer equally valuable land. There was one problem. The seller's obligation to compensate applied only to land the seller possessed when he stepped into the buyer's shoes as a defendant.[91] If before then the seller had traded all his land for sheep, he would not pay a penny. In lawyers' jargon, by getting rid of all his land he had made himself "judgment proof."[92]

10. (1316)[93]

> [1] When Adam sold a farm to Bogo he gave him a guarantee that was good for him or anyone to whom he sold the land.[94] Bogo sold the farm to Cosmo. When a stranger claiming to own the farm sued Cosmo,[95] Cosmo brought a writ of "warranty of charter" against Adam.[96] Since only an heir of the

---

of ten pounds to which persons who hunted in warrens were liable." Case at 87 footnote 3.

[91] The relevant time according to 2 Britton 102.

[92] When a maimed plaintiff sued, the defendant tried to become judgment proof by alienating all his land before a jury reached a verdict. Justice Roubury ruled the plaintiff could recover his damages from the subsequent possessors. 3 31a Rolls Series 322 (1303).

[93] 45 Selden Society 99.

[94] As Adam subsequently concedes.

[95] By a writ of entry. The writ said Cosmo had taken the land from someone who had no right to possess it.

[96] Unlike voucher to warranty, warranty of charter produced a judgment not for land but for damages. 42 Selden Society 165 (1311) (warranty of charters). Why did Cosmo skip Bogo? Perhaps Bogo's sale did not include Bogo's guarantee. Perhaps Bogo's sale included a guarantee but Cosmo decided Adam was more solvent. Since Bogo

buyer—not a subsequent purchaser—qualified to bring the writ of warranty of charter Cosmo's writ described Cosmo as Bogo's "heir."[97]

[2] Adam: When Cosmo explains what he's prepared to prove, he admits he bought the land from Bogo—he isn't Bogo's "heir," he's Bogo's subsequent purchaser. Since he has contradicted a criterion within the "warranty of charter" writ, the court should dismiss his case. If he says that's the only way he can use the guarantee I made, he's wrong. He should do what any buyer does. He should "vouch me to warranty." If this stranger proves he owns the farm, I'll make Cosmo whole.[98]

[3] Cosmo: There is one big difference between "warranty of charter" and "voucher to warranty." I can't "vouch" until the litigation is well underway. But I can bring a "warranty of charter" the moment I'm sued. If the court throws this case out, everyone knows what you'll do. Before I can "vouch" you, you'll sell off all your land so that you'll be judgment proof. The court should ignore the criterion that says I'm Bogo's heir.[99] The court should allow my case to proceed

---

is dead, perhaps Cosmo wanted to avoid the complications involved in suing the heir or widow.

[97] The writ of warranty of charter describes the plaintiff as either the buyer or his heir. *See* Early Registers of Writs, 87 Selden Society 78 (#148). Adam argues "You {Cosmo} demand this warranty as an assign, and the writ does not mention you are an assign." Case at 100. In other words, Cosmo said in court that he had bought the land from Bogo—he was Bogo's "assign." Because Adam says he has contradicted his writ, Cosmo's writ must have said he was either the first buyer or the first buyer's heir. He chose "heir."

[98] Interpreting "You have heard how he counts that {a third person} brought against him a writ of entry on which he could have vouched; and thereupon we could have entered into the warranty …" Case at 100.

[99] The paragraph interprets "If a writ of entry be brought against me, and my warrant alienate before he is vouched, he will not give to the value except of those lands which he had on the day of the voucher;

because I haven't contradicted my writ in a legally relevant way.

[4] *The Reporter*: The court let Cosmo use the "warranty of charter."[100]

Bereford believed the law embodied common sense. Sometimes he made a judgment without even talking about the criteria within the writs.

11. (1311)[101]

[1] Adam sued[102] the abbot for a hundred pounds, the sales price of the wool he had sold Bogo, a monk.

[2] Abbot: Unless you show this monk had written authorization to buy the wool we're not paying.

[3] Chief Justice Bereford: Wasn't he buying wool for the abbey, and didn't the abbey use it? Suppose I told my man to buy twenty pounds of spice on credit. He signs a receipt and I get the spice. Do you really think I could refuse to pay if I hadn't given him written authority?

[4] *The Reporter*: The abbot's lawyer made him settle.[103]

---

and therefore I bring a writ of warranty of charter etc. immediately after the writ is purchased against me; and if then he alienate before I can vouch him he will give to me to the value, if etc., of the tenements which he had on the day when the writ of warranty of charter was brought against him." Case at 101.

[100] In another case Bereford said that in a writ of warranty of charter, the words that say, 'Which he holds, and claims to hold, of him' are merely formal..."63 Selden Society 281 (1311?). That is, Bereford said the writ's statement he "bought" the land from the seller was just a fiction.

[101] 42 Selden Society 19.

[102] Writ of debt.

"Give a Good Writ"

By asking the court to ignore her failure to prove her writ's criteria, a plaintiff asked the court to engage in law reform. Sometimes the plaintiff did the same thing with a pleading called "give a good writ." When the defendant asked the court to dismiss her writ the plaintiff might reply, "Give me a good writ." The challenge was just rhetorical. The plaintiff did not expect the defendant to provide a better writ. The plaintiff meant that the court should refuse to dismiss her writ. She thought she had bought the writ closest to the facts she intended to prove. Her "Give a good writ" pleading contended the court should ignore the contradiction between her writ and the facts she intended to prove.[104] She had suffered an injury that deserved a remedy.[105] Since there was no better writ

---

[103] "*Toudeby* saw he must answer the monk's deed and the averment, and he made his client settle." Case at 20.

[104] When a defendant asked the court to dismiss the plaintiff's writ because she had not joined her sister, the plaintiff replied her sister was dead, and therefore she could not join her despite the apparent requirements of her writ. In rejecting the defendant's argument Bereford said "If you would abate this writ, give a better writ." 20 Selden Society 66 (1310). On rare occasions the defendant can identify a better writ. A writ claimed the possessor of land was dead even though he was living as a monk. "Defendant: I cannot have any other writ in Chancery. Justice Hengham: Yes you can. There are writs that say, 'On the day on which he died,' but there is also a writ that says, 'On the day when he took the habit of religion.' If you bring one writ when you should have brought another, the court will dismiss your writ." 5 31a Rolls Series 130 (1306). *See also* 20 Selden Society 185 (1310).

[105] The son of a second marriage sued to recover his right as the recipient of a gift to his mother and her child. A son from the first marriage had survived his mother, took possession, and then died. When a child of the second marriage sued to recover the land as his half-sibling's heir (a requirement of the formedon in the descender writ) the defendant said the writ had to be dismissed—he made an "exception to the writ"—because a brother does not inherit from his

to satisfy the needs of justice the court should approve the writ she had brought.[106]

Chancery sold a writ[107] that allowed a widow to recover her land that her late husband had sold. A woman invoked the give a good writ doctrine. She brought the widow's writ

---

half-sibling. Bereford said "Although you put forward your exception to abate the writ it is properly an exception to the action." By this Bereford means the pleading to dismiss the plaintiff's writ actually amounted to the contention that a half sibling had no right under a fee tail if his late half-brother had taken possession. Since no other writ would better serve the child's claim, the defendant's pleading amounted to a contention under the common law in this context a half-blooded child had no claim under the fee tail. Bereford concludes the substantive law allows such a child to recover. Therefore he approves the writ the child had brought on the theory he had brought the closest writ available—the defendant could not give another "good writ"—and under the common law, he deserved a remedy. 26 Selden Society 58, 61 (1310–1311). *See also* "Chief Justice Bereford: By making your conclusion in abatement of the writ, you mean that he ought not to touch the action. But take good care, for you can have one meaning and perhaps we may have another." 34 Selden Society 172, 173 (1312–1313). Bereford's meaning is further explained by another version of the report: "Chief Justice Bereford: (Be careful) whether you want to abide (judgment on that point); the answer which you have given is to oust them from the action, for in the case etc. they cannot have another demonstrance." *Ibid* at 175–176. Bereford means that although the defendant asserts that his objection is to the writ, his objection actually contends the plaintiff should not be able to recover in the king's court (the objection is "to the action"). Bereford warns the defendant he will rule against such a position. Sometimes, however, the court decided the injured plaintiff simply had no enforceable right. "Chief Justice Bereford: Well, we cannot provide for every hard case." 20 Selden Society 128, 130 (1310).

[106] In common with the other law reform techniques Bereford exploited the "give a good writ" argument had been used before he became the dominant figure on the court. See, *e.g.*, 2 31a Rolls Series 428 (1294). Bereford took existing law reform doctrines and enhanced their importance.

[107] *Cui in vita* and its variants.

even though the seller was neither dead nor her husband and the defendant had not actually bought "land."

12. (1313–1314)[108]

[1] After her marriage was annulled[109] Anna sued[110] Bogo to recover land that her "husband" had sold him.

[2] Bogo: Your writ claims land but in court you claim grazing rights. Grazing rights aren't land.[111]

[3] Anna: Can you give me a better writ?[112]

[4] Bogo: Chancery sells a writ to people who possess grazing rights—use that.[113]

[5] Anna: I've inherited these rights but I haven't used them. I've never put sheep onto the pasture. You say I should use a writ of "possession" but I'm not in possession. My writ's the best I could find.[114]

---

108 27 Selden Society 130.

109 Although the Latin title of the writ—*cui in vita ante divorcium*—suggests a divorce, in modern terminology the proceeding was an annulment, a declaration that no marriage had ever existed.

110 Writ of *cui in vita ante divorcium.*

111 Interpreting "Judgment of the writ whether she ought to have answer to such a writ, seeing that her writ runs *precipe quod reddat* pasture for eight sheep. Whereby she supposes that a right of pasture is of the nature of demesne; whereas it cannot be rendered, and cannot be demesne." Case at 132.

112 Interpreting "What writ ought she bring if you oust her from this writ?" Case at 131.

113 Interpreting "He can make his demand either by a writ of right or by a possessory writ. In this particular case the *quod permittat* is open to him." Case at 131.

114 The paragraph interprets "She relieth upon the seisin of her mother, in demesne and as of fee and right in regard of the land and meadow, and as of fee and right in respect of the pasturage." Case at

[6] Bogo: There's another problem with your claim. You say I guaranteed your grazing rights on a meadow I don't even own. The court can't enter a judgment that impacts somebody who's not in court.[115]

[7] Anna: Common Pleas didn't see that as a problem in another case. A farmer sued to stop someone from interfering with his cattle drive across a river. His writ said the defendant owned the river. In court the farmer admitted someone else owned the river. The court said the writ was good enough. When necessary the court ignores a false statement by a litigant.[116]

[8] Justice Stanton: Since Bogo can't show a better writ Anna can use this one.[117]

Another case also approved a doubly false statement within the same writ a widow brought to recover land her dead husband sold. First the court said a son of a dead widow qualified as a "widow." Then court said the seller qualified as "dead" even though he was alive.

---

135. That is, she can say her mother had possession (demesne) of the grazing rights but she can't say she herself did.

[115] Interpreting "[T]he *precipe quod reddat* cannot lie against a stranger, otherwise a profit might be recovered against him in the soil of one who was no party to the action." Case at 133.

[116] Interpreting "I remember when a man brought his writ of *quod reddat passagium ultra aquam* that was the water of another [than him against whom the writ was brought] and he asked if he that had hindered him were the lord of the water course, and he said that it was not so; but that he was hindered by a stranger, against whom he had brought his writ; and the writ was thereupon ruled to be good. So in this case." Case at 132.

[117] Interpreting "If you say she ought not to have this writ you must give her another, for she ought not to be left without recovery." Case at 132.

13. (1316).[118]

[1] When she married her first husband Anna already owned a farm. After their son Adam was born, her husband died. Anna remarried. Her second husband engaged in a fraud. For a penny he sold her farm to his friend; the friend sold it back to him for a penny. Anna couldn't do anything while Bogo was alive, and she died during his lifetime.[119] Adam then brought the widow's writ against his stepfather.[120] His writ said his mother's dead husband had sold her land during her lifetime.

[2] Bogo: The court has to dismiss this writ—I'm not dead.

[3] Adam: If I can't use this writ I'll be kept out of my inheritance indefinitely. I'll be deprived of my inheritance until my stepfather Bogo dies.[121]

[4] Chief Justice Bereford: We'll ignore the fact that Bogo's alive—the writ's good.[122]

Chancery sold a writ the owner of a hunting monopoly could use against other claimants to the

---

[118] 52 Selden Society 98.

[119] The husband and wife were one, and the husband was that one.

[120] Writ of *cui in vita*. Some of the standard forms for the *cui in vita* identified the widow's heir as the plaintiff. Early Registers of Writs, 87 Selden Society 292 (#793, #797). The extra step—the husband's sale to the accomplice who sold it back to him—was addressed by a standard form. *Ibid.* #795.

[121] Interpreting "If we are not answered on this writ, we are disinherited for the whole of Bogo's life." Case at 99.

[122] Interpreting "Bogo is sufficiently dead to the heir in this case, since there is no privity [between them], wherefore the writ is sufficiently good." Case at 99.

monopoly.[123] But Chancery did not sell a writ that the owner could against use non-hunters.[124] An earl resorted to the courts when some townspeople disrupted his sport.

14. (1311)[125]

> [1] The earl claimed a privilege[126] to hunt in the area adjacent to a village.[127] Trying to protect their tranquility, some villagers beat his dogs and confiscated a deer carcass. The earl sued[128] them for an enormous sum, a hundred pounds.[129]
>
> [2] Villagers: You don't have hunting rights here.[130]
>
> [3] Earl: My writ doesn't raise the question of hunting rights; my writ complains about a violation of the peace.[131]

---

[123] Cf. Early Registers of Writs, 87 Selden Society 179 (#309).
[124] The owner of the franchise could arrest those hunting in violation of his rights. "And note that he cannot attach the body [of the trespasser] unless he be found with the mainor, that is to say with greyhounds or conies or partridges &c. But quaere if he can take the trespassers' greyhounds, if they be roaming about in his warren without having caught anything? He may do so …" Note, 1 31a Rolls Series 136,138 (1292).
[125] 31 Selden Society 150. Also reported in 63 Selden Society 244 (1311).
[126] A free chase. The writ for a free chase must have conformed to the exemplar of a free warren writ, a writ brought against rival hunters. "To show why with force and arms they entered the free warren of the said A. at N. and hunted therein without his license…" Early Registers of Writs, 87 Selden Society 179 (#309).
[127] The right could apply to land the claimant did not own—in modern terms, it provided an easement to hunt on another person's land. Cf. "warren in his demesne lands or in other lands…" 1 Britton 75.
[128] Writ of trespass.
[129] From the case record at 150. A rich man tries to intimidate poor men.
[130] "The village is not within his free chase, ready etc." Case at 150.
[131] Interpreting "What do you answer as to the coming with force and arms and as to the battery of the hounds?" Case at 150.

[4] Villagers: Chastising your dogs and confiscating a deer carcass doesn't constitute a violation of the peace. Unless you have more your writ's no good.[132]

[5] Earl: There's got to be some way I can protect my rights. What writ do you suggest?[133]

[6] Chief Justice Bereford: The earl can use this writ but we won't ask the question the writ typically poses. This case isn't about a violation of the peace. This case is about whether the earl has hunting rights in the village. The jurors will tell us if he does.[134]

Bereford thinks the king's court needs to resolve this quarrel. Seeing no better writ Bereford lets trespass define a property right.

The King Scoffs at Technicalities

Bereford said the king thought "give a good writ" was an efficient way to overcome technicalities.

15. (1310)[135]

[1] Bogo sold a manor to Adam. Cosmo had a scheme to take possession of the manor. [136] He had a close

---

[132] Interpreting "Our exception is to the writ." Case at 150.
[133] Interpreting "Then suggest a good writ." Case at 150.
[134] Interpreting "The villagers say the village is not within your free chase, and, if that be true, {they are} quit of the trespass." Case at 150.
[135] 20 Selden Society 193. The order of the arguments has been revised. Bogo's brother has been named Babs to make the case easier to understand.
[136] Cosmo's relationship with Babs is described in inconsistent ways. In the first paragraph of version B Babs is said to be ignorant of the scheme, but a little later in the report Cosmo asks the court to dismiss Adam's writ "for it says that we conspired {to create this bogus

relationship with Babs, Bogo's sister.[137] He persuaded Babs to sue to enforce a security interest[138] in the manor she supposedly enjoyed because she had lent Bogo two thousand pounds before he sold the manor to Adam.[139] The loan and security interest were fabricated but since neither Bogo nor Adam got notice of the suit, Babs won.[140] Adam discovered the plot before Babs provided Cosmo possession of the manor,[141] and he had the judgment nullified.[142] He then sued[143] Cosmo with a writ of conspiracy.

[2] Cosmo: A conspiracy is an agreement to perpetrate a future evil. You refer to a past evil, the security interest. Your writ's no good.[144]

---

debt} for the profit of {Babs}, who is not named [as a party] in this writ." The text takes the simple (and perhaps accurate) approach that Cosmo used Babs as his agent to perpetrate the fraud.

[137] The facts so suggest (although in reality Babs is male). As a cat's paw, Babs betrays her brother. Although she might have been motivated by greed, she and Cosmo had to have been intimate before Cosmo would suggest the fraud.

[138] By a statute merchant.

[139] A valid security interest created before the sale to Adam would have priority over Adam's rights. 5 31a Rolls Series 92 (1305) (Note on debt).

[140] The report reads "without Richard's {*i.e.*, the brother's} knowledge." Case at 194. But the reporter constantly confuses Bogo and Babs, and Bogo's ignorance of the claim makes more sense than Babs' ignorance of the claim. The entry of the judgment suggests neither Adam nor Bogo knew about the scam litigation.

[141] "[to the intent that] Babs should grant them to Cosmo for the time of the debt." Case at 194.

[142] Bogo sued in King's Bench "until this statute {*i.e.*, the security interest created by the statute merchant} was attainted as false…" Case at 194.

[143] Writ of conspiracy.

[144] Interpreting "The writ supposes {a security interest created in the past} whereas every conspiracy and alliance ought to be precedent to what is conspired and devised; so we pray judgment." Case at 195.

[3] Adam: The security interest never existed. You engaged in a corrupt agreement to fabricate evidence about the past.[145]

[4] Chief Justice Bereford: Anything else, Cosmo?

[5] Cosmo: Adam says Babs was a confederate but he doesn't make her a defendant.

[6] {Chief Justice Bereford: He doesn't have to.}[146]

[7] Cosmo: In his writ Adam describes me as a "conspirator" and then as a "procurer." The writ contradicts itself.

[8] Chief Justice Bereford: Another worthless argument.

[9] Cosmo: Adam calls me a "procurer" but I'm not. Babs sued to enforce the security interest. I didn't. Only a litigant can "procure" a judgment.[147]

[10] Chief Justice Bereford: Although you weren't a party your knowing participation makes you a "procurer." Everyone knows the distinction between ignorance and knowledge. If I see my lawyer and ask him for advice, if he doesn't know I have a corrupt goal, he won't be responsible for having "procured"

---

[145] Interpreting "You conspired [to allege] that a statute was made … which statute was not made." Case at 195.

[146] Despite the argument the report continues. Bereford must have rejected the argument.

[147] Interpreting this colloquy: "Adam: You procured a suit against us, whereby under judgment of this Court we were ousted from our manors. Cosmo: Judgments are not to be 'procured'; they proceed from law. Chief Justice Bereford: If the judgment was not 'procured' by [you], still you knew the suit upon which the judgment was made, and their complaint is of your false alliance." Case at 195.

the result. He can't be held for what I do. But if he knows my evil intention he'll be liable as a "procurer."[148]

[11] Cosmo: Adam should have brought a writ of deceit, not a writ of conspiracy.

[12] Chief Justice Bereford: In all my years I can't think of anyone who has produced such a barrage of nonsense.[149] I've got a story for you. Thirty accusations were brought in Parliament against the Countess of Albermarle. Her lawyer stood up. These accusations, he said, are too varied and too vague. This case has to be dismissed. Two justices rejected his argument. Then Justice Hengham spoke up, {the very same Hengham who was soon fined ten thousand marks for malfeasance in office.}[150] To one judge he said "Have you forgotten when you rushed to hang a receiver of stolen goods and then the accused thief was acquitted?" Then he told the other judge "You too acted in foolish haste. You hanged an outlaw so quickly that the king let his family keep his land." Hengham then addressed everyone in the chamber. "The common law gives every person the right to fair notice and coherent charges. This writ has to be

---

[148] Interpreting "Chief Justice Bereford: If you are of my counsel, and I pray your counsel to set going some business, although the thing be bad in itself, if you do not know the evil, you will have no punishment for [giving] your counsel. So I say in this case. His complaint is that you knew the evil, and you procured its being taken in hand." Case at 196.

[149] Interpreting "Chief Justice Bereford: These seven years I never was put to study a writ so much as this; but there is nothing to what you say." Case at 195. The text treats "seven years" as a figure of speech.

[150] The text adds facts to which Bereford implicitly refers. In 1290 Ralph Hengham was dismissed from his post, and fined 10,000 marks. "Ralph Hengham," *Oxford Dictionary of National Biography* (entry by Paul Brand).

dismissed."[151] At this point King Edward stood up. Here's what he said. "I'm not going to interfere, but by the blood God shed, you're not getting out of here until you find a good writ to bring this woman to book!"[152] Cosmo, have you got something more to say?

[13] *The Reporter*: After an adjournment Cosmo paid Adam two hundred pounds.

Land Grants

Although Bereford's court changed legal doctrine to make the law reasonable, the court dealt with the sale of land differently. The country's wealth derived from land and land transactions were not done casually. The context demanded clarity. "Reasonableness" was too uncertain. The court said unless land deals satisfied the precise criteria within a limited number of writs the deals were unenforceable.

16. (1308–1309)[153]

[1] Claiming a farm, Cosmo sued[154] Adam. In court he described the grant that gave him his rights. He said

---

[151] Interpreting "But, if you had your way, this lady would answer in court for what she has not been warned to answer by writ. Therefore she shall be warned by writ of the articles of which she is to answer, and this is the law of the land." Case at 196.

[152] Interpreting "Then arose the King, who was very wise, and said: 'I have nothing to do with your disputations, but, God's blood! you shall give me a good writ before you arise hence.'" Case at 196–197.

[153] 17 Selden Society 166. The case does not disclose the identity of the person who has taken possession because the courtroom argument focuses on the plaintiff's right, not the defendant's. The text's assumption that Adam is the grantor's son makes the case easier to understand.

Adam's father gave the farm to Bogo and his surviving child, but if Bogo died childless, Cosmo got the farm.[155] Cosmo said Bogo died childless. His description satisfied his writ's criteria.

[2] Adam: Produce the deed.

[3] *The Reporter*: The deed didn't match Cosmo's description: "Adam's father gives the farm to Bogo and his surviving child. If Bogo dies childless, Adam's father gets it back for the rest of his life, and then Cosmo gets it."

[4] Adam: The deed has an extra step—my father gets it back. The contradiction between your writ and the deed means you lose.

[5] Cosmo: Chancery doesn't sell a writ that includes the extra step. But Chancery sells two different writs that together describe your father's plan. Chancery sells a writ that says he could give me the farm if Bogo died childless. Chancery also sells a writ that says he could take it back if Bogo died childless. Your father just put the two grants together. {The court should be reasonable and uphold the grant. The common law has always allowed each of the steps, and his intentions are clear. There's no reason to reject the grant.}[156] I've

---

[154] Writ of formedon in the remainder. The writ says the grantor gave land to a person and her surviving child, but since no child survived, the land belonged to a third person the grantor identified, the plaintiff.

[155] A fee tail. If the recipient dies without a surviving child either the land goes back to the grantor and his heirs (a fee tail with a reversion) or the land goes to a third person and his heirs (a fee tail with a remainder).

[156] The text makes explicit an argument Cosmo must have made.

> chosen the closest Chancery writ and the court should enforce this sensible deed.[157]
>
> [6] Justice Bereford: Do you think a seller can create whatever kind of interest in land he wants?[158]
>
> [7] Cosmo: He can if he uses clear language and the grant doesn't violate public policy.[159]
>
> [8] Justice Bereford: The grant violates an important policy. According to our rules, once the land comes back to the seller no subsequent interest can exist—he takes it back in absolute ownership. We won't enforce a deed that purports to give away the land, take it back, and then give it away again.[160]

Bereford insists on the letter rather than the spirit of the law. The court won't get involved in the business of interpreting whatever land grant someone concocts. Land transactions are too important to generate that kind of uncertainty.[161] The court insists that deeds must conform

---

[157] In addition to adding a rationale, the paragraph interprets "They challenge our writ because it makes no mention of the reversion; but reversion and remainder cannot stand together in one writ, for one can find no such writ in the Chancery. Wherefore etc. And again, if we were ousted from this writ, we should be barred forever, which would be a hardship, since no other writ can we find. Judgment etc." Case at 167.

[158] Interpreting "If the form [of the gift] were 'tailed' in a manner not allowed by law, do you think to be aided by a writ which is given by law?" Case at 168.

[159] Interpreting "But this is not contrary to law." Case at 168.

[160] The paragraph interprets "Yes it is; for if tenements which are given in fee tail have returned to the giver, then every kind of 'tail' is extinct. How then can you afterwards demand anything by means of the 'tail'?" Case at 168.

[161] Despite its insistence on clarity in land transactions the court rejected overly technical arguments. A litigant claimed a grant by A.

to a limited number of templates—the writs Chancery sells to enforce land grants.

in frank marriage to Robert and his daughter Matilda was defective: "And the 'his' was challenged; for the 'his' ought to be referred to the last person, and that was Robert, and consequently he married his own daughter: so it ought to have said, "With Matilda 'daughter of the aforesaid A.' Nevertheless the writ was held good, because the 'his' ought to be construed in the fittest way by which it could be understood." 5 31a Rolls Series 246, 248 (1306).

CHAPTER 3

The King, Parliament, and King's Bench

BY CREATING NEW COMMON LAW RULES Bereford's court invaded the authority of other branches of government. Both the king and Parliament—the executive and the legislature—made laws the court could not question. Other parts of government tasked with overseeing the legal system had power over Common Pleas. Chancery wrote the writs that controlled access to the court.[1] The Court of King's Bench had the right to review Common Pleas' decisions. Hemmed in from start to finish Bereford's decisions might have been just a subordinate judge's intemperate fulminations. Power, however, flows to those with an appetite for power. Neither the king nor Parliament fought to protect their authority against Bereford's innovations. As for the court's two significant competitors—King's Bench and Chancery[2]—Bereford outfoxed them both and took away their power.

---

[1] Occasionally a litigant could avoid buying a writ by procuring an order directly from the king, Parliament, or the Court of Common Pleas itself.

[2] The next chapter discusses his duel with Chancery.

The King

A monarch with absolute power could ignore court decisions.[3] Unless the king volunteered to respect his courts[4] nothing but an armed revolt could force his hand. Bracton thought scripture would convince the king to kneel before the law.

> But the king himself ought not to be subject to man, but subject to God and to the law, for the law makes the king. Let the king, therefore, attribute to the law what the law attributes to him, namely dominion and power, for there is no king where the will and not the law has dominion; and that he ought to be under the law, since he is the vicar of God, appears evidently after the likeness of Jesus Christ {who} was willing to be under the law, that he might redeem those who were under the law, for he was not willing to use his strength, but his reason and judgment. So likewise the Blessed Virgin Mary, the parent of God, the mother of our Lord, who by a singular privilege was above the law, nevertheless, in order to show an example of humility, she did not refuse to be subject to the institutions of law. So therefore {the king's} power should not be unrestrained...[5]

---

[3] "To a writ of right brought against the abbot ... it was answered the tenements were in the king's hands... Plaintiff: Although the tenements were seized into his hands ... you ought ... to answer. Justice Brumpton. ... inasmuch as we cannot entertain the suit while the tenements are seized, I advise you {to} send to Court and purchase permission; for we will hold no such plea before we are commanded to." 3 31a Rolls Series 170, 170–171 (1302).

[4] He often chose to litigate his rights. *See, e.g.*, 122 Selden Society 286 (1285).

[5] 1Bracton, *De Legibus et Consuetudinibus Angliae* 39–41 (Travers Twiss translation 1878).

Religious imagery or reference was noteworthy in its absence from Common Pleas judgments. But Bracton's exhortation apparently bore fruit when Edward I proclaimed his intention to abase himself.

1. (1290).[6]

> King Edward ordered the sheriff to arrest John Brampton and bring him before the king and his council.[7] He accused Brampton of forging his seal and orders. Upon hearing of the proceedings Brampton appeared.[8] He said the king had violated his right to due process of law. According to Brampton the common law provided three ways to resolve accusations of crime. The accused could be indicted by the {grand} jury;[9] the victim could challenge the accused to battle; an accused person taken in the act could be punished on the spot. None of these procedures had been used. Instead the king had just concocted an order to force him to appear.
>
> The king's council asked William Bereford to transmit the pertinent documents.
>
> The king proclaims to all his subjects that he and his council have dismissed the king's case. Brampton's

---

[6] Select Cases in the Court of King's Bench, 57 Selden Society 25.
[7] Interpreting "To have his body before the king … to do and receive etc." Case at 6.
[8] The text interprets "Afterwards the aforesaid John of Brampton comes and says…" to mean Brampton voluntarily appeared before the king's council.
[9] The presentment jury, the precursor to the modern grand jury.

> arguments about due process of law are right. The king's order is void. Brampton is acquitted.[10]

How remarkable. Edward submits to the law. Bracton had said the king should "attribute to the law what the law attributes to him, namely dominion and power, for there is no king where the will and not the law has dominion."[11] Too bad Bracton did not live to see the day when his words bore fruit.

Maybe the case is just a bit too remarkable. Edward brings an ill-conceived proceeding against some forger. Somehow the miscreant manages to have not just an ordinary court consider his fate; instead he appears before the king and the other rulers of the country. By coincidence Bereford is on hand to give advice. The decision is not put to bed in a court record. A proclamation goes out to the nation. Devoted to the rule of law, the king sets free a forger of royal documents. Perhaps Edward and his consigliere had decided to let the country know they were ruled by a constitutional monarch. Perhaps the case is really a press release. Brampton had the good luck to be the right forger at the right time at the right place.

Despite his part in this show Bereford does not seem to have taken it seriously. He admired the king's tirade against the Countess of Albermarle.[12] If the king told him

---

[10] Interpreting the final sentence in the report "And be it known that judgment is rendered here by command of the lord king and by ordinance of the same king's council." *Ibid.*

[11] 1 Bracton 39–41, *supra.*

[12] 20 Selden Society 193 (1310).

to jump Bereford never said "my lord, have you observed due process?"[13]

2. (1311)[14]

> [1] As his cousin's heir, Adam sued[15] the abbot to recover a farm.
>
> [2] Abbot's lawyer: The abbot has immunity from suit.
>
> [3] *The Reporter*: The lawyer gave the court a royal order that said "We have taken the abbot into our protection. While he's abroad during the coming year he can't be sued."[16]
>
> [4] Adam: The immunity's worthless. The king doesn't say the abbot is on state business. If the court upholds this the king can nullify any claim. The Magna Carta says the crown guarantees "to no one will we sell, to no one will we refuse or delay right of justice."[17]
>
> [5] Chief Justice Bereford: If the king tells us not to hear a case we won't. We sit in his place and we will do his bidding.[18]

---

[13] Elsewhere a cynical reporter observes "Note, the Justices did this rather for the King's profit than in accordance with law; for they gave this decision '*in terrorem*.'" 3 31a Rolls Series 502,506 (1302).
[14] 63 Selden Society 6.
[15] Writ of cosinage.
[16] "Except for circuit court inquiries and claims for widow's portions, recent dispossessions of land, and appointments to church livings." Paraphrasing the record at 8.
[17] Magna Carta c. 29 (1225) (3 EHD 345).
[18] Interpreting "The king, in whose place we are, has sent word to us that the abbot is quit of all kinds of pleas; and if the king had sent word to us that we should not hold any plea here, could we hold pleas against the order of the king? (*as if to say,* No.)" Case at 7.

In another case Bereford said "If you could appeal to legal principle you would be right, but against the king, who is above the law, you cannot rely upon legal principles."[19] If, however, Bereford believed the king's representatives had misinterpreted applicable law, Bereford would enforce the correct rules despite their erroneous contentions on behalf of the king.[20]

Even though Bereford acknowledged the king's unlimited power he had little reason to worry about royal interference with his campaign to revise the law.[21] The king's agenda included raising revenue, organizing armies, dominating domestic rivals, and treating with foreign powers. He did not have much time to meddle with his subjects private rights.

Parliament

Early in Edward's reign Parliament revised the common law extensively.[22] Maitland says that after Edward's death Parliament put off making further revisions.[23] He does not explain why. This book does.

---

[19] "If you could appeal to legal principle what you say would be well enough, but against the King, who is above the law, you cannot rely on legal principles." 41 Selden Society 73, 74 (1315). In another case the king's lawyer successfully argued, "The King is prerogative; so no prescription of time runs against him." "Right" 1 31a Rolls Series 68 (1292).

[20] *See, e.g.*, 43 Selden Society 38 (1313) and 54 Selden Society 45 (1317).

[21] From time to time the king might take cognizance of a case just by means of a royal request. *See, e.g.*, 29 Selden Society 90, 91 (1313–1314). A notable royal interference appears in 5 31a Rolls Series 52 (1305) discussed below.

[22] Statute of Westminster II (1285) (3 EHD 428).

[23] "Only some slight power of varying the ancient formulas {the writs} will be conceded to the chancellor; all that goes beyond this

Bereford took away the incentive to legislate. The legislators ignored private rights not for lack of power but for lack of interest.[24] A modern adage probably explains their thinking. "If it ain't broke, don't fix it."

In 1311 Parliament created a route for losing litigants to complain to Parliament.[25] Few litigants used it and just eleven years later the statute was repealed.[26] The following case shows how Bereford tried to persuade the legislators they did not want to know how he made sausage.

Today's guardian puts the ward's income into a trust fund. The medieval guardian[27] kept the ward's income for himself.[28] Upset that their children got nothing, landowners asked their lawyers for help. One lawyer had a plan. He had his client sell his land to a corporation. The corporation agreed to a two tiered payment. When the recipient was an adult the corporation paid more than the land was worth. When the recipient was a minor the corporation paid nothing. If the actuaries did their job right the overall payments would be fair market value. No one would lose. That is, no one but the guardian. He got what the corporation paid a minor: nothing. The lawyer did not think about unintended consequences. Lawyers are a conservative bunch for a reason. New ideas may

---

must be done by statutes, and, when Edward I is dead, statutes will do little for our ordinary private law." 2 P&M 564.

[24] Parliament even enjoyed the power to create writs itself, a power not often invoked. For an unusual example *see* 54 Selden Society 58 (1317).

[25] Parliament invited litigants to seek review of cases in which the justices were not unanimous. The New Ordinances, 1311, c. 29 (1311) (3 EHD 536).

[26] Statute of York, repealing the Ordinances of 1311 (1322) (3 EHD 543–544).

[27] The discussion speaks about a guardian in military tenure.

[28] But if the king demanded support for his military adventures, the guardian had to pay.

seem attractive but they always carry a risk of unintended consequences.

3. (1312)[29]

> [1] Since the Priory had always paid her late husband three pounds a year Anna sued[30] the prior for her widow's share, a lifetime right to a pound a year.[31]
>
> [2] Prior: According to the court settlement by which we did the deal we pay nothing while the recipient is a minor.[32] Your husband's dead and your son, his heir, is underage. We'll pay you when the boy turns twenty-one.[33]
>
> [3] Anna: {The common law protects widows.} If some transaction seems to eliminate her rights the courts ignore the provision. Suppose a father gives land to his son and his surviving child. The deal's language indicates the father gets the land back the moment the son dies childless. The son's widow still gets her share.[34]

---

[29] 33 Selden Society 81 (1312). The facts have been simplified. *See also* 63 Selden Society 30 (1311) and 34 Selden Society 46 (1312–1313) which appear to be different cases, but may in fact be different reports of the same case. Bereford also asks for Parliament's advice in 19 Selden Society 43 (1311), another obscure legal battle that would bore most legislators. In contrast 63 Selden Society 121 (1311) addresses a controversy they would have cared about.

[30] Writ of dower.

[31] "Dower," the widow's portion, provides a lifetime right to one third of the land her late husband possessed at any time during their marriage. Without discussion the court views an annual rent as "land."

[32] In military tenure by a sham judicial proceeding that created a judgment embodying the terms of the deal.

[33] The paragraph interprets "You cannot up to now claim aught, for see here a fine..." Case at 81.

[34] Interpreting "If tenements be given to a man and to the heirs begotten of his body ... yet even in such case the wife will have her

[4] Prior: You don't understand the court's rationale. The father can't take back the land because the widow might be pregnant—his son might still leave a "surviving child." {Once she takes her share he can't complain if she doesn't give birth. Once she has acquired a lifetime right, subsequent events can't defeat it.}[35] But your case is different. Let's say you married an underage boy whose father had just died. We wouldn't pay the boy anything and we wouldn't pay you anything if the boy expired before he turned twenty-one. Your case is the same.

[5] Anna: You want to talk hypothetical cases? Suppose my child was an adult right now. You'd pay me my pound. Suppose he then died survived by an infant. You'd have to keep on paying me even though you would have no obligation to pay two pounds to my son's underage child. This is the same.[36]

[6] Prior: Actually all these argument are beside the point. This problem isn't widows' rights. The problem is whether deals done by court settlements will be

---

dower, because the husband was so seised that he could endow her, notwithstanding the condition made by the donor…" Case at 82.

[35] The text adds the rationale.

[36] Interpreting "The wife would recover by the assize of novel disseisin, the nonage of the heir notwithstanding; and since she would recover, the nonage of the heir notwithstanding, because she had been seised, by parity of reasoning she ought now to be answered, notwithstanding the nonage of the heir etc. Judgment etc." Case at 83. The widow's lawyer tries to change the focus of the "possession" argument. In the case itself the widow never possessed a widow's share; her lawyer's hypothetical creates a widow who would in fact be in possession of a share. The widow's hypothetical is a variation on the fee tail rule. Once the widow got possession of her dower, she would keep it.

enforced. A statute says they must be.[37] The court can't ignore the statute.[38]

[7] Anna: Why should I be bound by the deal? My husband's father did the deal. He couldn't represent me. I wasn't even born. I've got no blood relationship with him. How can the court let someone like that shred my safety net?[39]

[8] Chief Justice Bereford: The statute seems to tell us to enforce the deal.[40] {But then we've always favored widows' claims.}[41] This is a difficult problem for which Parliament can provide helpful advice.[42]

[9] *The Reporter*: After debate Parliament said Anna wouldn't get her widow's share until her son turned twenty-one.

Bereford relentlessly pursues power. Uncharacteristically he defers his decision for advice from Parliament. He is thinking strategically. The case cannot have a satisfying outcome. The decision must shred either

---

[37] Statute "of fines levied" (1299) (3 EHD 491).

[38] Interpreting "She would be barred by the fine, as she is now." Case at 83.

[39] The paragraph interprets "since none other than the heirs are privy to the fine" case at 82.

[40] Interpreting "The statute enacteth that the provisions of a fine are to be maintained, notwithstanding that by the common law the wife ought to have dower…." Case at 83.

[41] An implicit point from the context.

[42] The paragraph interprets "But, because the circumstances are uncommon, there is need for much consideration; and so sue you out a bill to the Parliament." Case at 83. The statute that called for review by Parliament spoke of disagreements among the justices. The New Ordinances, 1311, c. 29 (1311) (3EHD 536). There is no apparent disagreement here. Bereford does not even acknowledge the statute as he submits the case to Parliament.

the security of land deals or the widow's safety net. In contrast to a modern legislature filled with lawyers the medieval legislators would hardly enjoy unravelling this knot. Nor would their decision have any lasting importance. The next lawyer who decides to cheat a guardian will include an express provision about widows' rights. Bereford wants Parliament to learn that tears can be shed over answered prayers. A few years later the legislators repealed the statute that gave them appellate authority.[43] Common Pleas, the honorable members decided, could keep its work to itself.

King's Bench

Although legal subtleties might not excite the appetite of king and Parliament, the Court of King's Bench focused upon complex problems and enjoyed appellate authority over Bereford's Court of Common Pleas.[44] Had King's Bench exercised effective review, King's Bench would have created the common law. Bereford would offer tentative theories; King's Bench would declare binding judgments.[45] To be supreme Bereford had to

---

[43] Statute of York, repealing the Ordinances of 1311 (1322) (EHD 544).

[44] Statute of Westminster II, c. 31 (1285) (3 EHD at 447). Holdsworth discusses King's Bench's authority under the statute in 63 Selden Society xxviii. Of King's Bench Sayles says, "To them also belongs authority to correct the errors of all the other judges…" Select Cases from King's Bench, 57 Selden Society xxxiv. King's Bench reviewed Common Pleas decisions before the statute was enacted. *See ibid.* c. For an example *see* 112 Selden Society 271 (1287). For a reference to a King's Bench reversal of a Common Pleas decision, *see* 20 Selden Society 46 (1310).

[45] The pervasive appellate authority King's Bench might have exercised appears in a case decided before the consent under duress tactic was widely used. 112 Selden Society 271 (1287) (Weyland, C.J., Common Pleas; Brabazon, J., King's Bench).

emasculate King's Bench. He did. He persuaded litigants to "volunteer" not to appeal.[46]

In taking King's Bench out of the picture Bereford took the strategy that allowed the jury to replace divine intervention as the decision maker. Until late in the twelfth century most criminal complaints began when a victim made an accusation.[47] The question of the defendant's guilt was then decided by an "ordeal" in which God intervened. God favored litigants who won battles, or carried red hot irons comfortably, or sank into welcoming ponds.[48] Some skeptics put a spoke in the divine wheel of justice. They told the king the supposed victim had made a malicious accusation and therefore their case was not ripe for the judgment of God.

4. (1206)[49]

> Adam accuses[50] Bogo of robbery {and challenges him to battle.}[51] Bogo pays the king to impanel a jury to decide if Adam made the charge maliciously. The jury says he did and Bogo is acquitted.

---

[46] When the court was not worried about reversal, the court would enter judgment. *See, e.g.*, 34 Selden Society 40 (1312). In 22 Selden Society 56 (1310) a litigant challenged the court to go on record. Justice Stanton took up the challenge. "If you say that as law, we will give answer enough. Justice Stanton: We say that as law, for life and death." After the court took up the challenge, however, the litigant agreed to go to the jury, thereby waiving a right to appeal.

[47] In 1166 the Assize of Clarendon created the alternative of government indictment.

[48] *See* T.F.T. Plucknett, *Concise History of the Common Law* 113–118 (5th ed. 1956).

[49] 1 Selden Society 51 (1206).

[50] An "appeal."

[51] The proof method by which the charge is conventionally resolved.

Soon bold defendants paid to have a jury decide not just malice but rather the ultimate question of guilt.

5. (1221)[52]

> Accused of robbery, Adam pays the king to impanel a jury to determine his guilt. The jurors say he is a robber. He will be hanged.

Adam may have been disappointed by the outcome but he had to climb the gallows anyway. He had asked for the verdict. At about the same time the jury took greater prominence. Other influences were diminishing the importance of divine intervention in secular litigation. In 1215 a church council told the clergy to stop supervising procedures to uncover God's will in criminal cases.[53] By a happy coincidence a version of the common law jury had recently made its debut.[54] But what could be done with defendants who refused to put their fate in the hands of the jury? In 1285 Parliament said they should be locked up until they decided to consent.[55]

6. (1302)[56]

> [1] *The Reporter*: Accused of various felonies, Adam wouldn't say if he wanted a jury.

---

[52] 53 Selden Society 589 (1221). The superiority of this method of proof so quickly achieved widespread approval that the Magna Carta guaranteed a criminal defendant's right to a jury trial. *See* William Sharp McKechnie, *Magna Carta* 359–367 (2d. edition 1914).

[53] *See* Maitland, *Introduction to Peas of the Crown for the County of Gloucester* xxxvi–xli (1221).

[54] *See* Donald Sutherland, *The Assize of Novel Disseisin* 5 (1973).

[55] Statute of Westminster 1, c. 12 (1275) (3 EHD 400).

[56] 3 31a Rolls Series 510. The text rearranges part of the report.

[2] The Justice: Can he talk?

[3] The Jury: He can, but he doesn't want to.

[4] *The Reporter*: The court said he needed to suffer penance {until he made up his mind}. He would be locked up and iron would be piled onto his body. He could eat and drink only on alternate days, and his thirst would be quenched by stagnant water.[57]

Consent

Common Pleas did not need to be so blatant. Why shout when you can whisper? A widow sues to get her rights.[58] Her son refuses to provide her anything—he points to a statute that says an adulterer forfeits her widow's portion. She says she was abused. If Common Pleas says abuse justifies adultery King's Bench might reverse the decision as licentious. But suppose the judge says to the son "She tells a tragic story. What should we do?" The court is not asking a question. The court is punching the boy on the chin. The court has decided an abused wife can leave and seek solace without forfeiting her widow's share. But the court does not want to go on record. If the son understands Common Pleas practice he will know he is supposed to answer, "A jury will say my father never abused my mother." Common Pleas has never ruled on content of the common law. The son has volunteered to stake his case on the factual question he

---

[57] Interpreting "He was adjudged to suffer penance, namely, that he should be put in a house on the ground in his shirt, laden with as much iron as he could bear, and that he should have nothing to drink on the day when he had anything to eat, and that he should drink water which came from neither foundation nor river." Case at 510.
[58] *See* 1 31a Rolls Series 182 (1292).

has formulated. He has consented to the jury, and he has no point of law to appeal to King's Bench.[59]

The reporters are interested in difficult cases and difficult cases have the greatest potential for appeal. Many reported cases end in fake jury submissions.

7. (1310)[60]

> [1] When Adam got married his father deeded a farm to him "and his surviving child." Later Adam convinced

---

[59] "Often in the course of pleadings arguments were put forward which failed to recommend themselves to the judges and were accordingly quashed. These rejected pleas were not entered on the roll and could not be made the basis of any future writ of error, which had to confine itself strictly to allegations of error in the record itself." 57 Selden Society c (1938) (introduction by G. O. Sayles). If he does not like the jury verdict, he can bring an attaint proceeding against them. But he has no way to complain about the court's hint.

[60] 22 Selden Society 165. The actual reason for the father's reconsideration is complex. At the end of the case the reporter says the gift was in fee tail to both Adam and his first wife, but when she died and Adam remarried, the father decided to redo the gift. A digression into these complications would serve no useful purpose. Therefore the text provides a simple explanation for the change. The text also ignores a legal complication in the case. It may be that Adam sold the land to Bogo with a guarantee that purported to bind his son. His son, however, can escape the guarantee because he is only bound to the extent that he has inherited from Adam, and he has not. "Bogo: We tell you that you are the heir of Adam. Son: We have nothing to do with Adam's deed because we do not demand through him nor as his heir {because my claim is based upon the gift my grandfather gave me.}" (case at 165). Justice Stanton: He claims an estate by the form {of the fee tail}. So it behoves you Bogo to say more than that he is his father's heir: you must say he inherited assets from his father or else he does not have to guarantee his father's outright sale of the farm to you." (case at 166). Finally the reader of the original report may experience some confusion because of the case reference to a "reversion." The text's simplification excises the problem because it gives Bogo outright ownership. In fact he bought only a life estate with a "reversion" (in modern jargon a "remainder") to a third person.

his father he needed to sell the place, a sale the deed banned.[61] His father executed a second deed[62] that gave Adam outright ownership. Adam then sold the place to Bogo. After Adam died, his son sued[63] Bogo. He said a jury would find his grandfather's first deed had given him an interest that no second deed could invalidate.

[2] Bogo: The common law doesn't let a jury decide this case. I've shown the court a deed. The only proof allowed against a deed is another deed. Twelve neighbors can't second-guess a document.[64]

[3] Justice Stanton: The son says he can't find the first deed—don't you think a jury should be able to decide what his grandfather did? What do you say, Bogo, wouldn't that be fair?[65]

[4] Bogo: Of course if you want to enter a judgment that twelve bystanders have more credibility than a sealed instrument on parchment, I'll bow to your wishes. But until you do I'm standing by the common law rule that no jury can contradict a deed.[66]

---

[61] Because it would abrogate his surviving child's interest.

[62] Stanton says "it may be after the charter in tail he made a charter in fee simple." Case at 165. The Selden Society editors footnote the passage with the comment "But there does not seem to have been any such charter." Footnote 3 page 165. The text adopts Stanton's view that a charter was executed.

[63] Writ of formedon in the descender.

[64] Interpreting "And as they have nothing for the form other than wind against our charter, which witnesses fee simple, we demand judgment whether they can have action." Case at 168.

[65] Interpreting "Justice Stanton: Will you accept the averment?" Case at 167.

[66] Interpreting "If you award it, we will take it willingly." Case at 167.

> [5] Justice Stanton: If you insist on a judgment you'll regret it.[67]

> [6] Bogo: Well, since you put it that way I'm not going to insist. I'll go to a jury. Of course this litigation will end with the statement that "the parties agreed to have a jury decide whether the grandfather made two gifts." Everyone knows that's the same as a court judgment that the common law rule allows a jury's speculation to contradict a deed.[68]

The conventional common law rule says a deed can be answered only by another deed. Stanton does not want to enter a judgment violating this rule but he has a good reason for thinking the son deserves a different rule. When someone makes a gift of land he gives the recipient the deed in case some controversy comes up later.[69]

---

[67] Interpreting both "You must concede it yourselves, for we do not award it." (version II at 167) and "Justice Stanton: If we award it, you well know at what peril it will be." (version III at 169). Maitland and Turner remark "On the one hand Stanton does not desire to decide a point of law, and on the other hand, Herle, fearing perhaps his client's displeasure, wishes not to make any voluntary concession." (footnote 2 at 167). Maitland and Turner do not understand that Herle wants the court to take responsibility for contradicting the axiom of evidence law that a deed can only be met by another deed. Instead they impute to Herle the improbable goal of client management.

[68] Interpreting both "We shall have what is equivalent of a judgment, for the enrolment will say 'let an inquest be made.' So it is all one." (version II at 167) and "Bogo: [Well] you will say 'Therefore be there a jury,' and that is an award." (version III at 169).

[69] "If you are the purchaser, the deed remains with you." 22 Selden Society 164 (1310). *See also* 41 Selden Society 85 (1315), 38 Selden Society 88, 89 (1312–1313) (III). Perhaps, however, Adam's father kept the deed because he had retained a reversion. In another case Justice Hertford so suggested as regards a gift in frank marriage. 2 31a Rolls Series 398, 402 (1294). Regarding a grant in fee tail

When Adam's father first gave him the farm he also gave him the deed. Once Adam got his father's second deed he threw the first into the fire. Why would he preserve evidence that showed he had cheated his son?[70] Stanton knows this but Stanton does not want to go on record with a bald statement that a jury can contradict a deed. King's Bench might not agree. He protects himself against appeal by making Bogo "consent" to a jury verdict about the missing deed.

Although the loser capitulates by asking for a jury he gains something[71]—time to negotiate a settlement.[72] The victor will take less than he deserves. Juries are

---

Bereford said "Peradventure the deed remaineth with {the grantor}." 36 Selden Society 139, 140 (1313). Stanton would have applied the same rationale nonetheless because Adam's father would have destroyed the first deed after Adam persuaded him to execute a second deed.

[70] If a donor of a fee tail makes a second gift in fee simple the second gift eliminates the donor's reversion but does not abrogate the interest of the recipient's issue. *See* 42 Selden Society 67, 70 (1311) (Bingham).

[71] Sometimes neither party is confident about the likely jury verdict, and the report chronicles their settlement. "Reporter: The case was submitted to the jury as defined by Justice Brumpton, but the parties were not confident as to the outcome, and therefore before the jury had a chance to render its verdict, they settled." 3 31a Rolls Series 228, 228–230 (1302).

[72] *E.g.*, "Justice Spigurnel: Await your judgments etc. And, as you know very well what judgment you will have, come to terms with {the clearly victorious party.}" 29 Selden Society 90, 92 (1313–1314). In addition to getting time to settle, the losing party avoids the penalties imposed upon a losing litigant. *See* 4 31a Rolls Series 258 (1304). Until the court enters judgment, there is no loser. By settling the loser avoids a judgment against him. In an unusual case a plaintiff insisted on a judgment, a judgment that went against her; but she apparently suffered no additional penalty. 2 31a Rolls Series 330, 334 (1294).

unpredictable. Life is uncertain—people die; [73] even worse, they go bankrupt.[74] A rational person will give a discount to experience the joy of immediate satisfaction.

8. (1302)[75]

[1] Adam sued[76] Bogo for cheating him in various ways. After Bogo lost a defense based upon a technicality[77] he conceded he owed eight years rent, but said a jury would find he didn't owe any more than that.[78]

[2] Adam: Your honor, tell him to pay me the eight years now. He's admitted he owes it and whatever happens I'm entitled to at least that much.[79]

[3] Justice Malore: You and Bogo have both asked for a jury. We won't enter a judgment until we hear their verdict.[80]

[4] Adam: That's not fair. I could wind up with nothing. If Bogo dies before the jury comes back my case will just be dismissed.[81]

---

[73] The victor will have to start all over. 45 Selden Society 133 (note #1) (1313–1316).
[74] That is, judgment proof. No proceeding like modern bankruptcy existed.
[75] 3 31a Rolls Series 30 (1302). Although Bogo is Adam's socage guardian, the text avoids so identifying him in order to postpone the discussion of the difference between military and socage guardians.
[76] A writ to force a guardian in socage to account.
[77] He said his late wife was the socage guardian, and the plaintiff had failed to join her executors as defendants.
[78] "For these eight years' rents … we are ready to account." Case at 32.
[79] "For what he has acknowledged we pray that he may render an account." Case at 32.
[80] Interpreting "You shall wait here until the inquisition is taken etc." Case at 32.

[5] *The Reporter*: Adam then told Bogo he would accept seven rather than eight years rent if Bogo paid immediately.

Duress

Lawyers benefit from cordial relationships with the judiciary but lawyers cannot sell out their clients. Lawyers knew that if they insisted upon a judgment rather than taking a jury verdict on a losing question their clients would suffer.

9. (1310–1311)[82]

[1] Adam sued[83] Bogo. He said Bogo refused to turn over a deed he had given him for safekeeping. When Bogo denied getting the deed, Adam produced character witnesses, and challenged Bogo to do the same.[84]

---

[81] Interpreting "See what a risk that would be, for by the death of Bogo, if he should die before the inquest is taken {*i.e.*, the jury returns its verdict} Adam's action would be at an end etc." Regarding the death of a litigant, Bereford elsewhere said, "This is an original writ, and the {defendant has died,} and therefore upon this writ a judgment cannot be made ... Justice Scrope: {The plaintiff} should sue a new original speedily, for this court cannot do anything else." 45 Selden Society 133 (note #1) (1313–1316). If the case involved multiple parties the dangers were exponentially larger. 1 31a Rolls Series 222–224 (1292).

[82] 26 Selden Society 15. The report's facts as reflected in the record suggest a complex intra-family dispute. Rather than speculate about the convoluted facts, the text ignores the context and just focuses on the legal question.

[83] Writ of detinue of charters.

[84] Interpreting "Counted in a detinue of charters, and said at the close of his count, 'If he wish to deny it he has good suit,' and he did not say in whose presence he delivered the charters." Case at 15.

[2] Bogo: I'll take that challenge. Here are my character witnesses.[85]

[3] Adam: That's not good enough. Three neighbors saw what we did. Since the facts have come to public attention the court should ask a jury what happened.[86]

[4] Bogo: You challenged me to character witnesses, and I accepted your challenge. That's the end of any discussion about the right type of proof.[87]

[5] Adam: I made a mistake in the way I pled my case but my inheritance of land turns on whether I can get the deed back. With so much at stake a jury makes sense. The court should let me change my mind about the correct form of proof.[88]

[6] Justice Stanton: Look, Bogo, he says there were witnesses. Shouldn't he get to a jury?

[7] Bogo: According to the pleading rules once I accept my opponent's challenge he can't change his mind.

[8] Chief Justice Bereford: I think you should accept a jury.[89]

[9] Bogo: Not unless your judgment forces me to.

---

[85] Interpreting "We are ready to deny that he delivered any charters to us to guard." Case at 15.
[86] Interpreting "We delivered our charters in the presence of A., J., and C." Case at 15.
[87] Interpreting "To that you will not come now, for in answer to what you have counted we have defended by our law." Case at 16. The word "law" refers to character witnesses.
[88] Interpreting "Detinue of charters is much in the nature of disinheritance. Judgment if such an action should be tried by wager of law." Case at 16.
[89] Interpreting "Will you have a jury or not?" Case at 16.

> [10] Chief Justice Bereford: Are we supposed to enter a judgment just because you want one?[90]
>
> [11] Justice Stanton: By the blood that God shed if you insist on a judgment you'll rue the day. If we decide Adam deserved a jury we're not going to call one. We'll just enter a judgment that you took the deed and refused to return it. You'll give it back and we'll make sure you pay damages and court costs.[91]
>
> [12] Bogo: Wait, give me a jury.[92]

Most litigants behaved.[93] Bereford taught the legal profession that they were wise to waive their right to appeal.[94]

---

[90] Interpreting "Ought we to make an award on every word you say, *meaning,* No?" [sic]. The Anglo-Norman text correctly puts the question mark after "*vous dites*."
[91] Interpreting "By the blood which God shed if we make an award, we will award you undefended."
[92] Interpreting "Ready are we etc. that he has delivered to us any charter." Case at 16.
[93] When a litigant wanted the court to enter judgment about the interpretation of a deed Bereford said if he insisted on a judgment, if the judgment went against him, he would not be able to say he had inherited nothing from the grantor, and therefore should not be bound by the deed. The litigant then asked for a jury. 5 31a Rolls Series 332 (1306). Another litigant tried to recover two years of an annuity by a writ of debt rather than by the conventional writ for an annuity. The defendant argued the plaintiff was attempting to recover a freehold by a writ of debt. Discouraging the plaintiff from using the writ, Bereford said if he insisted, the court's judgment for the accrued two years would extinguish any future claim for further installments. The plaintiff agreed to abandon his writ in order to refile a conventional annuity claim. 27 Selden Society 50 (1313–1314). The court's use of duress was openly described. "And, against his will, he {the lawyer} was made by the court to answer this." 5 31a Rolls Series 492, 494 (1307). "Justice Stanton: You have done well; for you did

10. (1313)[95]

[1] Adam's father sold a farm to Bogo. The deed said "I have sold my farm to Bogo and his heirs. My heir will guarantee the title forever."[96] When Bogo's heir got ejected from the land he asked the court to make Adam stand by the guarantee.

[2] Adam: I won't. The deed's first sentence says the farm has been sold to "Bogo and his heirs." The second sentence says "My heir will guarantee the title forever." As my father's heir I have to guarantee only "Bogo's title." The deed doesn't create a guarantee that Bogo's heirs can use.[97]

---

spontaneously what the law would have driven you to do." 17 Selden Society 54, 55 (1308–1309).

[94] *E.g.*, "Toudeby {arguing his client need not undertake a warranty} Sir, if you adjudge etc. {my client will undertake the warranty}. Justice Bereford: If we give judgment we shall give it with the benefit attaching {*i.e.*, if we enter the judgment you insist upon, you won't be able to present any other defense such as the argument your client never actually transferred the land}. Reporter: And at last he warranted {without the court entering a judgment}." 5 31a Rolls Series 332, 334 (1306).

[95] 43 Selden Society 15. In order to present the controversy in its simplest form the text avoids a discussion of the reason Bogo's son vouches to warranty. The report suggests that after Bogo's son inherited the farm Adam's mother sued him for her widow's portion. He then vouched Adam's son to warranty. Version I says Adam had enfeoffed Bogo, but version II says Bogo "proffered a deed with a warranty clause made by Adam's father." Case at 17.

[96] Interpreting "I and my heirs will warrant and defend against all men for ever etc." Case at 16.

[97] Interpreting "Nor are we bound by the warranty clause to warrant, for it does not specify any person whom we are bound to warrant, as, for example, it might have specified some definite person and his heirs and assigns; but since it does not specify anyone in certain we ask judgment whether we are bound to warrant {anyone other than Bogo himself.}" Case at 16. A grant imposed an obligation to

[3] Chief Justice Bereford: The deed says the title will be guaranteed "forever." "Forever" means all Bogo's heirs can use the guarantee.[98]

[4] Adam: I won't honor the guarantee unless you enter a judgment forcing me to.[99]

[5] Chief Justice Bereford: As you wish. Here's the judgment. Pay Bogo's heir what the sheriff says.[100]

[6] Adam: Your judgment has to be revised. The sheriff made a major mistake. Instead of figuring out what the land was worth all those years ago when father sold it he just looked at its present value.[101] The acres were a wasteland when father sold them. Bogo's father transformed the place. He dug marl into the soil and he put up outbuildings. When sold the place was worth four pence an acre. The sheriff mistakenly assessed it at twelve pence an acre, its present value. I'll pay, but I'll pay at the four pence rate.[102]

---

warrant "heirs and assigns." Justice Cave said the assign of an assign could not use the warranty. 1 31a Rolls Series 232, 234 (1292).

[98] Interpreting "The warranty clause says that you are bound to warrant…against all persons, and that makes it clear enough that the feoffee and his heirs are entitled to the warranty. Will you, therefore, warrant or not?" Case at 16.

[99] Interpreting "We will take your ruling as to that." Case at 16.

[100] Interpreting "Chief Justice Bereford ruled that he must warrant." Case at 16. The text simplifies the warranty's actual obligation of giving the buyer land worth as much as the land he lost.

[101] Cf. 104 Selden Society 146 (1320) ("For at the time it was only a toft … and now this toft is an inn so that it was worth forty shillings a year.")

[102] Interpreting "For each acre has been valued at twelve pence, while it was not worth more than four pence when it passed from our seisin, for it has now been well fertilized by digging-in marl, and good buildings have been erected when there were none at the time…." Case at 16.

> [7] Chief Justice Bereford: Maybe you're right but you wouldn't listen when we asked you to volunteer to go to the jury. You insisted on a judgment. If you had accepted a jury you'd get a reappraisal. But you refused. You'll pay the twelve pence rate.[103]

When an outsider came into Bereford's court his ignorance of the way the game was played provided an amusing spectacle a reporter chose to memorialize.

11. (1310)[104]

> [1] Anna owned a farm. After she married, her husband sold Bogo a lifetime right to her farm. The deed said his son Adam would pay Bogo if Anna took the farm back.[105] Bogo paid for the farm by giving the husband some woodland. The husband died and Anna took the farm back.[106] Bogo's lawyer asked Adam to compensate Bogo for the loss of his interest in the farm. But the lawyer made a mistake. He asked for the full value of the farm. He should have asked for only the value of a lifetime right.

> [2] Adam's lawyer: Bogo has asked for too much. According to the common law he forfeits the guarantee. Bogo can't get anything from Adam.

---

[103] Interpreting "If you had warranted of your own free will what you ask for would have been reasonable, but since you did not do this, but resisted the warranty until you were forced by our judgment to give it, you will not now have this benefit [of a re-evaluation]." Case at 16.

[104] 20 Selden Society 78.

[105] The guarantee applied to any hostile claimant. The text simplifies the context.

[106] By a *cui in vita.*

[3] Bogo: My lawyer made the mistake because he was just filing papers to begin the process of enforcing the guarantee. Once he had time to look more carefully he cut back our request to a lifetime interest. He didn't try to cheat you. I shouldn't be penalized.[107]

[4] Adam's lawyer: The law's the law.

[5] Justice Stanton: Shouldn't you act in good faith? Let's look at things as they stand. Bogo gave the woodland to Adam's late father. As his father's heir Adam has title to the woodland. Adam's mother Anna has also died. So Adam's inherited the farm too. Adam's got both the farm and the woodland and Bogo's got nothing. Doesn't that seem harsh?[108]

[6] Adam's lawyer: A lawyer's job isn't to decide what's fair. A lawyer's job is to help his client get everything the law says he deserves.[109]

[7] Chief Justice Bereford: Mr. Lawyer, any reasonable person would say Adam's getting too

---

[107] Interpreting "When a man vouches, the voucher [serves] no purpose but that of bringing his warrantor into court. And now you have come into court, and we have produced the deed of your ancestor {conveying a lifetime interest.}" 20 Selden Society at 79.
[108] The paragraph interprets "You should proceed in good faith. Are not you yourselves this day seised?" Case at 80.
[109] The paragraph interprets "We must serve our clients according to the law of the land." Case at 80.

much. The law is founded on reason.[110] Do you really think Adam can keep the chicken and the eggs?[111]

[8] Adam's lawyer: I guess you've decided so that's that.[112]

[9] Chief Justice Bereford: Wait, we need to have Adam's authorized agent accept the outcome. Is he here?

[10] Agent: Right here, Sir!

[11] Chief Justice Bereford: My good friend I'm delighted to see you. On Adam's behalf please provide his consent.[113]

[12] Agent: Certainly—just as soon as your judgment says I must.[114]

[13] Chief Justice Bereford What! Not until we enter judgment. By God Mr. Agent you're about to eat something more than a guarantee.[115]

[14] Adam's lawyer: {Sorry, Chief Justice! This fellow's clueless. We'll pay. We'll pay.}[116]

---

[110] Interpreting "Chief Justice Bereford: Reason requires that you warrant him, and the law is founded on reason, and good faith demands it since you yourself are this day seised of the tenements." Case at 80.

[111]Interpreting "They would like to have the eggs and the ha'penny as well." Maitland adds a footnote: "Or 'the chicken.'" Case at 79, footnote 1.

[112] "If that is your decision, so be it." Case at 80.

[113] "Fair friend, will you warrant?" Case at 80.

[114] Interpreting "Attorney: If you so decide." Case at 80.

[115] Interpreting "If you let it come to a decision, by the faith that I owe you, you will have to warrant with the sauce!" ("Si nous devoms fere sur ceo agard, par la fey qe jeo vous dey vous gar[rantirez] ove la sause!") Case at 80.

No Judgment, No Appeal

Common Pleas could indefinitely adjourn a plaintiff's case and he would have no way to complain.

12. (1308–1309)[117]

[1] Adam's lawyer sued[118] Bogo for the seventy-five pounds Adam had been promised if he didn't get a document by Easter.

[2] Bogo: Since I've come back to England I've tried to turn it over but he won't take it.

[3] Adam's lawyer: If that's the best argument you have the court should enter judgment against you.[119]

[4] Bogo: The court needs to know more. After we did the deal I had to go to France and I put my wife in charge. She failed to follow through but I didn't learn about her neglect until I got home three months after Easter.[120] Adam doesn't say he lost a penny. I've acted in good faith; the court should dismiss this case.[121]

[5] Adam's lawyer: If the agreement said nothing about the consequence of delay I suppose your defense

---

[116] Interpreting "Reporter: In the end Adam warranted, and conceded that they would give the recompense." Case at 80.

[117] 19 Selden Society 58. The text invents the date; the actual claim was for one hundred marks.

[118] Writ of debt.

[119] Interpreting "Judgment whether we ought not to be answered." Case at 58.

[120] Interpreting "On the day when we ought to have delivered it and for a quarter of a year afterwards we were beyond the sea, and we left the writing at home with our wife for delivery to you." Case at 58.

[121] Interpreting "You cannot show you were damaged for want of the writing; judgment."

might have some value.[122] But there's no ambiguity here—you agreed you absolutely would pay seventy-five pounds if my man didn't have the parchment in hand by Easter.

[6] Justice Bereford: I don't hear anything about Adam's loss. Seventy-five pounds for nothing? You're trying to get a penalty. We won't let you. Take the document and drop the suit.[123]

[7] Adam's lawyer: I wish I could. But Adam's agent here in court has no authority except to accept the full seventy-five pounds. I'd like to settle but I can't.[124]

[8] Justice Bereford: You're lying. No one tells an agent he can't do anything except accept full payment.[125]

[9] Adam's lawyer: I'm sorry but a judgment's the only way this case can end.[126]

[10] Justice Bereford: Camp out until doomsday—you'll never see a judgment from us.[127]

---

[122] Interpreting "If the writing were unconditional your answer would serve for any free man; but the writing is conditional…." Case at 58.
[123] Interpreting "Moreover, this is not, properly speaking, a debt; it is a penalty; and with what equity (look you!) can you demand this penalty?" Case at 59.
[124] Interpreting "[The plaintiff] is here by attorney, and the attorney is here to receive seventy-five pounds" Case at 59.
[125] Interpreting "[According to you then] the attorney was received [by the court] to receive and not to lose. I do not believe that he who received you [as attorney] received you in that form. Therefore accept the [tendered] writing." Case at 59. Maitland observes "The attorney, it will be remembered, is appointed '*ad lucrandum et perdendum*.'" Footnote 2 page 59.
[126] Interpreting "I cannot do that unless under a judgment of the court. If the law will suffer it, we will do it gladly." Case at 59.

A Judgment Reversed

Coerced consent gave Common Pleas virtual immunity from review. An unusual case shows a heroic effort to exploit political connections and persistence to reverse a judgment despite coerced consent.

Adam sued [128] the abbot to recover a manor he claimed as his uncle's heir. His writ required proof that no other relative had taken possession after the uncle's death. The abbot said Babs, the uncle's sister (and Adam's mother), had announced her claim to possession inside the manor. Justice Hengham said the common law required more than an announcement. [129] Rather than asking Hengham to enter a judgment about the law, the abbot said he would take a jury verdict about what Babs actually did.[130] After the jury said Babs did nothing but announce her claim, Adam won. The abbot could not appeal—he had consented to a jury. But he had friends. He got the king to tell Common Pleas to reconsider.[131] He got a judge from the Court of King's Bench to take a temporary seat on Common Pleas. The judge made sure that he alone heard the request for reconsideration.

---

[127]Interpreting "Were you to remain asking for our judgment, you would not come by your debt these seven years, for a judgment of the law is not to be given in that sort of way." Case at 59. The text interprets "seven years" as a figure of speech.

[128] Writ of mort d'ancestor.

[129] The abbot's prayer for "judgment of the writ" was rejected. Case at 54.

[130] Since "the assize came" (case at 54) the abbot must have joined issue on whether Babs had taken possession.

[131] The case is finally heard "Before the King." Case at 52.

13. (1305)[132]

[1] *The Reporter*: In the king's presence a Common Pleas' judgment is reversed.[133]

[2] Justice Roubyri of the Court of King's Bench:[134] The record shows that Bogo's corpse was laid out in state in the manor's central hall. Bogo's sister Babs was among the mourners. In the midst of the funeral she suddenly stood up and proclaimed she was taking possession of the manor. For about half an hour no one knew what to do. Then the abbot had Babs shown the door and the monks carried off their brother's corpse.[135] Justice Hengham ruled Babs hadn't done enough to take possession.[136] He was wrong—as her brother's heir she just needed to make her announcement.[137] The abbot should have won his case. Adam's writ forced him to show no one took possession after Bogo died but someone did. Adam's judgment is reversed.[138]

---

[132] 5 31a Rolls Series 52 (1305). Babs must be dead. Adam's lawyer had to choose between describing Adam as his mother's heir or as his uncle's heir. He chose his uncle's and won before Hengham; Roubyri suggests Adam should have sued as his mother's heir.

[133] "A judgment in an assize of mort d'ancestor reversed." Case at 52.

[134] *See* 5 31a Rolls Series xiii (preface by Alfred Horwood).

[135] Interpreting "That after the death of Bogo Babs while the corpse was in the bier, entered and took possession, claiming as heir of Bogo, and for half an hour in the day remained there, until, on the corpse being carried away, she still wishing to keep possession, came the said abbot and ousted her." Case at 54.

[136] Interpreting "Because it appeared to the said Sir Ralph and his companions that that small seisin and at that time was nothing {Adam} might well employ this writ {of mort d'ancestor}." Case at 54.

[137] Interpreting "We think the mere placing of the foot conferred seisin on the true heir…" Case at 54.

[138] Interpreting "Because we see… that Babs claiming etc. entered after the death of Bogo and was seised etc. … and thus the exception

Taking "esplees"—harvesting the fruits of the land—is the gold standard for possession. For the most part mere presence is not enough. Hengham insisted on esplees here; he insisted on esplees in another case.[139] A victorious plaintiff went to a manor with the sheriff[140] and proclaimed he was taking possession. After the lady of the manor ignored them he left without doing more. Common Pleas said he had acquired possession—an announcement on the site by a person who had won a court case was enough.[141] Hengham dissented. He said even a judgment creditor had to harvest the fruits of the land.[142] Hengham took the same hard line with Babs, a rigorous criterion that represented a minority view about the law. The abbot took the majority view, but his consent to the jury barred his appeal.[143] Through contacts and persistence he won nonetheless.

The quarrel between Roubryi and Hengham stands for something more important than the criteria for

---

of the Abbot {*i.e.*, the Abbot's legal theory that Hengham rejected} is affirmed by the verdict of the Assise..." Case at 54.

[139] 17 Selden Society 125 (1308–1309). The case does not focus on the victor acquiring a judicial writ authorizing entry, although he may have. Elsewhere Justice Inge suggests possession will be transferred by an announcement on the land but only if the victor has acquired a judicial writ authorizing entry. 43 Selden Society 88, 89 (1313). *See also* 1 31a Rolls Series 52 (1292) requiring delivery of seisin by the sheriff or bailiff, perhaps implicitly after a judicial writ.

[140] Unless a victorious plaintiff executed a judgment properly with livery by the Sheriff or bailiff she would commit a dispossession. *See* 1 31a Rolls Series 48, 52 (1292).

[141] While he was on the land he claimed.

[142] "Hengham, C. J. (in private). The possession was too naked, for he took no esplees." 17 Selden Society 125, 126 (1308–1309).

[143] "For if he found no other person in seisin, and he is next heir to the ancestor whose inheritance he claims, the bare setting his foot in the capital messuage of his inheritance is enough to give him seisin." 1 Britton 310–311.

possession. The abbot had to move heaven and earth to overturn Hengham's decision. His odyssey shows the consent ploy had paralyzed King's Bench's appellate authority.

CHAPTER 4
Chancery

CHANCERY STOOD AS A RIVAL CLAIMANT to power. Bracton said the king and his advisors had delegated Chancery the power to create new writs that implemented their implicit intentions.[1] As a man who looked back to the Roman Empire and forward to the end of the world Bracton saw the present as relatively static. His great treatise created a portrait of all of English law. He did not focus on the process of change. For him law reform was an unusual event. When necessary, he said, Chancery could create "personal" writs as a "special favor."[2]

Bracton made the courts a watchdog over Chancery. If a new writ went beyond Chancery's implicit authority the courts would strike it down.[3] The power to review laws was not a power to create laws. Bracton had nothing to say about conflicts between Chancery and the courts over the power to create law.

---

[1] "If a writ is brought without warrant of the law, it shall be sustained {by the courts} as long as it is consonant with reason and not contrary to the law, provided it has been granted by the king and approved by his council. ... it does not matter that the magnates have not given their assent expressly so long as they have not expressly dissented and no sufficient reason is shown why it should not be valid..." Bracton 414b.

[2] Bracton 414b.

[3] "A writ will abate if it has been brought against the law and custom of the realm..." Bracton 413b. Bracton expected the courts to do the abating.

Bracton died in 1268.[4] In 1285 Parliament passed a potentially revolutionary statute that gave Chancery greater power than Bracton had described. Had Chancery exploited the statute, Chancery might have claimed the law-making power that Bereford subsequently captured.

The Similar Case Statute

In paraphrase the statute said

> Parliament wants to help litigants whose cases do not fall within the letter of the law. If Chancery has already sold a writ for one case, and the clerks see a similar case involving the same law and remedy, the clerks should write a new writ.[5] Chancery now sells a writ against a person who wrongfully builds an embankment, but Chancery will not sell a writ against a person who takes the embankment from him. Chancery now sells a writ to protect a parson's grazing rights, but Chancery will not sell a writ that the parson's successor can use. In cases like these the clerks should write new writs. If they cannot agree they should ask Parliament for help.[6]

---

[4] Paul Brand, *Oxford Dictionary of National Biography.*

[5] "Instead from now on when a writ is granted in one case, in a like case requiring like remedy it shall be made as before" 3 EHD 442–443.

[6] Interpreting Statute of Westminster II, c.24 (1285) (3 EHD 428,442–443): "And whensoever in future it happens in the Chancery that a writ is found in one case, but in a similar case involving the same law and requiring similar remedy, it is not, the clerks of the Chancery shall agree in framing a writ, or shall adjourn the plaintiffs to the next parliament and shall write down the matters on which they cannot agree and refer them to the next parliament and a writ shall be framed by the joint opinion of the learned in law, that it may not happen hereafter that the court {*i.e.*, the royal council} long fails those who seek justice."

The statute responds to a problem Parliament had observed. The Chancery clerks—the staff—have not been willing to vary the laws they administer. The clerics apparently consider their collection of writs, their "Register of Writs," as a form of scripture, something inscribed on stone. Rather than trying to look at the spirit of the law, they look to its letter. Parliament tells them to be more creative.

The statute presents a naïve view of the law-making process. The legislators think the clerks can easily recognize a small variation. In practice things are not easy. Even the simple examples the statute provides quickly become puzzlers. The clerks should realize, Parliament says, that if they sell a writ against someone who builds an embankment they should sell a writ against a person who acquires it. Perhaps Parliament is speaking about a subsequent possessor who has knowingly taken possession of a wrongfully erected embankment. [7] Suppose he dies—should the clerks create a new writ to sanction his innocent widow or heir?

The clerks' day job consists of selling documents copied out of form books. They have no expertise in deciding whether one case is analogous to another. They get no help in making the decision. They hear only one side of the story. The defendant is not notified that the plaintiff has asked to buy a "similar case writ." He gets notified after the clerks have sold a writ. The clerks hear no adversarial argument about whether cases are similar. They are supposed to make the decision themselves. If they cannot decide they are told to do what no bureaucrat

---

[7] The EHD translation footnotes the translation of the statutory phrase "has changed hands" with the explanation "literally, is transferred from one to another." By not using the word "sale" perhaps Parliament intended to refer only to fraudulent transfers designed to impede the injured person's ability to use the courts.

ever likes to do: annoy the authorities by asking for help, help from Parliament.[8]

Parliament has not considered the statute's impact upon the relationship between Chancery and the courts. Bracton said the courts could strike down writs that exceeded Parliament's implicit delegation of power to Chancery.[9] The courts cannot strike down a writ Parliament has explicitly authorized. In contrast to the American system the medieval courts cannot say Parliament has violated a constitution. The medieval courts must enforce a writ Parliament has written. Perhaps by the statute Parliament has given Chancery explicit orders to sell "similar case" writs. Perhaps Chancery's similar case writs constitute Parliament's writs. The courts would have to enforce such writs. By saying a case was "similar" Chancery could create new common law rules that the courts could not review. The statute might dramatically change the relationship between Chancery and Common Pleas.[10] An open ended class of writs—writs concerning "similar cases"—would be exempt from judicial review.

---

[8] "If they can't agree they should ask for Parliament's help."

[9] Bracton 414b.

[10] The statute might have transformed English law. "[O]ur legal system would have developed along rather curious lines. We should have the common law courts reduced to the role of trying cases upon writs whose scope was beyond their criticism. The expansion of the law would have taken place, not in the courts, but in the Chancery which alone could have settled the form of a writ in unusual circumstances.... The theoretical implications of such a system must not detain us now, interesting as they are, for {the similar case statute} was soon systematically ignored, and the bench proceeded to exercise those mingled powers which from the fourteenth century until today have defied analysis." T.F.T. Plucknett, Case and the Statute of Westminster II, 31 *Colum. L. Rev.* 787–88 (1931).

The statute did not bring about a crisis. Perhaps the high officials in the Chancery might have sought power but the clerks did not. They did not want the job Parliament put on their plate—especially a job that every malcontent in the realm might ask them to do. They refused to change their behavior. They kept selling copies of existing writs. On occasion they might create new writs but they did not say anything about the similar case statute when they did. No one argued their new writs were immune from review. If Common Pleas mentioned the statute—and the court rarely did—Common Pleas interpreted the statute as if it spoke as directly to the courts as to Chancery. The statute said reasoning by analogy was good. The court agreed. The similar case statute died for two reasons. The clerks killed it by neglect. And the problem Parliament addressed itself died. Once Bereford took over the common law was no longer ossified.

The statute would have stayed dead except for a politically motivated judgment. In 1310 Common Pleas said a Chancery clerk had invoked the statute, and written a similar case writ. Common Pleas then enforced the writ without discussing whether the clerk had correctly identified a "similar case." The court's silence implied the clerk rather than the court would make the call.

Although the judgment was made by the Court of Common Pleas, the judge was Roger Brabazon, Chief Justice of King's Bench. He had taken a temporary seat on Common Pleas. As a lawyer Brabazon would see the dead statute's implications. As a politician Brabazon would see the statute's potential impact. A judgment giving life to the statute would disrupt the equilibrium that had settled upon the relationship among King's Bench, Common Pleas, and Chancery. The judgment might inspire the top authorities at Chancery to invade Bereford's authority to create new common law rules. A conflict between Chancery and Common Pleas had to be resolved somewhere. King's Bench might be the peacemaker. King's Bench might recapture the appellate authority it had lost.

In order to exhume the similar case statute Brabazon had to climb three mountains. No lawyer had any interest in bringing a similar case writ. No Chancery clerk had any interest in writing a similar case writ. Common Pleas had no interest in rendering a decision that would give Chancery power over the court.

No lawyer had any interest in using the statute because Bereford had transformed the common law. Lawyers had become adept at exploiting Bereford's penchant for law reform. Lawyers are conservative and they do not take a difficult road when they see an easier route. No sensible lawyer would try to buy an unprecedented writ—a "similar case writ"—when he could follow a conventional path to his goal. Bereford gave a liberal interpretation to writs; a lawyer had no need to ask the conservative clerks to create new law.

No clerk would sell a "similar case writ." For decades the clerks had shown they preferred just to copy writs out of their form book. The Register of Writs did not include a form for a "similar case writ." The clerks did not want to engage in the complex analysis the creation of a similar case writ required. Chancery's top people might want law-making authority but they did not write the writs. The clerks did. They had nothing to gain by buying a headache.

Finally Bereford the lion stood at the gate. He was power hungry and unprincipled. He would find some way to turn aside a similar case writ.

In 1310 Brabazon solved all three problems in a single stroke. He found a case Common Pleas was about to consider. He took a seat on Common Pleas and somehow kept Bereford from joining him. Brabazon then found a lawyer who had asked for a similar case writ and a clerk who had sold one. The lawyer was standing in front of him. The clerk was the one the lawyer had used. Neither the lawyer nor the clerk had expressed any intention to invoke the similar case statute. But when Brabazon told the lawyer he was going to win, the lawyer had no complaints.

The case concerned an underage ward. In contrast to the normal guardian[11] (who pocketed his ward's income for his own benefit) the peasant's guardian accumulated the ward's income and paid it to the ward when he became an adult. Some rich realists bought land in peasant ownership. They ignored the déclassé stench of peasant ownership so that their heirs could collect a trust fund upon attaining the age of majority. They did not think about fortune hunters.

1. (1310)[12]

> [1] Anna sued[13] Bogo for abducting her ward and putting him in a bad marriage. In court Anna said she was her son's peasant guardian.[14]

---

[11] *I.e.*, the guardian in military tenure. "Guardianship by reason of nurture" provides a third form of guardianship, a mother's right to retain her child during the period of nurture, a custodial right without economic benefits. *See, e.g.*, 34 Selden Society 31 (1312–1313).

[12] 19 Selden Society 157.

[13] The reporter's headnote says Anna brought a writ of ravishment of ward. Maitland adds a sentence to the headnote. "{The writ} has been devised by the common counsel of the clerks in the Chancery and falls within the Statute (Westm. II. C. 24) {the 1285 statute} which enjoins the making of writs *in consimili casu.*" Case at 157. Although the original headnote doesn't show the reporter understood Brabazon's agenda, Maitland's interpolation says he did.

[14] She admitted the land was held "in socage." Case at 158.

[2] Bogo: Both peasant and normal guardians have always had a writ to protect their interests.[15] Anna ignored that remedy. Instead she bought the fast track writ[16] that Parliament created so that a normal guardian can protect his lucrative rights.[17] A normal guardian sells the ward's marriage and puts the proceeds in his pocket. A peasant guardian puts it in a trust fund. Anna can't use a fast track writ. She neither qualifies under the letter of the law—she's not a normal guardian—nor under the spirit of the law. She hasn't lost any money.[18]

[3] Anna: Although I've brought a fast track writ I qualify to use it. In the similar case statute Parliament told Chancery to write variants on conventional writs.[19]

---

[15] Interpreting "There was no writ at the common law except the writ of right of ward…." Case at 158. All writs of right were slow moving.
[16] Ravishment of ward.
[17] In contrast to the writ of right of ward's focus upon the guardian's possessory rights (Early Registers of Writs, 87 Selden Society 237 (#556), the ravishment of ward statute (Westminster II, c. 35) focuses upon the financial injury a guardian suffers from the ward's bad marriage. 3 EHD 448. The ward also had to pay if he refused to marry. The so-called Statute of Merton, 1236, c.7 (3 EHD 353). The statutory remedy applied even if the abductor claimed no right to the guardianship. 2 31a Rolls Series 554 (1294).
[18] The paragraph interprets "There was no writ at the common law except the writ of right of ward, and for speedy remedy and the punishment of trespassers the writ of ravishment was ordained for those to whom the profit [of a wardship] belonged. And since in this case the profit would come to the heir when he came to full age, we demand judgment whether she, to whom no profit can come, can use this writ against us." Case at 158.
[19] Interpreting "The wrong is done to us, and it ought not to go unpunished, for Statute says 'let not the complainants leave Chancery without remedy.' And since this writ is delivered to us in the Chancery, and the infant has no action in this case, consequently, if we were not answered, the wrong would remain unpunished, we pray judgment etc." Case at 159. Although the paragraph suggests

> Parliament wanted the court to sustain writs that addressed problems analogous to those orthodox writs solved. My injury is no different from that suffered by a normal guardian by an unauthorized marriage. You say a bad marriage by a ward causes no financial loss to a peasant guardian. You're wrong. Suppose a peasant guardian puts up commercial buildings on her ward's city land. She can lay out the funds because she knows she will be repaid when the ward makes a good marriage. A bad marriage makes repayment impossible. I have a financial stake in my ward's marriage in the same way a normal guardian does.[20]

Anna had brought a "similar case writ," the reporter doesn't mean that. He uses ambiguous words because he doesn't understand Brabazon's agenda. Brabazon's comment that Anna's writ "is not founded upon the Statute concerning wardship…." (case at 160) shows that he himself concocted the idea that Anna had brought a "similar case writ." Prior to his startling conclusion the litigants' arguments tracked a well-worn path. The court had the power to validate a variant writ that addressed a problem analogous to an orthodox writ's usual target. On those rare prior occasions when Common Pleas had referred to the similar case statute, the court invoked the statute as makeweight support for its reasoning by analogy. Years before Bereford had validated a variant formedon writ. Chancery's writ spoke about an event that occurred before the effective date of the statute that created the writ. Bereford's decision invoked the "similar case statute" as the legislators' approval of his court's decision to validate the writ through reasoning by analogy. In referring to the similar case statute, Bereford used language that could be interpreted to mean the plaintiff had brought a "similar case writ." Brabazon has not rendered his decision. Bereford had no reason to speak with precision about the writ's etiology. The other parts of the case, however, prove the plaintiff had brought a formedon writ. 2 31a Rolls Series 320, 322 (1294).

20 The paragraph interprets "Suppose that a man holds but a half-acre in socage and dies leaving an heir within age who is ward to the next friend {*i.e.*, his mother Anna}, then the guardian can sell the marriage; and when the heir attains full age, they shall account together, so that if [the guardian] has put the value of the land into a marriage, that expenditure will be allowed. So it seems that [the

> [4] Chief Justice Brabazon (of the Court of King's Bench sitting for the occasion on Common Pleas): Anna, you don't need to concoct some justification to qualify to use a fast track guardian's writ. You don't have to convince the court your case is sufficiently analogous to a normal guardian's case. The writ your lawyer bought isn't a fast track guardian's writ. He had the clerk sell him a "similar case writ." We'll enforce it.[21]

On its face Brabazon's opinion does not seem particularly important. He says that he will approve the writ because Parliament has told Chancery to create it. He does not say anything about the writ's immunity from review. Brabazon's threat manifests itself only in Bereford's reaction just as some sub-atomic particles appear only in the disturbance they create. The disturbance occurred quickly.[22]

2. (1310)[23]

> [1] Anna's father gave her only a lifetime interest in a manor. At her death, Bogo got the place. Anna violated the restrictions on her interest by selling the

---

marriage] does belong to the guardian sufficiently. Judgment etc." Case at 159–160.

[21] Interpreting "Brabazon, C. J. Forasmuch as Statute says 'that a plaintiff leave not Chancery without remedy,' and this writ has been given by the common counsel of the Chancery according to the plaintiff's case, and is not a writ founded upon the Statute concerning wardship, we adjudge this writ good." Case at 160.

[22] The three critical cases were all decided in 1310.

[23] 20 Selden Society 16. The actual facts involved a grant to Anna and her husband for their joint lifetimes with a remainder in fee simple to Bogo's father whose heir he has become. Case at 16.

manor outright to Cosmo. Demanding immediate possession of the manor, Bogo sued[24] Cosmo.

[2] Cosmo: Let's look at the writ you've brought. Parliament passed a statute providing a remedy when a bad widow tries to sell more than she has.[25] A widow gets a lifetime interest in part of her husband's land. Parliament said if a widow tries to sell her interest outright her husband's heir can sue the buyer immediately. He doesn't have to wait for the widow to die. You've brought a bad widow writ against me. But you don't qualify to use a bad widow writ. You aren't a husband's heir—your interest comes directly from the grant Anna's father made. Furthermore Anna didn't sell a widow's interest.[26] She just sold the lifetime right her father gave her.[27]

---

[24] A bad widow writ. Statute of Gloucester c. 7 (1278) (3 EHD 417). According to the reporter's opening summary Bogo brought "his writ of entry founded on the Statute…" The similar case statute is not "a writ of entry," a writ that condemns the defendant for having entered land based upon an improper transfer. The bad widow writ is a writ of entry. The bad widow statute says "the heir or other person to whom the land ought to revert after the {widow's} death … shall at once have recovery … by a writ of entry made therefor in the Chancery." 3 EHD at 417.

[25] Statute of Gloucester c. 7 (1278) (3 EHD 417).

[26] Interpreting "But the Statute does nothing for you, who are a remainderman and consequently outside the statutory case." Case at 17.

[27] Interpreting "The statute gives recovery only where a woman holding in dower alienates in fee, and then the reversioner is to have his recovery at once. If you wish to be aided by the Statute, that must be by some certain words comprised in the Statute.… Judgment, whether you ought to be answered to this writ." Case at 17.

[3] Bogo: The similar case statute tells Chancery and the courts to exercise discretion. The facts are close enough for me to use a bad widow writ.[28]

[4] Chief Justice Bereford: Bogo, at common law you can't sue Cosmo until Anna dies. You don't want to wait that long. But you don't qualify to use the bad widow writ. You aren't an heir and Anna isn't a widow. You lose.[29]

[5] *The Reporter*: Bogo went to Chancery to complain about Bereford. The leaders of Chancery ordered Bereford to appear at their offices to explain his conduct. At Chancery Bereford just repeated what he had already said in court.

[6] Barneby, Master of Chancery:[30] Bereford you don't seem to understand the theory behind Bogo's law suit. Even though you say he's brought a bad widow writ he hasn't. He's brought a similar case writ. You have to validate his writ.[31]

---

[28] Interpreting "Albeit the Statute does not make mention of the case of a tenant for life, one cannot but suppose that if he alienates, the reversioner at once has a recovery, for [another] Statute wills that in like case like remedy be ordained." Case at 17.

[29] Interpreting "On what will you rely: Statute or common law? At common law you have no writ; and, if you rely on Statute, it must be on some words comprised in the Statute. But the Statute does nothing for you; it only says that if a tenant in dower alienates, the reversioner [can recover at once.]" Case at 17.

[30] Maitland explains "Robert de Bardelby was one of the principal Masters in Chancery." Case at 19, footnote 5.

[31] The paragraph interprets "The Statute of Gloucester wills that, if women holding in dower alienate, the reversioner shall at once have his recovery; and Westminster the Second wills that *in consimili casu* etc." Case at 19.

> [7] Chief Justice Bereford: Bogo can win. But not until you sell him a writ that expressly invokes the similar case statute.[32]

This episode seems to constitute a triumph for Brabazon's theory. But in his apparent humiliation Bereford has followed an important strategy. Brabazon said the peasant guardian's writ had implemented the similar case statute. Her writ did not say anything about the similar case statute. Any plaintiff who bought a questionable writ could say Chancery had sold a similar case writ. Brabazon created a wide arena for conflict between Chancery and the Court of Common Pleas. Bereford puts the battle ground into a small area. "Sell a writ," Bereford says, "that expressly invokes the similar case statute." Bereford will not have to deal with Brabazon's similar case theory except in those cases in which the clerks choose to write a novel similar case writ. He rejects Brabazon's theory, but Brabazon cannot reverse his decision. In keeping with Bereford's speech in Chancery the clerks will sell Bogo a writ that invokes the statute. Bogo will ride his similar case writ to victory. He cannot appeal a victory to the Court of King's Bench.

A minor setback, Brabazon may have thought. Bereford can have his little moment. I have provided

---

[32] Interpreting "Make the writ and we will maintain it." Case at 19. The text omits Bereford's remark "Blessed be he who made that statute!" Case at 19. Readers are likely to think Bereford has expressed admiration for the statute. As the context makes emphatic he hasn't. Chancery has insulted the great Chief Justice by ordering him to come to the Chancery's office and abase himself. Bereford invests great effort to prevent the statute from being used. As the next case discussion demonstrates, he makes a preposterous interpretation of the statute to prevent anyone from invoking it. His remark really means "Damn the son of a bitch who wrote the statute!"

lawyers a roadmap to invoke Chancery's discretion. A lawyer who wants to have Chancery modify the law will tell the clerks to write a writ expressly based on the similar case statute. Bereford will strike down the writ and tell the lawyer he has to waive his right to appeal by consenting to a jury. The lawyer will refuse to waive his right—he will know that King's Bench is on his side. He will demand judgment, and then take Bereford's ruling up to me. I will take the writ Bereford has nullified and cram it down his throat.

Bereford had thought about that too. He uses a "poison pill" strategy that American lawyers recommend today to defang stock market raiders. When corporate management fears a hostile takeover, management creates a by-law that lets them sell bargain price stock to the raider's rivals. The raid never gets off the ground. The raider sees he can never win control because the buyers of bargain stock will always be a step ahead of him. Lawyers call the by-law a "poison pill." Once the raider sees it, he will never buy the corporation's stock. [33] Bereford puts a poison pill into the similar case writ. Despite Brabazon's plans no lawyer will buy the writ.

3. (1310)[34]

> [1] After Anna died her widower, Adam's stepfather, got a lifetime right to her land.[35] Anna's son Adam would get the land after his death. The widower then

---

[33] *See* M. Kahan, How I Learned to Stop Worrying and Love the Pill: Adaptive Responses to Takeover Law, 69 Univ. of Chicago L. Rev. 871 (2002).

[34] 20 Selden Society 106. The text assumes the surviving husband was Adam's stepfather. The text simplifies the facts by making the legally irrelevant change of postponing the sale until after Anna's death. The text changes the order in which Bereford presents his analysis.

[35] He became tenant by curtesy once a child had been born.

sold more than he had—he sold the land outright to Bogo. Adam did not want to wait for his stepfather to die to strike down the bad sale. He sued[36] Bogo immediately. He bought a bad widow writ that said his stepfather had violated the bad widow statute when he sold the land.

[2] Bogo: Adam's writ says a widower has violated the bad widow statute. At the risk of stating the obvious, a widower isn't a widow. The writ's no good.[37]

[3] Adam: This isn't a new situation. In the past Common Pleas has let an heir use the bad widow writ when a widower sold his lifetime interest outright.[38] But if I have to justify the writ, Parliament has told Chancery to create, and the courts to approve, writs for "similar cases." A widower is a widow in a different gender.[39]

[4] Chief Justice Bereford: You say you bought a "similar case" writ but you didn't. Your writ doesn't refer to the similar case statute. You bought a bad widow writ. The writ says a bad widower violated the bad widow statute. Your writ's no good.

---

[36] The writ of entry the bad widow statute created. The writ said "into which Bogo has no entry save by Anna's widower … who alienated against the form of the bad widow statute." Case at 108. He sues in his capacity as his mother's heir to recover the land his stepfather sold.

[37] Interpreting "This writ is [professedly] founded on the Bad Widow Statute, whereas there is no Statute ordained for this case. So we demand judgment of the writ etc." Case at 108.

[38] Interpreting "For the same reason the Chancery grants that if a man holding by the curtesy or for life alienates in fee, [the reversioner] shall recover by the form of the said Statute. And this writ we have always had and used, and you [Sirs] have maintained it." Case at 108.

[39] Interpreting "So, since tenant in dower and tenant for life are of like estate, it seems that the writ is good." Case at 107.

This is a good time to tell lawyers what the similar case statute means.[40] If Chancery sells a similar case writ for a case that is not both similar and strange we will dismiss the writ.[41]

This court has some more advice. Adam's lawyer should not have bought a writ that said a widower's sale violated the bad widow statute. The bad widow statute does not say anything about bad widowers.[42] The lawyer should have bought a writ that said the widower's sale to Bogo violated Adam's rights. The writ should not have said anything about why the sale violated his rights. Then we could have reasoned by analogy. A widower's sale certainly seems analogous to a widow's sale. Adam does not lose this case because he complained about a widower's sale. He loses this case because the Chancery clerks said the widower's sale violated the bad widow statute.[43]

---

[40] The concise report presents Bereford's "strange case" analysis without any camouflage. In his remarks in full Bereford would have added some specious reasoning to sanitize his power grab. Perhaps he would have said: Of course we'll respect the statute. But we have to interpret it. Parliament did not want the clerks to write writs for every type of similar case. Parliament just wanted them to write writs for a single type of similar case. Parliament wanted them to write similar case writs for cases that were both similar and strange.

[41] The paragraph interprets "as to what you say about 'let the clerks in the Chancery agree,' that is to be understood of writs in strange cases (*ceo est a entendre des brefs en estrange cas*)...." Case at 108.

[42] Interpreting "You allege the bad widow statute for the case, and the words of the statute do not accord with your case, whereas they and your writ should be accordant." Case at 107.

[43] The paragraph interprets "if your writ had not those words 'by the form of the Statute,' it would have some colour and might be maintainable." Case at 108. The paragraph explains Bereford's cryptic passage in lay language. Bereford might have added "We can't reject a writ Parliament has created but Parliament did not create such a writ."

{Adam's lawyer should not have asked them to interpret the statute.}

[5] *The Reporter*: A few days later Barneby, Osgodby, and the other leaders of Chancery[44] ordered Bereford to show up at their offices.[45] After some discussion they rewrote the clerk's writ so that it relied directly upon the similar case statute.[46] {Adam then brought this writ to Common Pleas and won.}[47]

From a litigant's perspective a victory is a victory. Adam will not—cannot—appeal. From the perspective of a lawyer advising clients, Adam's victory does not matter. The court's legal theory is what counts. A lawyer who reads this case will never buy a similar case writ. Bereford has put a poison pill into the writ. He says his court will reject any writ for a similar case that is not strange. The test is incomprehensible—how can something be simultaneously similar and strange? But Bereford's meaning is not. His court will reject every

---

[44] Interpreting "Bardelby and Osgodby and the other examiners of the Chancery…" Case at 109.

[45] Aware of the previous case, Adam's lawyer did what good lawyers do. If some strategy has worked in the past that's the strategy they use. Why reinvent the wheel by appealing Bereford's outrageous decision to Brabazon. The lawyer has no dog in the fight between Bereford and Brabazon. He just wants his client to win.

[46] Interpreting "And they amended the writ … "ought to revert to [the demandant] by the form of the Statute provided in a like case (*in consimili casu)*—so he says—and whereof he complains that the said etc." Case at 109.

[47] The report says nothing about what happened after the clerks wrote the similar case writ, but Adam must have won. Bereford would again avoid an appeal to Brabazon by letting the plaintiff win.

similar case writ. Lawyers do not invest their client's money in certain defeat at trial.[48]

Bereford tells them they have a better alternative—a writ that says nothing about Chancery's legal theory. The lawyers have a long history with both Bereford and the clerks. Bereford is bold; the clerks are timid. The lawyers will take their chances with Bereford and reasoning by analogy; they will not ask the conservative clerks to create a similar case writ.

Bereford tells lawyers that Chancery is out of the law reform business. Chancery's power under the similar case statute is dead. Chancery power to exercise discretion in interpreting the writs Parliament creates is also dead. The clerks have to quote the statute. Chancery has lost the power to force Bereford to accept its interpretation of the common law.

Bracton and Parliament both put Chancery in the driver's seat. Bereford has pushed the clerks out the door. He has taken the wheel.

Aftermath

Brabazon had thrown things into chaos. Bereford overcame the threat. Now the time was right to go back to things as they were.[49] Bereford's cases denied Chancery the

---

[48] No test case will ever subject Bereford's decision to review. Brabazon's friends may find a litigant, but they won't find a lawyer. Only a tiny group could appear before Bereford. None will commit suicide by arguing in favor of Chancery's power to innovate writs that Common Pleas cannot review.

[49] Which included ignoring the similar case statute. When a successor parson invoked a statute referring to the death of his predecessor, a predecessor who was alive but deprived, the court validated the writ without reference to the similar case statute. 65 Selden Society 9 (1318).

authority to write statutory writs that included facts that deviated from the statute.[50] But Bereford did not mean to deny his own court a similar discretion.[51] Common Pleas exercised its law-making authority by encouraging lawyers to buy statutory writs even though their clients' facts did not qualify according to the statutory language. Common Pleas could then choose to reform the law by saying the deviant facts did not contradict the statutory language.

---

[50] In 1312 Bereford repeated his rule. "Chief Justice Bereford: If additional words are inserted in a writ the form of which is given in a statute, the writ is bad." 33 Selden Society 94, 95 (1312). The plaintiff had added the words "force and arms" to a statutory guardianship writ probably because he hoped to have the defendant arrested. In contrast when Bereford thought a case involved no danger that Chancery would claim immunity from review, he invoked his own court's discretion to approve Chancery writs that deviated from the standard form. He allowed a plaintiff to include "force and arms" in a Chancery common law replevin writ. "Were it not [allowed,] every rascal in the country might take his neighbor's beasts, and, when he was to be attached, he would go fleeing from place to place." 22 Selden Society 195, 195–196 (1310).

[51] A 1313 case shows Bereford's willingness to validate a writ attacking an outright sale by a widower of his curtesy (lifetime) interest as analogous to the Statute of Gloucester's bar of such transfers by widows. In speaking of the plaintiff's writ, the reporter says "*ceo bref est garrante pur semblable cas…*" By translating the phrase as "the present writ is warranted by the provision for writs in *consimili casu*" the Selden Society editor suggests Common Pleas decided the plaintiff had bought a Chancery writ that relied upon the similar case statute. The suggestion is incorrect. The medieval reporter's use of "semblable cas" refers to the court's reasoning by analogy rather than Chancery's invocation of the similar case statute. 43 Selden Society 161 (1313).

4. (1318)[52]

[1] After his father gave a farm to him and his surviving child,[53] Adam tried to cheat his son Arthur by selling the land outright to Bogo. The deed said Arthur wouldn't sue Bogo. After Adam died Arthur sued[54] anyway.

[2] Bogo: Your father guaranteed you wouldn't sue.

[3] Arthur: A statute says I can ignore the guarantee because I haven't inherited anything from him.[55]

[4] Bogo: To be precise the statute says your father's "heir" can ignore the guarantee. You aren't suing as your father's heir. You're suing to enforce a gift your grandfather made to you. You can't use the statute.[56]

[5] Chief Justice Bereford: Arthur, tell us how you qualify to use the statute.[57]

---

[52] 61 Selden Society 34. The actual gift was in fee tail by Arthur's great grandfather to his daughter. Adam is the daughter's heir. Case at 34.

[53] Fee tail.

[54] Writ of formedon in the descender.

[55] "His son shall not be barred {unless} an inheritance has descended to him from his father." Statute of Gloucester c. 3 (1278) (3 EHD 416).

[56] Interpreting "Answer is given you in writs of mort d'ancestor, cosinage, ael and besael; and this is a writ of formedon, whereof the Statute makes no mention...." Case at 37. The text generalizes Bogo's defense. The text imputes a general intention to the legislators. The four referenced writs all relate to an heir's claim based upon his ancestor's possession. The text therefore says the statute gives the defense of no inheritance to a plaintiff who claims as an heir. By his writ of formedon Adam claims not as an heir, but rather as a direct recipient of his grandfather's gift.

[57] Interpreting "If a statute be made to amend the common law, then you must show [in what it is] to your advantage." Case at 35.

[6] Arthur: The writ says my father has tried to impose a guarantee upon his heir without leaving enough to pay for it. Just because I've admitted in court I'm not suing as my father's heir the court doesn't have to dismiss my case. The court can look to the general policy behind the statute and then say my statement doesn't contradict my writ. I'm not suing as my father's heir but the legislators would have wanted me to escape his guarantee.[58]

[7] Bogo: The court can't. When Parliament creates a writ by statute no one can vary the language of the writ in any way.[59]

[8] Justice Mutford: We've got more discretion than that. Statutes should be interpreted in light of their general purpose. Take the bad widow statute. The legislators just talked about widows' sales. But we can let a plaintiff use the statute when a widower makes the sale. Legislators often use specific examples as a

---

[58] For purposes of simplification the text generalizes an argument Arthur bases upon technicalities. "Moreover, in the common law, the writ of mort d'ancestor was given in cases where the writ of formedon in the descender now lies; so since this writ is in place of mort d'ancestor, it will have the same advantage that it would now have in mort d'ancestor etc." (Case at 37) and "Our writ serves us in place of mort d'ancestor; so we are sufficiently within the circumstances of the Statute." Case at 39. Arthur's formedon in the descender writ is the writ a grandchild would use to enforce a gift his grandparent made directly to him. The writ enforces the interest of the "surviving child."

[59] Interpreting "Scrope: No. A statute is a strict law, and cannot be treated nor construed by analogy to other law, [but attention must be paid] only to the words in the statute; and the Statute has nothing to say about this case." Case at 39.

way to explain their general intentions. They can't anticipate everything that will come up.[60]

[9] Bogo: You're completely contradicting what this court said eight years ago. The court said a plaintiff couldn't use the bad widow statute to attack a widower's sale. The court said if the plaintiff thought the cases were similar the plaintiff needed to buy a similar case writ. Arthur needs to go back to Chancery and buy a similar case writ.[61]

[10] Chief Justice Bereford: No, this writ is good enough. This court reasons by analogy. The legislators wanted a person who hadn't inherited anything to escape his ancestor's guarantee. Arthur's father tried to impose the guarantee upon him but didn't leave him

---

[60] Interpreting "Justice Mutford: We have it in the Statute of Gloucester itself that, if a woman holding in dower alienates in fee that which she holds by way of dower, the heir to whom the reversion belongs will now have his recovery by a writ of entry. It does not speak of tenements for a term of life or by the law for England. Yet if {a widower sells land outright} they to whom the reversion belongs will have the recovery; so it seems to me that for this very reason [the claimant] should be helped, because they who made the Statute could not bear in mind every case that might occur." Case at 39. When Mutford says the litigants "will have recovery" he is referring to the very cases the plaintiff invoked in the text's second bad widow case, 20 Selden Society 106 (1310). The plaintiff said "For the same reason the Chancery grants that if a man holding by the curtesy or for life alienates in fee, [the reversioner] shall recover by the form of the said Statute. And this writ we have always had and used, and you [Sirs] have maintained it." Case at 108. In that case Bereford ignored the plaintiff's reference to precedent. Here Mutford invokes the precedents because they suit his purpose.

[61] Interpreting "Scrope: Before now, in such cases, a man would bring a writ of entry founded on {the Bad Widow Statute}, and the writ would be abated; but later he was helped by another statute, that of Westminster II, which says: *in consimili casu* … etc." Case at 39.

> the assets he needs to pay it. The guarantee doesn't bind Arthur. Legislators can't list every type of case. Parliament expects this court to give statutes a liberal interpretation.[62]

With Brabazon's mischief contained Common Pleas found it convenient to return to a comfortable relationship with the clerks. As Bereford had said in his similar but strange decision, Common Pleas had no objection if they wrote new writs. Just so long as they did not attempt to make their writs immune from review by purporting to ground their novel writ in a statute. If a clever clerk did not try to force the court's hand Common Pleas might applaud his innovations.

The common law did not do much to help a renter. The lessor retained legal "possession" despite the renter's physical presence. Since the renter did not "possess" the land [63] he could not use the writs of possession. [64] Chancery sold a writ he could use against the lessor's agent or buyer.[65] But Chancery sold nothing the renter could use against a stranger who threw him off the land. One distraught renter found an innovative clerk.

---

[62] The paragraph interprets "[T]hey could not put all cases therein, but those cases that are most hard, and you must understand by this that it includes cases that are less hard." Case at 36. Bereford probably viewed the named writs as the "most hard" because they allowed an heir to invoke an ancestor's possession; the plaintiff's case is "easier" because he claims an interest given him directly.

[63] "Justice Bereford: The term is only a chattel…." 5 31a Rolls Series 164 (1306).

[64] The assize of novel disseisin provided possessors effective recovery. "Chief Justice Weyland: If the lessor had alienated the land before the term was over, the {lessee} would not have recovered by the assize of novel disseisin." Anon, 112 Selden Society 360, 61 (1278).

[65] Or the lessor himself. The writ of *quare ejecit infra terminum*. *See* 34 Selden Society 222 (1312–1313) (writ used against lessor's buyer).

5. (1312–1313)[66]

[1] Adam leased a farm to Bogo for a dozen years. A stranger—Cosmo—threw Bogo off the farm. Bogo sued him with the renter's writ.[67]

[2] Cosmo: The writ's invalid. Some clerk modified the standard renter's writ by dropping the language that I'm acting as the lessor's agent or buyer. A clerk can't do that. The court has to strike down his invention.[68]

[3] Justice Inge: The standard writs work only against an agent or buyer.[69] On their face they don't help Bogo. Tell

---

[66] 34 Selden Society 226. The plaintiff is in fact the son of the renter. Despite the clerk's sensible innovation, Chancery stopped selling the writ. For centuries common law courts struggled to solve the renter's dilemma. *See* A.W.B. Simpson, *An Introduction to the History of Land Law* 87 (1961). Another early innovation allowed the lessee to use the writ of covenant against the lessor when the king's escheator ejected the lessee even though the escheator did not act as the lessor's agent. 19 Selden Society 84 (1309).

[67] Described by the reporter as a *quare ejecit infra terminum*. Case headnote and text at page 226.

[68] Interpreting "This writ is not conceived in the right form, for this is neither a writ of covenant nor a writ *quare eiecit infra terminum* and we do not think that we ought to answer to such a writ, not conceived in proper form (*hors de forme*), without common assent of the council." Cosmo argues the clerks need express authorization. Bracton says implicit authorization is enough. "If a writ is brought without warrant of the law, it shall be sustained as long as it is consonant with reason and not contrary to the law, provided it has been granted by the king and approved by his council… it does not matter that the magnates have not given their assent expressly so long as they have not expressly dissented…" Bracton fol. 414b. The Bereford cases responding to Brabazon's threat said express consent was necessary. Now that the threat is gone Common Pleas reinstates Bracton's theory of implicit authority.

[69] The writs of covenant and *quare eiecit infra terminum*.

me what writ Bogo should have bought. If you can't name one, we'll validate this clerk's variant.[70]

[4] Cosmo: My alleged invasion will catch Adam's attention. He won't want me on the land. He'll sue me for dispossession. Then Adam will put Bogo back on the land for the rest of his lease.[71]

[5] Justice Inge: Bogo has a right to the years left on his lease. {Bogo can't rely on Adam. Adam's been paid. He's not going to waste his time and money on a lawsuit that just helps Bogo.}[72] Since you can't name a better writ, this clerk's writ is valid.[73]

---

[70] Interpreting "Justice Inge: A writ of covenant does not lie against a stranger, and the *quare eiecit* is given against a stranger 'on the occasion of a certain sale' {*i.e.*, a sale by the lessor.} Therefore if a stranger, of his own wrong, eject me from my term, what writ would you give me?" Case at 226.

[71] He adds if Adam doesn't put him back in possession, Bogo can sue Adam. Interpreting "[I]f (Bogo be ejected) by a stranger (acting) on his own authority the lessor will recover the free tenement by assize and then {Bogo} (will recover) his term against the lessor by writ of covenant." Case at 227. The "useful" writ Cosmo gives Bogo (the writ of covenant) is worthless unless Adam brings a novel disseisin (*i.e.*, "the assize") against Cosmo.

[72] The text adds the rationale.

[73] Interpreting "Inge, J.: This writ is conceived in a case where the termor is ousted by a stranger, and not on the occasion of a sale. And therefore answer." The text interprets Inge's comment to refer to the novel writ Bogo bought. The Selden Society editors don't understand the "give a good writ" doctrine. Therefore they twist the passage into nonsense. They explain Inge's reference to "this writ" by the footnote "*I.e.*, the writ or writs mentioned by Cosmo." Footnote 3 at 227. If the editors are right that Inge is referring to the writs of novel disseisin and covenant that Cosmo suggested Bogo should have brought, how can Cosmo—as Inge demands—answer those writs. Bogo did not bring them. The case outcome supports the text's interpretation. By presenting a factual defense to Bogo's writ, Cosmo concedes its validity. Cosmo says he will go to a jury on his alleged

The clerk's solution to the renter's dilemma made sense. Once Brabazon's threat was dead the court was happy to hear its junior partner's bright ideas.

After reestablishing a comfortable relationship with Chancery, Common Pleas might even reject a writ with an offer to help the clerks if they could not figure out the correct writ to write.

6. (1312–1313)[74]

> [1] Adam bought a farm and sold Bogo a lifetime interest in the place. When some oaks were improperly harvested Adam sued[75] Bogo to recover possession. After Bogo failed to appear, Adam asked the court to enter judgment that he could retake the farm. Cosmo then asked to intervene in the case.
>
> [2] Cosmo: Adam originally bought the farm from someone who had given me a security interest in the place when I loaned him money.[76] After he didn't pay I sued to enforce the security interest, and a court gave me a judgment {that put me into possession instead of Bogo} until the profits from the farm paid off the

---

facts that Adam had previously enfeoffed his son, and after his son's death, his son's heir (the son's sibling) enfeoffed Cosmo. Cosmo doesn't say Bogo's writ is defective; Cosmo apparently proposes the theory that Bogo couldn't have acquired the "possession" his novel variant renter's writ asserted because Adam's sale to his son invalidated any subsequent rental agreement he made.

[74] 34 Selden Society 96 (1312–1313). The actual facts by which Cosmo acquires the security interest are complicated. The text creates a concrete example of waste.

[75] Writ of waste.

[76] The original creditor had created a security interest under the Statute Merchant in conjunction with the sale of six sacks of wool.

debt.[77] The court can't interfere with my possession on the basis of a suit Adam has brought against Bogo, a person who isn't even in possession now.

[3] Adam: All the court needs to investigate is whether I leased the land to Bogo, and whether the oaks were cut down. Nothing else matters.

[4] Chief Justice Bereford: You have to answer Cosmo's claim that he recovered possession of the farm as security for the debt incurred before you bought the place.

[5] Adam: That's not fair. The oaks were cut down, and the only writ Chancery sells to remedy this problem is a writ I have to bring against my tenant. Cosmo isn't my tenant.[78]

[6] Chief Justice Bereford: You were stupid to buy the farm from someone who had already encumbered it with a security interest. Do you think this court has to protect you from your own folly?[79]

[7] Adam: Although Cosmo had a right to take possession because of his security interest, that security interest gave him no right to cut down the

---

[77] The text adds information from the Statute of Merchants that the reporter had no reason to include. *See* Statute of Merchants (13 Edw. I), 1285 3 EHD 457.
[78] Interpreting "Sir, if we be ousted of this writ we are without recovery, for we cannot bring a writ of waste against others than the tenant for term of life, to whom we leased." Case at 97.
[79] Interpreting "Do you think that the court is bound to safeguard (you) from damage in every foolish purchase you can make? No." Case at 97.

oaks. I must have some kind of remedy to recover the wasted land.[80]

[8] Justice Stanton: Then go to Chancery and buy the correct writ.

[9] Adam: I've got no idea what writ that would be.

[10] Chief Justice Bereford: We don't have the time now to provide you legal advice about your problem. You need to ask Chancery to solve the problem. But if they can't come up with a solution then we'll be willing to give you some help with them.[81]

---

[80] Interpreting "Albeit that these tenements were burdened before we purchased, still he that is seised now by virtue of the recognizance can now commit waste." Case at 97.

[81] Interpreting "Chief Justice Bereford: We are not now at leisure to discuss your writ now, but go the Chancery and try to have a remedy there. And if you (should) need our help, we shall gladly help you there etc." Case at 97. Bereford advised litigants about the language to put into a judicial settlement. 19 Selden Society 146 (1309).

CHAPTER 5
Pleading

THE BEREFORD COURT exploited its creative power in many ways. The court created common law rules by deciding questions about "pleading," the apparently value-free traffic rules that tell the litigants how to present their cases in court. The court used decisions about pleading to announce new common law rules, to favor disadvantaged groups, and to facilitate efficient use of court time.

The Creation of Legal Rules

The parties make in-court statements about the facts they intend to prove. At any point a party can reply to her opponent's statement by saying "So what? You rely on some facts. But the common law does not give those facts any significance. Therefore I should win." The pleading forces the court to turn a general common law rule into a precise rule about specific facts.[1]

---

[1] The common law "demurrer" now appears in much American litigation as a motion to dismiss under state rules modeled on the federal rules of procedure section 12 (b) (6), the failure to state a claim upon which relief can be granted.

1. (1307)[2]

[1] Adam sued[3] Bogo for legal services.

[2] Bogo: I pay you an annual retainer[4] but when I recently asked for your help you turned me down. The common law says a contract breaker can't sue to enforce the contract.[5]

[3] Adam: I stopped being your lawyer. So what? You have refused to pay my past bills. The common law lets a lawyer under contract stop working because of non-payment and still collect his past accounts.[6]

[4] Justice Howard: Bogo you stopped paying. Adam's right. The common law lets him collect for what he's done.[7]

Prior to this case no one knew what the common law said about a lawyer's obligation to a non-paying client. In dismissing Bogo's pleaded defense, Howard gives specific content to a general rule.

---

[2] 5 31a Rolls Series 402. For another dispute about a lawyer's annual retainer, *see* 33 Selden Society 1 (1312); for a dispute about an annual retainer for medical services, *see* 36 Selden Society 80 (1313).

[3] Writ of annuity.

[4] Interpreting "For a yearly rent for services performed and to be performed." Case at 402.

[5] Interpreting "We prayed him to serve us in that plea, and he would not: therefore since he has failed to do the thing which is the cause of the grant of the annuity, we do not think he can demand it." Case at 404.

[6] Interpreting "And we pray judgment ...if he can, by anything which he has pleaded, bar us of the annuity." Case at 404.

[7] Interpreting "The court doth adjudge that he do recover the ten marks accrued due before the writ issued, and also the amount which he has since accrued due, and also his damage etc." Case at 404.

Pleading forced Common Pleas to give specific content to the concept of "war." Sued for breaking a peacetime rule, the defendant asks the court to dismiss the case. The country was at war.[8] But—as American lawyers say—the salami can be sliced thinner. Battles rage but some people are at peace.[9]

2. (1278–1279)[10]

> [1] Lady Anna sued[11] Sir Bogo for violating the peace. He invaded her compound and took forty oxen, twenty cows and a hundred pigs. Then he broke into her house and took gold, silver, woolens, and linens. Finally he carted her off to his prison where she languished until he received a hundred pounds ransom.
>
> [2] Bogo: You say I violated the peace. There was no peace. The countryside was at war.
>
> [3] Anna: The Statute of Kenilworth says peacetime rules applied among the king's allies.[12]

---

[8] Cf. "Robert said that John never had possession of that land, but got possession of the land by abatement fifteen days before the battle of Lewes, and afterwards died in the said battle, in time of war… Justice Mettingham: Thereby you mean to say that he did not die seised in his desmesne in time of peace." Mort d'ancestor, 2 31a Rolls Series458 (1294).

[9] Cf. "The phrase 'time of war' is to be understood only of opposite parties..." 1 31a Rolls Series 192 (1292). However in a reporter's note a lawyer so asserted but the reporter dissented. Note, 1 31a Rolls Series 156 (1292).

[10] 122 Selden Society 63 (1278–1279).

[11] Writ of trespass.

[12] Interpreting "She asks for a decision in accordance with the statute of Kenilworth as to whether or not the parties are to be regarded as having been at war." Case at 64.

[4] Bogo: You weren't on his side. You harbored two rebels, both arsonists and murderers.

[5] Anna: Those men are my brothers, the king's loyal subjects. As clergymen they came to see me to discuss my rights as a widow. But I never asked for their help.

[6] *The Reporter*: The court asked the jury whether Anna supported the royal cause; and if she did, whether she invited her brothers to her manor.[13]

Sometimes a pleading dispute was really a dispute about whether a secular or church rule applied to a controversy. A person's legitimacy might turn on a phrase. One phrase would send the case to church court and legitimacy; another, to secular court and illegitimacy.

3. (1312)[14]

[1] Claiming he had inherited a farm Adam sued[15] his younger brother Bogo.

[2] Bogo: You were born out of wedlock so you can't inherit the farm.

[3] Adam: According to the rules of pleading you can't say I was born "out of wedlock." You have to call me a "bastard."

---

[13] Interpreting "Whether the lady was a participant in the war as he alleged or not; and whether the executors had come at her request or not...." Case at 65.

[14] 33 Selden Society 161. The order of argument within the report has been changed. The case is also reported in 36 Selden Society 210 (1313). 36 Selden Society 158 (1313) addresses the same problem.

[15] Writ of right.

[4] Bogo: If I plead "out of wedlock" the court will ask the jury to decide if you're legitimate. If I plead "bastard" the court will ask the church to decide. The jury applies the secular rule that a child born before his parents' marriage is illegitimate. The church applies its own rule that the parents' subsequent marriage makes the child legitimate. The common law favors the secular rule.[16] I can plead you were born "out of wedlock."[17]

[5] Adam: That's the usual rule. But I haven't brought the usual writ. I've brought the most conclusive land writ there is, the writ of ownership. If the church decides a person's status the question has been answered once and for all.[18] If a jury decides a person's status the question can be reopened. My conclusive land writ entitles me to the most conclusive answer.[19] You've got to call me a bastard.

[6] Bogo: The ruling class was outraged when the church said some {older sons born before their parents' married had a valid claim to the land their

---

[16] Interpreting "Whence it doth appear that it would be against the common law for such [as are born before wedlock] to take inheritance..." Case at 162.

[17] Interpreting "Our answer falleth within the jurisdiction of this court, so that this Court can try whether or not you were born out of wedlock; and we shall not go to Court Christian in a matter of which this Court can have jurisdiction." Case at 164.

[18] *See* 29 Selden Society 206 (1313–1314) (note VI) *See also* 19 Selden Society 110 (1309), 5 31a Rolls Series 64 (1305). A bishop's ruling about the validity of a marriage in dower litigation would also bind everyone. 5 31a Rolls Series 64 (1305).

[19] The paragraph interprets "If this were a possessionary writ he would certainly be entitled to make the answer that he now maketh; but, since this is a writ of right, he ought not to be able to make an answer which goeth to the possession, but he ought to make one which goeth to the right, that is, in accordance with our writ." Case at 164.

younger brothers had apparently inherited.}[20] They passed a statute that told the courts to apply the secular rule. I don't have to plead you are a bastard.[21]

[7] Chief Justice Bereford: This court has always let the younger boy keep his inheritance by pleading his older brother was born "out of wedlock." I'm not going to create a different outcome just because Adam has used a writ no one uses anymore.[22]

[8] Adam: You're contradicting a recent case. An older brother took possession after his father died. The younger boy threw him off the land. When the older brother sued the court forced the younger boy to call him a "bastard." The church court said that since the

---

[20] Interpreting "The Statute of Merton declareth that such as are born out of wedlock shall be not be capable of inheriting … while those of Holy Church hold that such as are born before wedlock are capable of inheriting. And it was said there by the commonalty that they would not change the law of England…." Case at 164. The text imputes legislators' self-interest as a force behind Parliament's insistence on the continued application of the secular rule.

[21] Interpreting "We do find in the Statute of Merton how when the Bishops etc. held that the Church counted them as legitimate that were born before wedlock, the Barons answered that they would not change the customary laws of the realm."

[22] Interpreting "In a writ of mort d'ancestor, cosinage, ael etc. would it not be a good answer to say that you were born out of wedlock?—*intimating that it would be.* And, if it were so found here, would you now be received to claim etc.?—*intimating that he would not be.* And, if of your own conceit you have waived your possessionary writ and gone to your writ of right, hath the tenant lost his answer? – *intimating that he had not.*" Case at 164. The possessory writs Bereford identifies were the conventional way to recover land; the writ of ownership was avoided at all costs.

parents married after his birth he was no bastard, and he got the land back.[23]

[9] Bogo: A single pleading rule sometimes serves two different purposes. Ordinarily an older brother loses because Parliament does not want a child born before marriage to inherit. But there's another policy. Parliament wants to discourage self-help.[24] The boy used self-help in the case you're talking about. The court had to choose between two policies. The court thought discouraging self-help mattered more. The court said the boy had to call his older brother a bastard so that the boy wouldn't profit from his violence. The older brother got the land back when the church court said the parents' marriage made him legitimate. That case doesn't apply to us. I took possession when father died. The court will let me plead you were born out of wedlock so the jury will say I'm the true heir. I'll keep the land I've peacefully taken as my inheritance.[25]

---

[23] The paragraph interprets "In the Michaelmas term of the fourth year we saw in a writ of entry that the defendant could not be received to make such an answer as above, but was compelled by the Court to say fully that the claimant was a bastard." Case at 165. The excerpt necessarily implies that the older brother first took possession, the younger brother then ejected him, and then transferred the land to a third person. As the person who first took possession, the older brother then brought a writ of entry against his younger brother's transferee. The text simplifies the case by eliminating the transfer.

[24] Parliament created the assize of novel disseisin. Its long shadow is manifested in contemporary reference to the maxim "possession is nine points of the law."

[25] The paragraph interprets "He is in a better condition to rebut you by exception than he would if he were bringing an action, for the law is more favourable to maintaining his tenancy than it is to you who are bringing an action … for the condition of the possessor is better than that of the claimant." Case at 165.

[10] Chief Justice Bereford: The boy's right.

Another pleading rule gave a man the ability to have a "surviving child" even though he never engendered a child.

4. (1312–1313)[26]

[1] Anna's cousin gave a farm to Bogo and his "surviving child." Anna sued[27] Cosmo claiming her right to inherit the farm because Bogo had died childless.

[2] Cosmo: I'm Bogo's surviving son. I've got a better right than you to the land.[28]

[3] Anna: You can't be Bogo's son—Dan's your father.

[4] Cosmo: So what? I'm in possession of the farm, and I can plead everyone knew that Bogo had accepted me as his son. I don't have to plead we had a blood relationship.[29]

[5] Chief Justice Bereford: Cosmo's right. He has pled the proper facts to show he qualifies as Bogo's "surviving child." Even if he isn't related by blood to Bogo, Bogo made him "his child" when he publicly accepted him as his son.[30]

---

[26] 34 Selden Society 218. Anna sues through her husband. Case record at 221.
[27] Writ of cosinage.
[28] Interpreting "After {Bogo's} death {Cosmo} entered as son and is 'in' as heir." Case at 220.
[29] The paragraph interprets "The son of Bogo, accepted and recognized. Ready etc." Case at 220.
[30] Interpreting "Chief Justice Bereford: If he wants to plead wisely he cannot give another answer in his case than he has done, for the one

Through the use of pleading rules the court created a common law of adoption. Anna's cousin's gift suggests he wanted the farm to stay in his bloodline forever.[31] Bereford favors adoption, favors it to the point of saying Bogo's adopted child satisfies the dead cousin's intentions better than Anna herself, the cousin's actual blood relative.[32]

The Disadvantaged

Common Pleas manipulated pleading rules to favor widows, children, and the poor.

5. (1310–1311)[33]

> [1] When Anna sued[34] Bogo for her widow's portion Bogo did not show up. On the day set for judgment, Bogo's lawyer appeared.

{the blood relationship} and the other {Bogo having accepted and recognized Cosmo) tend to one effect." Case at 221.

[31] The text assumes the grantor cousin was related by blood to Bogo. The blood relationship is often but not necessarily the background to a gift in fee tail. 3 31a Rolls Series 388 (1303) discusses a gift in frank marriage by the Earl of Cornwall to a recipient without any suggestion of a blood relationship.

[32] One case suggested the doctrine applied only to the children of a woman whom the "adoptive" father married. Raising the specter that "a Frenchman might after my death enter my land and say he entered as son and heir," Justice Hertford insists "there must be color that he is {the decedent's son} but now {the claimant} makes him a stranger {by pleading} his father never married his mother: and therefore there is neither color nor presumption that he is the son."2 31a Rolls Series 616,618 (1294). The child was described as "the son of one Serle who was vicar of the church of N." Case at 616. Other cases impose no such requirement. *E.g.*, 17 Selden Society 186,187 (1308–1309).

[33] 26 Selden Society 132.

[34] Writ of dower.

[2] Bogo's lawyer: I see Anna is represented by an agent rather than one of my fellow lawyers. Mr. Agent, could you repeat Anna's claim?[35]

[3] Agent: As you certainly know, Anna is claiming …[36]

[4] *The Reporter*: The agent stopped talking when he saw Justice Stanton wink at him. Then he saw the light.[37]

[5] Agent: I'm not going to repeat Anna's claim. I want the court to enter judgment because of Bogo's past failures to appear.[38]

[6] *The Reporter*: Stanton saved Anna. If her agent had kept talking he would have waived Bogo's defaults.

[7] Bogo's lawyer: Then I say her writ's no good because she has sued Bogo alone but he and his wife bought the land together. Since Anna hasn't made Bogo's wife a defendant her writ is no good.

[8] Chief Justice Bereford: It's too late to plead that. You've missed court dates and unless you have some excuse you lose.

[9] *The Reporter*: Many lawyers thought the court would let a defendant ask for dismissal at any time if

---

[35] Interpreting "Scrope: What do you ask?" Case at 132.
[36] Interpreting "The attorney began to state his demand."Case at 132.
[37] Interpreting "The attorney began to state his demand. And afterwards Justice Stanton winked at him." Case at 132.
[38] Interpreting "The attorney said afterwards: 'I betake myself to the default strictly': for if he had stated his demand he would have released the default and pled on the principal matter." Case at 132.

> the plaintiff had failed to join a party. Bereford's new rule now sets a different standard.[39]

The reporter implies Bereford has revised general rules, but Bereford has probably revised the law only for widows. Delay deprives them of a right they cannot get back. The court can give a renter extra time if his lessor has interfered with his term of possession. The court cannot tack on years at the end of lifetime right.

The court exploited a varied arsenal to protect widows.[40] The court advised widows and allowed them to repudiate their mistakes.

6. (1311)[41]

> [1] Anna sued[42] Bogo for her widow's portion of three houses and six shops in London.[43] When Anna's late husband sold Bogo the investment properties he guaranteed that his son Adam would compensate Bogo if Anna took a widow's share. Bogo had Anna's suit adjourned so that he could notify Adam in Norfolk and Suffolk[44] that he intended to enforce the guarantee.[45] Months later when the case resumed Bogo had a new reason for delay.

---

[39] Interpreting "Chief Justice Bereford … until you have purged that default you cannot be received to abate the writ. (This seemed strange to many, but now is the law.)" Case at 132.

[40] Delaying tactics were limited in claims for a widow's portion. 63 Selden Society 261 (1311).

[41] 26 Selden Society 167.

[42] Writ of dower.

[43] Case record at 168.

[44] *See* case record at 168.

[45] He was vouched to warranty.

[2] Bogo: We'll have to start all over.[46] Anna has remarried and she and her new husband need to bring a joint claim.

[3] Anna: {I haven't remarried,} and anyway it's too late for you to claim I have. Once you brought my son in you waived your right to further delay.

[4] Chief Justice Bereford: Perhaps, Anna, you are not taking the best strategy. You want the case to go forward on the merits despite Bogo's new attempt at delay. If we let the case go forward you'll get your widow's share but your son will pay for it.[47] Here's another idea. If you haven't in fact remarried, plead that. If the jury agrees we'll immediately award you your widow's share. Bogo will have no way to enforce the guarantee against your son—the case will end before he can ask for that. His delaying tactics will make him pay the share himself.[48]

[5] Justice Stanton: Follow the Chief's advice, Anna. Plead "I agree to go to a jury on the question of my alleged remarriage. Where and when did this supposed remarriage take place?"[49]

[6] {Anna: That's just what I plead.}[50]

---

[46] Once Anna made a new claim, Bogo would again vouch the son, and again the son would have to be notified. Maybe, Bogo thinks, I'll have good luck: Anna could die suddenly, and I'll escape liability.
[47] He will follow through with vouching the son to warranty, and the son will pay him for what Anna gets.
[48] The paragraph interprets "Does he not wish to resort from his voucher, and to answer you for himself? I think that it is an advantage for you for him to risk his land against your writ." Case at 168.
[49] The paragraph interprets "Justice Stanton: Where was he married and when?" {sic} Case at 168. The Anglo-Norman correctly states "ele."
[50] The reporter omits this answer, and instead jumps to Bogo's reply.

[7] Bogo: You remarried last Easter in the Church of the Holy Cross in Southampton.

[8] Anna: I haven't left London since my husband passed.

Common Pleas also intervened to protect children.[51]

7. (1293)[52]

[1] The prior's predecessor sold Bogo's father a farm. When the father died, the prior said he was Bogo's guardian and sued[53] Bogo's mother Babs because she would not give up the boy.

[2] Babs' lawyer: Your predecessor's deed says he sold the place in peasant ownership. [54] Peasant ownership means that Babs is her son's guardian.

[4] Prior: Bogo's father paid military assessments. That changed the farm into normal ownership.[55]

[5] Babs' lawyer: He never made those payments.

---

[51] Improper use of court procedure against minors was a serious offence. The court imprisoned an attorney for bringing a proceeding to outlaw defendants who turned out to be minors. 5 31a Rolls Series 6 (1305) (parceners).

[52] 2 31a Rolls Series 178.

[53] Writ of wardship.

[54] Socage tenure.

[55] Interpreting "The ancestor of Bogo who was underage held of him by foreign services, that is to say, when Escuage runs etc. and by homage; and that ... John his predecessor was seised of the Escuage." Case at 180. The text uses the phrase "normal ownership" to refer to military tenure.

[6] Justice Hertford: Stop. You're committing malpractice. Why are you talking about what the father did? A jury might find he made the payments and then the prior would be the guardian and confiscate Bogo's income. You should just say the deed trumps everything —it doesn't matter what the father did. If you had an adult for a client he would pay for your incompetence. But we take minors' rights seriously. We'll let you change your pleading so that the boy will receive some assets when he becomes an adult.[56]

[7] Babs' lawyer: The deed trumps everything.[57]

[8] Prior: The court is wrong—if the father paid, the status of the land is transformed.

[9] Justice Hertford: You apparently want a judgment on whether the priory can exact some unjustified payment from the father and then take the son's income as a bonus. We will give you a judgment, a judgment that you have no right to be the boy's guardian.[58]

---

[56] The paragraph interprets "Justice Hertford: You do bad service to your clients; you only take care to get to an averment; you have pleaded badly; you have offered an averment that his predecessor was not seised of the Escuage; and if it were not to the disherison of the infant who is underage, you should not resort to another answer." Case at 180.
[57] Interpreting "They cannot deny their deed…" Case at 180.
[58] Interpreting "Think you that even if your predecessor had the wardship of his father tortiously, even if he was tortiously seised of the Escuage by distress, you should have the wardship in opposition to your predecessor's deed? Certainly not. Babs' lawyer: The Prior has admitted the deed. Judgment. Reporter: It was adjudged {Babs won}." Case at 180.

Bereford added the poor to the court's protected classes but he could not help a farmer who committed himself to a losing position.

8. (1311)[59]

[1] Adam's writ[60] said Bogo had broken the law[61] by taking his plow animals.[62] In court Adam repeated his writ's allegation that Bogo had confiscated his "oxen."[63]

[2] Bogo: Since in court you say I took "oxen" I say the jury will find I didn't. I took cows.[64]

[3] Adam: The court should interpret my statement to mean you took my draft animals. You can't make the jury question the particular kind of animal you took.[65]

---

[59] 31 Selden Society 18. The text adopts American usage by substituting "oxen" for "bullocks."

[60] Replevin founded on *Statute De Districcione Scaccarii*. Headnote at 18.

[61] *Statute De Districcione Scaccarii*. *See* case at 18, footnote 1.

[62] "Our writ runs 'Of the beasts of the plough.'" Case at 18. If he could confiscate other property, the lord could not take plow beasts. By confiscating a plow animal at either planting or harvest, a landlord could force his tenant to waive a valid defense. Under the modern American version of this doctrine a creditor cannot take tools the debtor uses in his trade.

[63] "We will aver that you took the beasts of our plough, to wit, bullocks etc." Case at 18.

[64] Interpreting "You have counted that we took the beasts of your plough, to wit, oxen. Ready etc. that we not take oxen, but four cows." Case at 18.

[65] Interpreting "If you want to be received to the averment you must traverse our plaint, and deny it; that is you must say that you did not take our beasts, without saying more; and then we will accept that; but what you say, that you took our cows, is an affirmation and outside this plea, and is no answer to this writ." Case at 18.

> [4] Bogo: After you posted bond you got your cows back pending the court decision.[66] If I win I'll have a right to get those animals back. If I tell the sheriff to get my "oxen," he won't find any. You chose the word "cows" and you've got to live with the consequences.[67]
>
> [5] Chief Justice Bereford: He's right, Adam. You caused your own grief. I know many poor farmers can't keep oxen. Why didn't you say "Bogo took my plow animals—the cows I use to pull my plow"? Then we would have asked the jury if he took your cows.[68]

Efficiency

Although the court manipulated pleading rules to favor certain groups most pleading rules were designed to make efficient use of court time.[69] The courtroom was not a coffee klatch. But the court allowed some tentative debate.

---

[66] Interpreting "In order that we may have return" (case at 18) and "you have deliverance of the cows by this writ." Case at 19.
[67] Interpreting "We say it that we may get return, for you have deliverance of the cows by this writ." Case at 19.
[68] Interpreting "There are many folk of the neighbourhood who put cows to plough for want of oxen, and if this be your case you could have said 'The beasts of the plough, to wit, cows,' and then your counting would be sufficiently good.—And afterwards the defendant's averment that he did not take the oxen of the plaintiff's plough but four cows was received."" Case at 19.
[69] Sometimes the court itself entered a pleading on behalf of a litigant because the litigant herself could not offer the plea without disastrous consequences, and the court wanted to use the litigation to resolve a question. "Chief Justice Bereford: We grant aid *ex officio*, but we shall cause an entry of the averment which you tender to be made, to save you your answer if at some other time the fine be alleged against you {so that the court's granting aid will have no *res judicata* effect upon you in another proceeding.}" 38 Selden Society 69, 76

9. (1311)[70]

[1] Adam sued[71] Bogo for breaking down his wall and carrying off the stones.

[2] Bogo: The earl's court ordered removal of the wall. I was just enforcing the judgment.[72]

[3] Chief Justice Bereford: Can anyone other than the court's chief officer enforce its judgment?[73]

[4] Bogo: Anyone—I'll go to the jury on that.[74]

[5] Adam: You're wrong. Only the chief officer or the complainants can enforce the judgment.[75]

[6] Bogo: Actually the chief officer told me to act as his agent.[76]

(1312–1313). Also reported at 41 Selden Society 91 (1315). A woman claimed ownership of land against a man who defaulted, and his minor son petitioned to intervene claiming his father had received a fee tail. "The Justices adjudged an inquest, *virtute officii* (because the infant could not be a party while he was underage), to know whether the father was enfeoffed in fee simple or not." 2 31a Rolls Series 44 (1294) (*cui in vita*).

[70] 42 Selden Society 136.

[71] Writ of trespass.

[72] "It was awarded by the court that this wall should be pulled down … and so we came etc. with others … as well we might…." Case at 137.

[73] Interpreting "When such a presentment is made is it to the court or the steward of the court that the award belongs?" Case at 137.

[74] Interpreting "Sir, to the whole court; and if they wish to remain in judgment as to this, we will remain." Case at 137.

[75] Interpreting "They do not say that Bogo was one of the presenters nor one of the bailiffs of the leet, nor anything else which gives him authority for pulling it down. Of this we ask judgment." Case at 137.

[76] "By command of the bailiff" Case at 137. Although the English text reads "we came as one of the presenters," Turner's observation "perhaps as one of the tithingmen" (footnote 1 page 137) shows his view that Bogo did not necessarily claim to be a complainant. The

[7] Adam: You've changed your story—the court should dismiss your case.[77]

[8] Chief Justice Bereford: Until now the court has given you both the latitude to air your theories. It's time for you both to commit. Be careful. We will hold you to every word you say.[78]

[9] Adam: {In that case, I'll abandon my pleading about the earl's court's judgment.} I'm ready for the jury on an easier question. No one has cause for complaint because I built the wall on my land.

[10] Bogo: The wall stuck out into the royal highway.

[11] Chief Justice Bereford: So the earl's court's judgment is now irrelevant.[79] I'll just ask the jury if the wall encroached.

In contrast to this case the court typically insisted that any firm stance that an opponent challenged created a precise issue for the jury. An American scholar described judicial enforcement of strict rules of pleading as "the sporting theory of justice."[80] He did not mean it as a compliment.

Anglo-Norman says "*nous sumes com un des parceners*" but Turner footnotes "*sic* (an error *for presentours*)..." Case at 137 footnote 17.

[77] Interpreting "Still we ask judgment of the avowry, for you see how they avow this pulling down, by reason of a presentment, and they do not say that Bogo was one of the presenters nor one of the bailiffs of the leet, nor anything else which gives him authority for pulling it down. Of this we ask judgment." Case at 137.

[78] Interpreting "Chief Justice Bereford: Trust no more to the favour of the court; but be advised about your plea; for the court from now will record how you reply etc." Case at 137.

[79] Interpreting "Now, you have waived your presentment." Case at 137.

[80] *See* Roscoe Pound, The Causes of Popular Dissatisfaction with the Administration of Justice, Annual Convention of the American Bar

10. (1307)[81]

[1] Adam sued[82] an abbey for two pounds and a horse that he had loaned Bogo the monk.

[2] Abbot: Bogo couldn't bind us. The common law rule doesn't let a monk bind his monastery {unless he has written authorization.}[83] Anyway look at the facts. Some rogue pretended to represent us and borrowed money and a horse {as part of a plan to break his vows and run away.}[84] If we never received what he borrowed we can't be liable.[85]

Association 1906. Justice Mettingham criticized a litigant for trying to take advantage of a misspelled name in a writ. "It is not the fault of the client, but is the fault of our clerk ... so we tell you that the process is sufficiently good; and you are not courteous in speaking in that fashion." 2 31a Rolls Series 224 (1293) (note).

[81] 5 31a Rolls Series 566 (1307). The text substitutes two pounds for an uncertain sum.

[82] Writ of debt.

[83] Interpreting "One can never charge an abbat on the deed of his monk unless the goods have come to the profit of his house; for you have no other cause in this case for demanding against the abbat." Case at 568. Four years later an abbot argued his monk could bind an abbey only if he had written authorization. Bereford said he was wrong. 42 Selden Society 19 (1311). The text interprets "no other cause" as a reference to written authorization. Cf. "Chief Justice Bereford: If the cellarer or anyone holding office in the House take things which go to the profit of the House, the Prior will be answerable therefor." 37 Selden Society 131, 132 (1314).

[84] The text adds the argument about Bogo's premeditation. Perhaps the argument is implicit in the report. The facts suggest premeditation, and the abbot's lawyer was likely to have mentioned it.

[85] The sentence interprets "Toudeby: Also he was an escaped monk, and he carried off the money with him, so that it never came to the profit of the house, ready etc." Case at 568. As the court interprets Toudeby's remarks, the lawyer has made two factual assertions. First the abbot denies Bogo had the authority to bind the abbey. Second the abbot says his abbey cannot be bound unless the monk turned over the loan proceeds and then later stole them.

[3] Justice Hengham: Was Bogo an ordinary monk?[86]

[4] Adam: No—he was management.[87]

[5] *The Reporter*: Justice Stanton and Justice Hengham chatted a bit. Then Stanton asked Adam if he denied that Bogo ran off.[88]

[6] {Adam: No, I know he did. But the abbot says Bogo couldn't bind the abbey. That's the factual question I'll take to the jury. They'll find Bogo's position gave him the right to bind the abbey.}[89]

[7] Justice Stanton: The abbot made two points. He said Bogo couldn't bind the abbey, and he said Bogo ran off with the horse and the money. That gave Adam the right to choose between the two. He's chosen Bogo's authority. We'll ask the jury about that.[90]

---

[86] Interpreting "Justice Hengham. What situation had he in the house?" Case at 568. Cf. 122 Selden Society 37 (1269?).
[87] Interpreting "He held an office there." Case at 568.
[88] "To Hedone {Adam's lawyer} Do you admit that he is an escaped etc." Case at 568. The report ignores Hedon's answer – he must have admitted Bogo escaped.
[89] The abbot makes his two points, and the report says only that Adam answers Bogo was management. The overall case report provides the text's basis for its description of Adam's full answer. If a party pled several points his opponent could choose any one of the points as the issue for the jury. *But see* "The Reporter: Note that where the party impleading offers an averment on two or three points ... the other party can not traverse one point without the others." 1 31a Rolls Series 374,376 (1293).
[90] In the overall context of the case (including in particular Hengham's question whether Bogo held an office) this paragraph interprets "Justice Stanton ... Do you wish on both sides that this averment should run. .... Therefore I say, that if {Adam} will admit that {Bogo} escaped, the averment {by the abbot that Bogo could not bind the abbey} shall run {that is, will go to the jury} ...." Case at 568.

> [8] Abbot: Wait. I've changed my mind. Even if Bogo had the authority to bind the abbey we aren't liable unless we received the proceeds of the loan. If I'm right about the law the court should just dismiss the case. Adam admits Bogo ran off with everything.[91]

> [9] Justice Stanton: No, it's too late for you to ask us to rule on the law. You denied Bogo could bind the abbey and Adam challenged you on that. The case will be resolved on that question alone. We'll enter judgment after the jury tells us about Bogo's authority.[92]

When Justice Hengham asked about Bogo's position Adam realized he would apply the rule now called "apparent authority."[93] The abbey could be bound by a person whose position induced public belief that he represented the abbey. The abbey's lawyer had dug their grave and Adam pushed them into it.

Pleading rules also gave a party the power to define the question for the jury[94] and sharpen the focus of the judgment.[95] Focus was important because subsequent

---

[91] Interpreting "Judgment then if by the deed of an escaped monk you can demand anything against the abbat." Case at 568. A request for "judgment" asks for a court ruling on the law instead of a jury submission.

[92] "Nay, you have pleaded and offered an averment, and are at issue." Case at 568.

[93] *See, e.g.*, Hely-Hutchinson *v.* Brayhead Ltd. 1 QB 549, 583 (1968). Bereford adopts the doctrine in 42 Selden Society 19 (1311).

[94] In arguing about the reason for a lapse of time in presenting to a church living one party asserts the negligence of the abbot created a delay, and Justice Siddington responds "We will never proceed to take a jury in that form, as it is uncertain how it was his failure. Therefore it is necessary to specify how." 123 Selden Society 404 (1289).

[95] For exceptions *see* 41 Selden Society 204 (1315) and 1 31a Rolls Series 242 (1292). A defendant argued that the plaintiff had not been married to her supposed late husband (an issue for the church) and

cases might be resolved on the basis of the precise language of the judgment.[96]

11. (1304)[97]

[1] Claiming a hundred pounds of damage the prior sued[98] the bishop because he had rejected the prior's nominee for a parsonage.

[2] Bishop: The nominee was unqualified.[99]

[3] Prior: You've got to be more specific.

[4] Bishop: He was illiterate, illegitimate, and underage.

[5] Prior: You can't choose three alleged defects—you have to decide on a single question for the jury. This court's judgment will create a final statement about my candidate's qualifications.[100] An ambiguous judgment will harm him.[101] {If your complaint is about

---

that she had claimed more land than he possessed (an issue for the jury). The court decided the church should first decide the question of the marriage; and then, if necessary, the jury would decide the question of possession. 33 Selden Society 31 (1312).

[96] Through the doctrine of *res judicata*, the subject of a subsequent chapter.

[97] 4 31a Rolls Series 30.

[98] Writ of *quare incumbravit.*

[99] "He did not present a suitable person…" case at 32.

[100] The necessary submission to the church authorities appears in the passage "He presented a suitable person, ready etc. where and when etc." Case at 32. The phrase "ready etc., where and when etc." refers to a submission to the church authorities.

[101] Interpreting "But consider whether he shall be received to aver these three causes; for the judgment to be by you now given will be hereafter an authority in every *Quare non admisit* in England; therefore consider if he shall be received to aver the three causes etc." Case at 32–34.

age or education, time can cure things. But if he is illegitimate he can never be a parson.}[102]

[6] {*The Reporter*: The court forced the bishop to focus.}[103]

Education

The court would bend pleading rules[104] if a lawyer could provide a persuasive reason.

12. (1306)[105]

[1] After he became an adult Adam sued[106] Bogo to recover a farm. He said that his sale of the property was voidable because he was then a minor.

[2] Bogo: I gave you my woodland as the purchase price. If you still possess the woodland you can't take the farm back.[107]

---

[102] The text adds the rationale.

[103] The reporter does not say that the prior's argument prevails. He does not have to—the architecture of the medieval report means that an unanswered argument wins. The convention saves time and parchment. Sometimes reports deviate from this general rule. For example the case reported at 33 Selden Society 132 (1312) includes five versions. In the first four Bereford approves a voucher after disclosing earlier doubts; the fifth report ends with his assertion that the obligation to warrant would be a hardship. The fifth report is probably an incomplete account which terminates during Bereford's preliminary discussion before judgment.

[104] Parties agreed to a jury to decide if a deed had been entrusted to a named stakeholder. When the jury identified a different stakeholder, but said that stakeholder was obligated to provide the deed to the named stakeholder, the court treated the verdict as applicable to the named stakeholder. 1 31a Rolls Series 212 (1292) (Detinue).

[105] 5 31a Rolls Series 192. A litigant convinced Bereford himself to change his position in 52 Selden Society 110 (1316).

[106] Writ of *dum fuit infra aetatem*.

[3] Justice Hengham: Bogo, I think you should plead that Adam confirmed the deal by keeping the woodland after his twenty-first birthday. Whether he still has the property doesn't matter.[108]

[4] Bogo: Right. Adam still had the woodland when he turned twenty-one.[109]

[5] Adam: I didn't have the place at that birthday. I'll go to a jury on that.[110]

[6] Bogo: Wait, I think I see now what he did. While he was still a minor Adam traded the woodland for another property. He knows the jury will say he didn't possess the woodland when he became an adult. I'd like to change my pleading. The jury will find he had the woodland or its equivalent[111] when he turned twenty-one.[112]

[7] Justice Malore: When you put it that way, Bogo, I see you're right. That's the correct question for the jury.[113]

---

[107] Interpreting "The demandant received a messuage in exchange. You are seised, if you have not alienated it." Case at 192.

[108] Interpreting "You must say that Adam was seised of the subject of the exchange after he was of full age and agreed etc." Case at 192. The text assumes the land was held in military tenure, and therefore Adam's age of majority would be twenty-one.

[109] Interpreting "After he was of full age he alienated the tenements which he received in exchange, ready etc." Case at 192.

[110] "We were not seised after we attained full age, ready etc." Case at 192.

[111] If it was not, Adam says Bogo could recover the woodland from the purchaser. "{he} would have {his} recovery…" Case at 192.

[112] The paragraph interprets "And if {Adam was} underage at the time of alienation, {he} would have {his} recovery; judgment etc.; for it is not right that {he} should have both." Case at 192.

[113] Interpreting "Malore: Answer if you {Adam} received certain tenements in exchange or not." Case at 192. By "exchange," Malore is referring not to the original exchange of Bogo's woodland for Adam's farm, but rather to the underage exchange Adam made of the

[8] Adam: But your honor I said I was ready to go to the jury when Bogo said I had the woodland on my birthday. He challenged me; I took up the challenge; that's that.[114]

[9] Justice Malore: I've bought Bogo's argument. You can either deny you did the trade or I'll enter judgment against you.[115]

[10] *The Reporter*: Adam capitulated.[116]

Mistakes Can Hurt

A lawyer has to understand both the strengths and weaknesses of her client's case.[117] Her client will lose if she cannot see clearly.

---

woodland for some other property. Malore appears to assume the other property is as valuable as either the woodland or the farm.

[114] "We are pleading to that which they have given us, for they have said that we were of full age and consenting etc., and we say Not so, ready etc." Case at 192.

[115] Interpreting "Malore: Answer to this statement that you received certain tenements in exchange."

[116] "{I} did not receive any tenements in exchange, ready etc." Reporter: And the other side said the contrary." Case at 192.

[117] After pleading in defense to a claim his widowed client had kept land after a lease had expired, a lawyer asked the court to dismiss the case because the plaintiff had sold the land outright to the late husband The court said that plea was too late—once the lawyer identified his client's interest as dower, he could not plead the land had been sold outright. He had to vouch the husband's heir. 33 Selden Society 244 (1312).

13. (1306)[118]

[1] *The Reporter*: An inept lawyer cost his client a third of his land.[119]

[2] Anna sued[120] Bogo for her widow's share of a farm. She said her late husband possessed the farm during their marriage. Bogo's lawyer said a jury would find he didn't.

[3] The Jury: When Bogo's mother died his stepfather got a lifetime right to her farm.[121] Bogo would get it when he died. The stepfather tried to cheat Bogo by selling the place outright to Anna's husband.[122] Bogo got a court judgment striking down the sale. {Since Anna's husband took possession wrongfully Anna shouldn't get a widow's share.}[123]

---

[118] 5 31a Rolls Series 348. The text recasts Malore's narration into the standard dialogue format. The case report speaks of both "P. to whom the reversion of those tenements belonged" and the defendant "E." The reporters' identifications of parties by initials often causes problems, and to simplify the presentation of the case the text replaces P and E with "Bogo" upon the plausible assumption he was the heir of the deceased woman whose husband sold the farm.

[119] More precisely, a third for the lifetime of the widow.

[120] Writ of dower.

[121] A curtesy interest.

[122] At the end of the stepfather's life estate, Bogo would get the "reversion."

[123] Interpreting Malore's statement describing the jury verdict: "because we {the court} find that {Anna's late husband} was seized in his demesne as of fee, although his estate was other than what is found by this verdict, and we cannot give judgment on the plea otherwise than in the form in which it is pleaded…." Case at 348.The text interprets "other than what is found by this verdict" to imply the jury said the husband's possession—his estate—was defective, and therefore Anna had no right to dower.

[4] Justice Malore: Although the jury thought they understood the law that applied to the facts they were wrong. Possession is possession. Anna's husband had "possession" even though his possession was wrongful. When Anna sued Bogo his lawyer shouldn't have asked for a jury. He should have just presented the judgment and asked the court to dismiss her case. We would have. Bogo's lawyer lost this case by his incompetent pleading.[124]

Another bad lawyer also chose a loser instead of a winner.

14. (1313–1314)[125]

[1] Anna sued[126] Bogo for putting her off a farm.

[2] Bogo: To sue me for dispossession you have to show you had possession. You never did. I inherited the place when father died and I've possessed it ever since.[127]

[3] Anna: I inherited the farm—you didn't. You were born before father married mother. In the eyes of the law you're no one's child.[128]

---

[124] Interpreting "And this {Malore} said because if {Bogo's lawyer} had disclosed the case and prayed for judgment, —inasmuch as Bogo recovered these tenements as his right by judgment etc., and the estate which her husband had was fully defeated—if she ought to have dower of those tenements, thereby of a truth he might have barred her etc." Case at 348–350.

[125] 29 Selden Society 90. "Anna" stands in for three sisters, each represented by their husbands.

[126] Assize of novel disseisin.

[127] Interpreting "He himself entered … as his son and heir, and has continued his seisin up to the present time without wronging or disseising" Anna. Case at 90.

[4] Bogo: A jury will say I'm the rightful heir.

[5] The Jury:[129] Here are the facts. Bogo was born two years before the parents married. Anna was born after the marriage. Then the father died. Bogo, Anna, and their mother all lived together on the farm before and after the father's death. Both Bogo and Anna claimed to have inherited the farm.[130] Then Anna and her mother left the farm voluntarily to live in the mother's widow's residence. Bogo stayed put. We don't know what our verdict should be. Can the court help us?[131]

[6] Justice Spigurnel: Bogo asked for a verdict about whether he inherited the farm. Your verdict shows he didn't. He was born before they married. That's all we need to know. You've done your job and now we'll do ours. Bogo dispossessed Anna.

[7] Bogo: That can't be right. The jury said Anna voluntarily left to live in our mother's widow's residence. I wasn't guilty of any act of dispossession.

[8] Justice Spigurnel: You're right about the facts. But you lose anyway. When siblings sit together on their

---

[128] Interpreting "Adam can be no one's heir, seeing that he was born out of wedlock; and Anna prays that this may be inquired of by the country." Case at 90.

[129] The report of the jury verdict is ambiguous. It says Bogo and Anna entered after the death of their father. The text assumes the jurors meant they stayed on the farm. Then the verdict states "claiming the right of succession by descent" from the father. Case at 90. While the claim might seem to relate only to Anna, the next sentence says Bogo assigned his mother dower, and that act of assignment shows Bogo himself claimed a right of succession by descent. Only someone claiming possession of the land could assign dower.

[130] Interpreting "Robert the younger {Bogo} and also the aforesaid {daughter} entered upon the tenements, claiming the right by succession by descent from … their father." Case at 90.

[131] "We pray your aid." Case at 92.

> dead father's farm in legal theory the true heir takes possession.[132] So Anna got possession. Your lawyer was wrong to say she didn't. Now as for the act of dispossession, you're right Anna left willingly. The dispossession didn't happen then. The dispossession happened in this courtroom because of the way your lawyer pled your case. According to our rules if you wrongfully deny a person's possession, that pleading constitutes an act of dispossession.[133] Your lawyer's bad defense dispossessed Anna. If your lawyer knew how to practice law you would have won. He shouldn't have said you were the heir. He should have just denied you dispossessed Anna. Before he made his inept pleading you hadn't.

In the next pleading battle the court loses its patience with a disreputable litigant who conjures up a series of worthless defenses. Although the case discusses a still controversial question—"the place of the wrong"[134] —

---

[132] "Since {Anna claims} on {her} own seisin, and we have several entering and claiming the right of succession, the seisin belongs to the one who has the greatest right ...." Case at 92. By this theory Spigurnel takes the dispute out of Bereford's rule that a child born before marriage can take possession, and stay in possession by forcing his sibling claimant to call him a bastard, an imputation the church courts will reject. 33 Selden Society 161 (1312). Bereford refers to a case in which only one sibling has in fact purported to take possession. Where several have Spigurnel's rule applies, and therefore Spigurnel can say "[T]he plaintiff {the younger sibling} will not be compelled to say explicitly that the tenant {the older sibling} is a bastard..." (Case at 92).

[133] Cf. "Note that if tenements be leased for a term of years and the lessee hold them beyond the term he is guilty of no disseisin; but if the lessor {sues} and the termor pleads against him, he becomes, ipso facto, a disseisor." 29 Selden Society 207 1313–1314).

[134] *See*, for example, Gordon *v.* Parker, 83 F. Supp. 40, aff'd, 178 F. 2d 888 (1st Cir. 1949). In twentieth century American contract law many cases distinguished between the place of making and the place

the reporter probably wanted just to provide a few laughs for his readers.

15. (1294)[135]

> [1] Lady Anna sued [136] Bogo in Cumbria for transmitting to the Archbishop of York a document that purported to be her nomination of him to a Cumbrian parsonage. The Archbishop had his doubts about the instrument,[137] but after Bogo's confederates reassured him, he ordered Bogo's installation in the parsonage.[138]
>
> [2] Bogo: The court should dismiss her case because she doesn't say where the document was written.
>
> [3] Anna: In Cumbria.
>
> [4] Bogo: You can't refer to an entire county. Be more specific.
>
> [5] Anna: Your honor, Bogo is so deceitful you shouldn't allow him to seek refuge in a series of worthless pleadings.[139]

---

of performance. *See*, *e.g.*, Seeman *v*. Philadelphia Warehouse Co, 274 U.S. 403 (1927). The issue is raised in 36 Selden Society 119, 121 (1313) and 1 31a Rolls Series 320 (1292) (annuity).

[135] 2 31a Rolls Series 388. The text invents "Cumbria" to stand for the reporter's "C." The confusing report suggests two proceedings: one to the Sheriff of York to acquire and transmit the fraudulent nominating document, and another against Bogo for deceit. The report does not clearly distinguish the two proceedings.

[136] Writ of deceit.

[137] "The Archbishop suspecting that the letter was fraudulently obtained, delayed the institution." Case at 368.

[138] "Was instituted and had corporal possession." Case at 388.

[139] Interpreting "Sir, we have counted against them for deceit, to which they answer not." Case at 388.

[6] Justice Mettingham: Bogo, Parliament asked the Archbishop to send us this forged document. The king has taken note of a plague of counterfeit seals of prominent subjects. What about it? Doesn't this document purport to be Lady Anna's nomination of you?

[7] Bogo: Just a moment, Sir, I need to look at the skin carefully. Ah, thank you! Your honor, the lady complains I was installed in Cumbria because of a deceit perpetrated in York. Shouldn't she have brought her claim in York? She needs to start all over.[140]

[8] Justice Mettingham: I didn't ask you where she should have sued. I asked you to comment on the content of this forgery.

[9] Bogo: Patience—first things first. Please rule on my argument that the lady brought the case in the wrong place.[141]

[10] Justice Mettingham: Are you listening? Haven't I just asked you if you will admit this document purports to nominate you?[142]

---

[140] Interpreting "Spigurnel prayed a sight of the writing and he had it. And he answered to the party, and said that in this writ he ought not to be answered; because he supposes by his count that the church is in the county of C., and that the disinheritance was committed in that county; and he ought to have purchased a writ directed to the Sheriff of that county and not to the Sheriff of C. whereupon we pray judgment." Although the sentence structure suggests "that county" refers to "C," that interpretation creates a conflict with the following reference to "and not to the Sheriff of C." Later passages in the case show that Bogo argued the case should have been brought in York.
[141] Interpreting "We will answer fully to the Court. And do you abate this bad writ." Case at 390.
[142] Interpreting "Do you admit that deed?" Case at 390.

[11] Bogo: Yes, your honor, in due time I'll comment on that question. I have some relevant memories. This document seems to be the one that a fellow I knew only as "John" gave me in Cumbria. He said the lady had acted in some haste {so that she could meet the six month deadline for the nomination}.[143]

[12] Anna: Now that Bogo has begun his lies about what he did at least he's given up on the jurisdictional arguments.[144]

[13] Bogo: Hardly. I wasn't talking to you. I was just giving a civil response to the honorable court. When I address you, you can make your arguments.[145]

[14] Anna: Enough of this. Just to get on with it I'll talk about jurisdiction. You committed both the forgery and the deceit in Cumbria. The court should enter judgment against you.[146]

[15] Justice Mettingham: If these events occurred in Cumbria Anna was right to sue there.

[16] Bogo: Your honor, you need to think more deeply about this. Just for purposes of argument let me suggest a hypothetical case. In Cumbria I forge a nomination to a Cumbrian parsonage but I hide this piece of work in my purse while I consider my

---

[143] Interpreting "One John brought that writing to us at C. for the purpose of maintaining the right of the lady, and in the lady's name."
[144] Interpreting "Would you abate our writ now that you have answered to the deceit?" Case at 390.
[145] Interpreting "We have answered to the Court and not to you; therefore that answer, as far as we are concerned, ought not to prejudice us." Case at 390.
[146] Interpreting "We complain of forgery and deceit committed in the county of C., to which they answer not etc."

options. No one could sue me in Cumbria – until the Archbishop gets the document in York no one's been hurt. Anna has to sue me there.[147]

[17] Justice Mettingham: For the last time, plead something else.

[18] Bogo: Your honor do you really want to insist? Naturally if you give this problem some more thought and then decide to stick to your position I'll answer in due course.[148]

[19] Justice Mettingham: Enough. Guard, put him in custody! He'll find out what's what tomorrow.[149]

---

[147] Interpreting "If he had made the writing in the county of C., and had not delivered it but had kept it in his purse, you could not have challenged it: so it follows that the cause arises from delivery, which was in the county of York; and where the cause arises there he shall bring his writ; and the cause here arose in the county of York and not in the county of C.; and his writ is directed to the sheriff of C.; so we pray judgment." Case at 390.

[148] Interpreting "If you so adjudge, we will give a sufficient answer." Case at 390.

[149] Interpreting "Justice Mettingham Serjeant, guard that clerk. Reporter: And they had a day on the morrow." Case at 390.

CHAPTER 6
Proof

MEDIEVAL PROOF LAW didn't focus on the way litigants presented evidence to the jury. Medieval proof law told the judge what type of proof he should apply to the dispute.[1] At one time he had a wide choice. Juries co-existed with "ordeals," techniques that identified the person God wanted to win. Accused criminals were dunked into ponds that God ordered to accept the innocent; others had their flesh burned so that God could impede the bad man's ability to heal. In the early thirteenth century the church condemned the ordeals.[2] Despite Rome's belief that no man could force God to disclose his will English law continued to use battle to decide claims to own land[3] and "oath helpers" to decide some other contests.[4] Battle worked not because might was right but because God had to intervene to favor the righteous. But battle could be fought without a priest on the scene. "Oath helpers" also forced God to intervene. After swearing to his version of the facts a litigant produced his supporters. They then

---

[1] One decision said a plaintiff could rely upon a document for part of a debt and oath helpers for the rest. The reporter disagreed. 1 31a Rolls Series 66 (1292) (debt).

[2] *See* F. W. Maitland, Introduction to *Pleas of the Crown for the County of Gloucester* xxvi–xli (1884).

[3] In civil litigation battle could be waged by champions. *See* 123 Selden Society 324 (1286).

[4] The plaintiff's oath helpers were called "suitors." The defendant's oath helpers were called "compurgators."

recited a formula that said they believed their man was righteous. They didn't claim to know anything about the facts. They just said they respected the litigant. If God let them recite their oath smoothly God said they supported a righteous man. If they failed to make the statement correctly God said their man was a liar.[5] Just like battle, this ceremony could take place without the participation of a priest. Although both these ancient methods survived Bereford's court never supported them on religious grounds. Instead the court limited their use, or re-worked them to implement a rational policy, or replaced them with the jury.

Battle

Common Pleas refused to expand battle beyond its historical limits.[6]

---

[5] By the ancient theory of compurgation a badly recited oath reflected divine intervention. Perhaps by the Bereford era this last gasp of divine intervention no longer existed and the character witness requirement just measured litigants' competing abilities to produce supporters, a test with some rational basis in a tight knit community. None of the Bereford era reports explains the theory behind oath helper proof.

[6] When a lady brought a *quod permittat* writ that led to the defendant's challenge to do battle she then withdrew her plea so that the case ended in a non-suit. 43 Selden Society 134 (1313). Her lawyer probably intended to bring a subsequent possessory writ with proof by a jury. By dismissing her claim he deprived the proceeding of res judicata consequences. The Selden Society editor does not see this strategic goal. *See* 43 Selden Society ix–x (introduction by William Bolland).

1. (1304)[7]

[1] Adam sued[8] Babs and her husband Sir Bogo for raping his wife.

[2] Bogo: Dismiss the case—a woman can't commit rape.

[3] Justice Howard: If she's an accessory, that's enough.[9]

[4] *The Reporter*: Sir Bogo then threw down his glove and told the court he would battle to prove his innocence. Adam threw down his own glove. They both wanted to fight. The justices wouldn't have it. The common law, they said, wouldn't let them battle.[10]

Character Witness Proof

From a modern perspective, when the plaintiff reinforced his case with "suitors" who asserted he was righteous and when the defendant brought his own witnesses, his "oath helpers," to assert the same, the litigants had presented "character witnesses." While proof by battle had no rational component, a rational person might believe a litigant's character indicated the likelihood he spoke the truth. In addition the court had

---

[7] 4 31a Rolls Series 316. The text changes the sequence of the arguments.

[8] A writ of trespass based upon the Statute of Westminster II, c. 34 (1285) (3 EHD 447).

[9] Interpreting "Although she could not ravish her, she could assent to it; therefore answer over." Case at 320.

[10] Interpreting "And then said Bogo that, if the Court would allow, he was ready to affirm by his body as became a knight that he was not guilty, and he threw down his glove to the Court. And Adam offered in like manner to prove the affirmative. And the Justices refused that issue, because they had no warrant to receive such an issue."

discretion to set the number of helpers. The reasonable court might ask a litigant with a bad case or reputation to produce more character witnesses than his opponent.[11] As a general matter, however, character witness proof was easily satisfied. The court could smooth a favored litigant's path by letting him use character witness proof.

2. (1310)[12]

> [1] Adam's executor, the representative of his estate, sued[13] Bogo for refusing to pay for a ton of wool. The executor had no document to prove the debt. He brought nothing but character witnesses to court.[14]
>
> [2] Bogo: I swear I didn't owe Adam a penny. I'll match his executor's character witnesses with my own.[15]
>
> [3] Adam's executor: The court shouldn't let you use character witness proof. There's no point in comparing our oath helpers—I don't know anything about what happened.[16] But people in the community would have

---

[11] According to Fleta a defendant in a writ of debt had to produce twice as many oath helpers as the plaintiff. *See* 4 31a Rolls Series xxxiii (citing Fleta, lib. 2, c. 63).

[12] 22 Selden Society 21. Several executors sued.

[13] Writ of debt.

[14] Inferred from Bereford's hypothetical about a creditor claiming a hundred pounds with nothing but "suit."

[15] "Ready [to make our law]." Case at 21. Typically "ready" means "ready for a jury." Here the reporter means "ready to produce character witnesses," as the executor's response shows.

[16] Interpreting "To the law you cannot get; for we are executors." Case at 21.

> known about a transaction for so much wool.[17] The court should impanel a jury.[18]
>
> [4] Chief Justice Bereford: Suppose executor you said Adam lent Bogo a hundred pounds. If you didn't have a document we would let Bogo rely exclusively upon a character witness defense. If we take that approach with a large debt, why shouldn't the same approach be taken with a smaller transaction?[19]
>
> [5] Justice Stanton: If Adam had been alive Bogo could have relied on character witnesses. I don't think his case becomes stronger just because he's dead.[20]

Rather than expressing respect for character witness proof the court expresses skepticism about the plaintiff's case. The claim that Adam sold a ton of wool without getting a signature doesn't ring true.

Common Pleas wanted to decide cases on the merits, not on technicalities. By letting a defendant prove lack of notification by character witnesses the court avoided entering a default judgment.

---

[17] The controversy was about six sacks of wool, a total weight of nearly a ton. *See* Nigel Saul, *A Companion to Medieval England, 1066-1485* 281–283 (1983).

[18] Interpreting "Besides, this is a big affair of which the country may have knowledge." Case at 21.

[19] Interpreting "If you surmised that he was bound to the testator in a hundred pounds, and only had suit {*i.e.*, character witnesses} whereby to bind him to the debt, he would be at his law {*i.e.*, he could defend by character witnesses}. Why then should he not 'at-law' himself for that which is less, namely for six sacks of wool." Case at 21.

[20] Interpreting "Show us why he should be in a worse position {than} he would be against the testator…" Case at 21.

3. (1313)[21]

[1] Adam sued[22] "the Prior of Stone Priory." After Prior Bogo defaulted Adam asked the court for judgment. The prior's agent appeared. He said Bogo had never gotten notice. The court said Bogo himself had to tell that to the court.[23] Before Bogo had a chance to show up church officials removed him from office.[24] Adam then asked again for a default judgment. Bogo's successor Cosmo appeared.

[2] Cosmo: My character witnesses will prove Adam never gave the Prior of Stone Priory good notice.[25]

[3] Adam: Their assertions are irrelevant. Of course you can say you never got notice—when I sued you weren't the prior. Why would I give you notice?[26] Maybe Bogo's no longer prior but he's still alive. Bring him to court and let him produce the character witnesses.

[4] Justice Inge: Adam you asked the court to tell "the Prior of Stone Priory" to say he didn't get notice. You asked for the office holder. You didn't ask for a named

---

[21] 36 Selden Society 172.

[22] Writ of entry.

[23] An agent could not "wage law" on his behalf. The next court date was postponed "because the Justices did not come." Case at 173.

[24] He was "deposed." Case at 173.

[25] Interpreting "The Prior who had been lately created … offered his law, in respect of the first default, that he had not been summoned, to the which default the claimant betook himself." Case at 173.

[26] Interpreting "For at that time he that now offereth himself was but an obedentiary of the same House, and therefore he can safely make his law that he was not summoned…." Case at 173. The *Oxford English Dictionary* defines "obedientiary" as a monk with administrative duties.

> individual. Any prior qualifies. Lawyers need to choose their words with care.[27]

As for theory the case is an exercise in absurdity. Cosmo's veracity has no relevance to whether Bogo got notice. The court has another agenda. Perhaps Bogo was removed because of alcoholism or dementia. A modern court could waive Bogo's default but a medieval court would find that difficult to do. The court manipulates the rules so the priory can present a defense on the merits.[28]

The court disapproved of character witness proof when important questions were at stake.[29]

4. (1311)[30]

> [1] Adam sued[31] the clergyman Bogo.[32] Adam said Bogo had violated the king's prohibition against bringing a secular claim in church court. He said Bogo had asked a church court to punish him for an alleged assault on a member of his staff.

---

[27] "Seeing that you bring your writ against the Prior etc. who made default and was re-summoned by his name of dignity... let men learn to [be wary how they] bring a writ against a Prior by his name of dignity [only]." Case at 178.

[28] For another case avoiding a technical default, *see* 70 Selden Society 126 (1319). Perhaps the court's judgment can be justified in another way. As an obedientiary perhaps Cosmo should have known whether the priory had been notified.

[29] But Bereford rejected a litigant's argument that character witnesses couldn't be used because an adverse decision would send him to prison. 39 Selden Society 104, 105 (1314).

[30] 63 Selden Society 121.

[31] Writ of attachment upon the prohibition.

[32] The text infers clerical status from the context and the description of Bogo as "Master."

[2] Bogo: My own character witnesses will show I never brought the suit.[33]

[3] Chief Justice Bereford: An improper extension of ecclesiastical jurisdiction hurts everyone. Are you really going to insist character witnesses can exonerate you from such a wrong?[34]

[4] Bogo: Adam's got nothing but character witnesses. The common law guarantees my right to match his with mine.

[5] Chief Justice Bereford: Do you want me to ask Parliament if you can whitewash your contempt of the king's order by trotting out a few underlings?[35]

[6] Bogo: Whatever you say I'm getting a judgment on my common law rights.

[7] Chief Justice Bereford: If we decide Adam's entitled to a jury, we won't impanel one.[36] We'll just enter judgment against you for having brought a secular claim to church court.[37]

---

[33] Interpreting "Ready are we to deny it against him and against his suit." Case at 121. "Suitors"—Adam's "suit"—are character witnesses. Interpreting "Sir, we did not sue any plea ... ready are we to deny it etc." in conjunction with "Willoughby: You shall not arrive at your law…." Case at 121.

[34] Interpreting "This is in derogation etc. and to the damage of all the people of the realm, and you are not willing to make another defense. Be well advised."

[35] Interpreting "Parliament is at hand and we will put the matter before Parliament to know whether a man can arrive at his law etc. concerning such a high and heinous matter." Case at 122.

[36] The appropriate proof for a trespass writ in royal court.

[37] Interpreting "If we award it, you will arrive at no other answer." Case at 122.

[8] Bogo: I give up. You want a jury; I'll take a jury.

Bereford thought Bogo's attempt to take a claimed act of violence to the church was a "high and heinous"[38] act: the king's interest in keeping the peace was imperative.[39] When a litigant said his opponent had taken a secular debt to church court, Bereford let character witnesses decide if he had.[40]

Bereford didn't have much respect for character witness proof.

5. (1310?)[41]

[1] Adam sued[42] to recover livestock he had put on Bogo's winter pasture.[43] He brought nothing but character witnesses to court.

[2] Bogo: Since you don't produce a written contract[44] I'll produce character witnesses to show I never took that livestock.

[3] Chief Justice Bereford: By God we won't let you hide behind character witnesses when the jury may know something. Any man can find a handful of

---

[38] Case at 122.

[39] Justice Stanton states the conventional rule of character witnesses proving whether an improper claim has been brought in church court in 33 Selden Society 118 , 119 (1312).

[40] 20 Selden Society 134 (1310).

[41] 19 Selden Society 195.

[42] Adam "complains" that Bogo wrongfully detains his chattels. Perhaps he brought an informal proceeding; perhaps he brought a writ of detinue.

[43] Perhaps a plausible interpretation of "to keep from Michaelmas to such a day." Case at 195.

[44] Interpreting "Suit arraigned and confessed in court does not bring a man to any other answer than wager of law…." Case at 196.

scoundrels who will perjure themselves. Do you really think we'll go with a rule that turns every handshake deal into an invitation for fraud?[45] Since you've got nothing else to say, Bogo, you lose.

Despite his contempt for the institution, Bereford tried to turn it into a useful tool when no other form of proof was feasible. A jury couldn't be asked about a deal done in private. Bereford tried to make character witnesses a sensible alternative.

6. (1293?)[46]

[1] Adam sued[47] to collect a five pound debt. He didn't have a written contract.

[2] Bogo: Your naked assertion I borrowed the money isn't enough.

[3] Adam: I've got character witnesses too.[48]

[4] Bogo: If the court says character witnesses are sufficient I want the court to interrogate them.[49] {I

---

[45] Interpreting "Now God forbid that he should get to his law about a matter of which the country may have knowledge, for then with a dozen or half-dozen ruffians ('ribauz') he might swear an honest man out of his goods. And if we were to award the law in this case, other folk in the country might take an example by this to award the law in every case where the party has only suit." Case at 196.

[46] 19 Selden Society 195 Regarding the date, *see* 19 Selden Society 195, note 4. The loan was in fact for ten marks. For another case referring to the interrogation of the oath helpers, *see* 27 Selden Society 45, 46 (1313–1314).

[47] Writ of debt.

[48] Interpreting "We have tendered suit, and to this you do not answer." Case at 195.

[49] Interpreting "They have offered nothing but their suit. We pray that it be examined." Case at 195. Whether Bogo asks to have the

think they might know something that favors me and the court shouldn't just let them make an oath that you're honest.}[50]

[5] Adam: Character witnesses aren't subject to interrogation—they just shift the burden onto you to make some sort of answer.[51]

[6] Justice Bereford: When a creditor has nothing but character witnesses the defendant has three options.[52] He can ask for a jury, he can present his own character witnesses, or he can ask the court to interrogate the

---

court or a jury examine the character witnesses is unclear. Bereford provides Bogo the opportunity "to put himself upon your suit that you have tendered, which is equivalent to the country." Case at 195. Other reports from the Bereford era show that the court on occasion interrogated the jury ("the country") by putting precise questions to them (a procedure today known as a "special verdict.") *See, e.g.*, 22 Selden Society 188 (1310). Bracton recommended judicial interrogation of the jury "so that it will not be said that Jesus was crucified and Barabas set free." Bracton fol. 143–143b. Sometimes the court itself determined the age of litigants by making its own "inspection." 39 Selden Society 26 (1313) (age of dower claimant). A judicial rather than jury examination of the character witnesses would be more efficient and effective. For these reasons the text interprets Bereford's comment "which is the equivalent of the country" to mean the court will interrogate the character witnesses just as it sometimes interrogates the jurors.

[50] The text adds the rationale.

[51] Interpreting "There is no need for that, for suit serves no purpose but to testify to that which the party has said and make him entitled to an answer." Case at 195.

[52] Applying the case context to Bereford's general remark "in this case the defendant can choose three ways…." Case at 195.

> plaintiff's supporters.[53] Bogo has chosen the third and since Adam won't take up his offer he loses.[54]

Since Bogo denies he borrowed the money he can't ask for a jury. According to his story there was nothing for them to see. Settled law said Bogo had to meet Adam's supporters with his own. Bereford rejects the past, and provides the best chance to find out the truth. Perhaps Adam's men will say he has no history as a money lender. Perhaps their description of Adam's relationship with Bogo will contradict the story he lent five pounds on a handshake. Perhaps they will reveal bad blood between the two. Bereford suggests a procedure that might bring something of value to light.

THE JURY

The Jury of Knights

Although the jury became the poster child for the common law's commitment to rational proof an early type of jury took up the role of God's spokesman.[55] When a plaintiff claimed the ultimate right to own land[56] —a right God would recognize—he challenged his

---

[53] Interpreting he can "put himself upon the country; to be at his law; to put himself upon your suit that you have tendered, which is the equivalent to the country." Case at 105.

[54] The report does not explain why Bereford enters judgment, reporting simply "So the Court awards that you take nothing by your writ, but be in mercy, and that Bogo go quit." The text interprets that silence to imply Adam demanded a judgment upon his theory that Bogo had no right to have his suitors examined.

[55] Perhaps the great council at Windsor in 1179 authorized the grand assize. G.D.G. Hall, *Glanvill* 181 (1965). A litigant could present evidence to the grand assize. 43 Selden Society 101 (1313) (7).

[56] By bringing the writ of right, the writ of ownership.

opponent to battle. The defendant could avoid battle by asking to have a panel of knights—the "grand assize"—resolve the dispute instead. In contrast to the conventional jury the grand assize decided no specific facts. Instead the panel declared one party had "the better right" to the land.[57] God gave no reason for favoring a litigant in battle. In theory the grand assize also spoke from behind the clouds.[58] But Common Pleas poured in some sunlight. A defendant could produce evidence about a particular claimed defect in the plaintiff's chain of title.[59] And the defendant could force the knights to render a judgment about such a focused question.[60]

---

[57] The process is discussed in a reporter's note. 3 31a Rolls Series 116 (1302).

[58] The panel of knights acted as God's instrument: the defendants "put themselves on God and the grand assize." 112 Selden Society 216, 217 (1285).

[59] In defending against a claim for land ownership a litigant proposed to prove to the grand assize that his ancestor properly developed a portion of the claimed moorland. Justice Herle allows the proof: "All this is matter for the grand assize, because the grand assize must be advised for their verdict..." He compares the problem to the valid introduction of proof regarding a grant made by an underage or incompetent person. 104 Selden Society 138, 140 (1320).

[60] In repudiating a litigant's argument that a quitclaim couldn't act as a bar in writ of right the court observed "Justice Bereford: Does not the mise join on the words of the quitclaim? Justice Roubry (on the same point). This is a mise based on words of the quit-claim." 5 31a Rolls Series 66, 68 (1305).

7. (1316)[61]

> *Reporter's Note*: When Adam claimed[62] he owned a farm Bogo paid a few shillings for a special procedure.[63] The court asked the knights a question Bogo had formulated: did Adam's grandfather die in possession of the farm?[64] When they said he didn't Bereford and Scrope entered judgment for Bogo. The case was over before the knights had a chance to say who had the "better right."[65]

The court didn't stop there. The knights had been standard proof for over a century. Common Pleas gave defendants the option to plead in a way that eliminated them completely.

---

[61] 52 Selden Society 145. Other examples of the procedure appear at 5 31a Rolls Series 66, 68 (1305), 33 Selden Society 25, 26 (1312) (the same case appears again at 104 Selden Society 138 (1320)), and 33 Selden Society 42, 45 (1312). In the latter case the court takes payment to tell the grand assize to focus upon a particular question. The report indicates that if both parties agreed, the question would go to an ordinary jury. "Scrope asked the defendant to agree to an inquest {that is, an ordinary jury} instead of the grand assize, by reason of the smallness of the tenements." 33 Selden Society 45, 46 (1312). In version II the defendant refuses to consent; in version III she agrees.

[62] Writ of right.

[63] "Half-a-mark."

[64] "Whether the ancestor of the plaintiff, of whose seisin he counted, was seised in the time of such a king." The report does not identify the particular ancestor; the text chooses a specific example.

[65] Interpreting "And he was non-suited after the mise had been joined, without waiting for the verdict of the grand assize." Case at 145.

8. (1302)[66]

[1] Claiming to own a farm Adam sued[67] Bogo in a local court. Bogo quickly asked Common Pleas to take the case because the local court had denied him justice.

[2] Adam: The case can't be ripe for removal. I brought my case on September 7th and you had it removed on September 22nd. {There's no way you could have been denied justice in that short period. The knights couldn't even have been impaneled.}[68] This court can't take jurisdiction before the local court has even had a chance to look at the case.[69]

---

[66] 3 31a Rolls Series 198. The medieval reporter mixes up the names of the lawyers. Lanfar represents Adam; Mutford represents Bogo. The first two Lanfars are correct (Adam asks to see Bogo's request to have Common Pleas take jurisdiction, and then he says the request was made too soon); the third Lanfar should be Mutford (only Bogo would ask for a view); the fourth Lanfar should be Mutford (Bogo says Adam's father sold him the land); and the last two Mutfords should be Lanfar (Adam says Bogo should go on record saying the deed is bad, and then Adam says the answer is impermissible because he is entitled to the knights.)

[67] Writ of right.

[68] The text adds an obvious argument. The protracted process for impaneling the knights is discussed at 4 31a Rolls Series 386 (1305). A reporter's note gives a vivid sense of the glacial movement: After observing a fresh election isn't required if some knights on the panel die, the reporter says "But if as many as half the knights die, then will a fresh election … be held." 61 Selden Society 290 (1318).

[69] Interpreting "The Original said 'given at Launceston the 7th day of September' and Pone said 'given at Dover the 22nd day of September.' Bogo: Judgment, since he cannot in such a short space of time have sued in the Lords' {sic} court, and have shown error in the court etc." Case at 198.

[3] Justice Brumpton: Yes we can. Bogo's allegation of justice denied gives us jurisdiction.[70]

[4] Bogo: Thank you. Now as for the merits, Adam says he inherited his father's farm, but he didn't. His father sold me the place. Here's the deed. Unless Adam disputes the deed I win.[71]

[5] Adam: I've sued for ownership. If I deny the deed the court will put the question to an ordinary jury.[72] That takes away my right to the grand assize. Unless Bogo agrees to the knights I win.[73]

[6] *The Reporter*: The court rejected Adam's argument and forced him to agree to have twelve ordinary people decide whether the deed was valid.[74]

---

[70] Interpreting "Answer over." Case at 200. That is, we will take jurisdiction. What answer have you got to Bogo's defense?

[71] Interpreting "Whereas he demands of the seisin of C. descending to B., and afterwards to himself, we say that B., through whom he counts, released and quit-claimed to us all his right; judgment, etc." Case at 200. Although the report says nothing about Bogo presenting the deed in court, he must have. He asks the court to render judgment, and he couldn't make such a request unless he had presented the deed.

[72] Interpreting "Which deed, if it be denied, must be tried by an inquest." Case at 200. *See also* 5 31a Rolls Series 36 (1305) (Quit claim a bar in a writ of right) ("he was driven by Hengham to answer to the quit claim").

[73] Interpreting "And so he has not given such an answer as this {ownership} writ requires, judgment etc." Case at 200.

[74] Interpreting "And his answer was not allowed: and then he denied the deed." Case at 200. The judgment entered on their verdict will probably have as conclusive an effect as that entered on a verdict by the knights. "Note: In a writ [of right] patent after the mise of an inquest, instead of a grand assize … the claimant was nonsuited. And this was the judgment, that the tenant hold in peace, quit of the claimant and of his heirs for all time etc." 61 Selden Society 4 (1317).

The Magna Carta banned the use of a royal writ to block the local lords' right to hear ownership claims.[75] Brumpton's fiction makes a mockery of a constitutional guarantee. Outrageous in theory, his decision had little impact on the ground. Developments after Magna Carta had already put local courts' authority over land ownership in limbo.[76] In an institutional version of Darwin's "survival of the fittest," royal justice flourished as local justice died.[77] Litigants preferred the efficient and rational writs of possession.[78] The knights had become vestigial organs.

The Jury from the Vicinity

Common Pleas made the jury the preferred fact finder.[79] The jury probably grew out of a panel the king

---

[75] "The writ called *Praecipe* shall not in future be issued to anyone in respect of any holding whereby a free man may lose his court." Magna Carta c. 34 (1215) (3 EHD 320).

[76] The court also created a doctrine of waiver that prevented a litigant from asserting the private court's jurisdiction if the court owner himself did not. 112 Selden Society 290 (1287).

[77] Maitland's metaphor. "A struggle for life is keen among them and only the fittest survive." 2 P&M 561.

[78] Beginning with the creation of the assize of novel disseisin during the twelfth century. *See* D. Sutherland, *The Assize of Novel Disseisin* 5–8 (1973).

[79] A deed, however, was preferred to a jury. "{A}s the writing had a suspicious look, for the seal and its annex were hanging by a thread, he prayed judgment if he ought to answer such an instrument." The case then went to a jury. The reporter says "he who proffered the writing was not challenged by the court, which seems strange. Quaere." 3 31a Rolls Series 152 (1302). *See also* 5 31a Rolls Series 370 (1306) (Record) (after no credible witness to the deed testifies the jury condemns it). If the defendant denied the validity of a writing the jury would hear the question, and if the writing referred to witnesses, the claimant had to present those witnesses to the jury.

created to decide land disputes.[80] Although local courts had the right to hear "ownership" claims, the king took jurisdiction over claims to possess land. "Possession" was not "ownership."[81] The royal court adopted a novel fact finding method. Twelve men from the vicinity spoke the truth about the facts.[82]

The Jury Replaces Character Witnesses

Despite the rule that character witnesses could be met by character witnesses, Bereford demanded more if important rights were involved. Parties doing a deal sometimes gave a document to a third person, a stakeholder. The document provided a solution for a contingency the parties hoped would never happen. A well-advised person got the stakeholder's commitment in writing. A dupe took less.

---

2 31a Rolls Series 436 (1294) (Note). Others besides the witnesses could provide information to the jury. 4 31a Rolls Series 184 (1304) (Note re debt). A jury couldn't contradict a court record. "Chief Justice Bereford: You can have no averment against the record, for if you could have an averment to the contrary all our rolls would be falsified, and that would be against justice." 26 Selden Society 20, 21 (1310–1311). Only an official record could prove a judgment. 1 31a Rolls Series 406 (1293) (Note).

[80] The assize that decided questions of dispossession, "disseisin."

[81] The rationale for the king's assumption of jurisdiction is discussed in Sutherland, 27–31, *supra*.

[82] Writ of novel disseisin. *See* Early Registers of Writs, 87 Selden Society 258 (#645) ("twelve free and lawful men of that neighborhood.") The jurors in novel disseisin took this oath: "I will not on any account fail to say the truth according to my knowledge; so help me God and his Saints." 1 31a Rolls Series 440 (1293) (Novel disseisin).

9. (1310)[83]

[1] Adam offered to sell Bogo a three year lease of a manor. Bogo was afraid some stranger might claim to own the place. As a renter he couldn't enforce his rights against anyone except Adam.[84] Adam allayed his fears by agreeing to execute a backup deed that made Bogo owner of the manor.[85] The deed would be kept in reserve to provide Bogo a good defense if someone sued claiming superior title to the farm. In the presence

---

[83] 20 Selden Society 123. The text's introduction interprets the reporter's comment "The case was this—that one R. had demised a manor to B for term of three years, and to insure him the term had made him this charter and delivered it into an equal hand etc." Case at 124. 31 Selden Society 148 (1311) probably provides another version of the case. The reports purport to be decided within a year of each other, both concern an action for detinue of charter for a manor (described as "C" in volume 20 and "P" in volume 31), both have the same dramatis personae of Bereford, Willoughby and Passeley (volume 20 adds Hedon), and both choose the jury over character witnesses. As Maitland observes the reporter's use of the identifying letters "R" and "B" contradicts his use of the letters elsewhere in the report. Case at 124 footnote 3. Reporters often mix up the parties they identify by initials. The text replaces the reporter's initials with the identities the context suggests.

[84] According to conventional law his only remedy would be against Adam. Two years later Common Pleas would vindicate a lessee's claim against a third person. 34 Selden Society 226 (1312–1313).

[85] The procedure also provided protection to the lessee against the lessor. A lessor sued a stakeholder to get possession of a deed; the stakeholder said he was obligated under the agreement to give the deed to the lessee if he was ejected by lessor within the three year lease term. Apparently the lessee was still in possession, and the stakeholder was unclear about his obligations. "The term is not yet ended, and if you {the justices} be of opinion that the charter should be delivered … here is the charter, to be done with as the Court shall direct." 37 Selden Society 216, 217 (1314). A stakeholder could also in effect interplead the entrusting parties. 37 Selden Society 217 (1314) (Note).

of witnesses they gave the deed to an escrow agent, Cosmo.[86] Bogo's fears became real. When a stranger sued claiming title Bogo asked for the deed. Cosmo denied ever having received it.[87] Bogo sued.[88]

[2] Cosmo: He's got nothing but character witnesses. Here are mine.[89]

[3] Bogo: That may be conventional doctrine regarding character witnesses but if I don't get the deed I'll lose the manor and its land. The subject is too important to be decided by a swearing contest. A jury should be called.[90]

---

[86] "Some [manuscripts] add 'in the presence of certain named persons.'" Footnote 2, case at 123. In the version at 31 Selden Society 148 (1311) Adam argues, "You received the charter in the presence of several persons, and of this the jury can have proof." 31 Selden Society 148 (1311). According to Bereford's doctrine regarding events of which the jury can have knowledge, this allegation by itself would warrant the impaneling of a jury. *See, e.g.*, 19 Selden Society 195 (1310?).

[87] Cosmo is probably Adam's corrupt confederate.

[88] Writ of detinue of charter.

[89] The challenge presented by ambiguous reports appears in the following passages. "Passeley: We will aver that you had [the charter] by our bailment. Willoughby: You say that you bailed the charter. Ready etc. Stanton, J.: When saw you such an issue in a writ of detinue of charter? Willoughby: We have seen the one [issue] and the other. Moreover, in a writ of mesne we could get to our law…" Case at 124. While ordinarily Willoughby's statement "Ready etc." means he is ready for a jury, here his statement "ready" means "ready to present my character witnesses." Not only does the context require such an interpretation, but his reference to being at his "law" (*i.e.*, ready to produce character witnesses) shows he uses "ready" to mean "ready to produce character witnesses."

[90] Interpreting "[P]erchance the detention of it might occasion our disinheritance. Judgment, whether [you can be received] to your law. [*another manuscript adds:* Besides, in it there is a clause of warranty, which touches 'the right.' Therefore etc.]" Case at 123.

> [4] Chief Justice Bereford: Too much is at stake to penalize Bogo for his stupidity. You've got to agree to go to a jury.[91]
>
> [5] Cosmo: Not unless you enter a judgment.[92]
>
> [6] Chief Justice Bereford: You insist, do you? If we enter a judgment you'll eat more than that.[93]
>
> [7] Bogo: Jury please.

Adam's victory probably turned on the fact that witnesses observed Cosmo's receipt of the document. Bereford preferred the jury if events took place in public but he had difficulty drawing a line. An agreement to sell six sacks of wool on credit was private but an agreement to store five sacks was public.[94] A lawyer argued "If a question involves public facts then character witnesses can't be used," but Bereford replied "Your maxim is too broad. In some cases we'll call a jury, but in others we won't."[95]

---

[91] Interpreting "[It is true that] he who bailed a charter to you without taking a letter did a foolish thing. [But] you must accept the averment." Case at 123. In a comparable case involving a bond for one hundred pounds, a stakeholder, and a request for a jury, Justice Spigurnel rejects the request observing "It was foolish to let your staff slip from between your fingers."27 Selden Society 19, 22 (1313–1314).

[92] Interpreting "If you so award." Case at 123.

[93] Interpreting "Chief Justice Bereford: If we award it, it will be with the sauce! (*ceo serra ove la sauce*!)" Case at 123.

[94] Compare 22 Selden Society 21 (1310) with 19 Selden Society 15 (1308–1309), perhaps reports of two different cases, or perhaps two reports of one case.

[95] "Justice Bereford: Your maxim, when you say that a man shall not be received to his law touching a matter the country may have knowledge, is too large. In some cases he shall and in others he shall not." 19 Selden Society 15, 17 (1308–1309).

Parties to a loan could cut notches onto a wooden rod —a tally—to prove both the debt and payments.[96] Sometimes the parties attached their seals. Bereford created a hierarchy of proof: juries at the top, tallies in the middle, character witnesses at the bottom.

10. (1313–1314)[97]

> [1] Adam sued[98] Bogo. He presented a sealed tally to the court.
>
> [2] Bogo: I never notched that tally—Adam could have whittled it himself. I'll bring some character witnesses to disprove it.[99]
>
> [3] Adam: You can reject it by a jury but not by less.[100]
>
> [4] Bogo: No. Character witnesses can always repudiate the wooden rods.[101]
>
> [5] Chief Justice Bereford: But Bogo, the tally has your seal on it.[102]

---

[96] The tally might be split in two so each party had protection against fraud. *See* 27 Selden Society 35 (1313–1314).
[97] 27 Selden Society 57.
[98] Writ of debt.
[99] Although Miggeley refers to his request to be at his law (*i.e.*, to present oath helpers) later in the discussion, his reference shows he made this defense from the outset.
[100] Interpreting "Is this your deed ('*vostre fet*') or not?" case at 57. Adam is challenging Bogo to say "I did not execute the deed." This factual denial would then go to the jury.
[101] Interpreting "We are not bound to answer this." Case at 57. Meaning I will not deny your assertion because that would constitute consent to go to a jury.
[102] Interpreting "What do you say as to your seal…?" Case at 57.

[6] Bogo: So what?[103] But if the court insists I'll take a jury.[104]

[7] Chief Justice Bereford Thanks, Bogo. I hope you don't think we're strong-arming you. That's not our practice.[105] I'd like to give practicing lawyers some advice. Bogo asked to have a jury decide whether he executed the tally. He could have asked the jury to decide whether he borrowed the money. That would have been a better choice.[106] Tallies can be so easily altered. Documents are much more reliable proof.[107]

---

[103] He adds "If I put my seal to an escrowet and write no letter, the fact of putting my seal there does not charge me." Case at 57.

[104] Interpreting "Bogo demanded *oyer* of the deed and had it … later he said "Not our deed, Ready etc." Case at 58.

[105] Interpreting "I am very glad that you have taken this issue without throwing any responsibility upon us {by insisting that the court render a judgment about character witness proof}, for we shall never force you to make such an averment." Case at 58. "Averment" here means consent to a jury. Bereford often uses duress to force consent. Why then does he deny it? Two years earlier a statute provided a right to appeal from Common Pleas to Parliament. The New Ordinances, 1311, c. 29 (1311) (3 EHD 536). Probably the statute responded to pressure from those who thought the trick of enforced consent to a jury gave Common Pleas improper immunity from review. Bereford's denial of coercion sounds like a witness giving self-serving testimony. "The lady doth protest too much, methinks."

[106] Interpreting "For the defendants might have said: 'We owe him naught. Ready etc. and so have gone to a jury.'" Case at 58.

[107] Interpreting "For what has been inscribed [on a tally] can be shaved off and something different from what was there before can then be put in its place at the will of the custodian of the tally, without anyone being able to detect it, which is not the case with a writing." Case at 58.

JURY OVERSIGHT

The Jury's Knowledge

Modern jurors know nothing except what they hear in court. In contrast medieval jurors had to investigate the facts on their own. [108] Bereford era reports show lawyers[109] could try to influence the jury. As the era began they needed court permission.

11. (1285)[110]

> [1] Adam sued[111] Bogo for ejecting him from land.
>
> [2] *The Reporter*: After the jurors took their oath Adam's lawyer spoke to them. When the judges heard about it they disapproved. They said the lawyer's job was done when he had finished talking to the court. Only judges were supposed to speak to the jurors. The court said, however, that a judge might give a lawyer permission to approach the jury.

Other cases from the same year casually mention lawyers speaking to the jury.[112] In later cases lawyers

---

[108] *See, e.g.*, Curia Regis Rolls, III, 118 (Common Pleas 1204); Curia Regis Rolls, V, 258 (Common Pleas 1208). To some extent a jury might refuse to answer a question because of ignorance. Asked about the conduct of multiple defendants, a jury told the court "Sir, we were far away from the place where the disseisin was effected, and therefore we do not know if {some of the defendants} were there or not." The court rendered judgment only against the defendant the jury observed. 1 31a Rolls Series 168,172 (1292).

[109] Parties themselves might present evidence to the jury. *See* 122 Selden Society 318 (1285).

[110] 122 Selden Society 275.

[111] Writ of novel disseisin.

[112] *See* 122 Selden Society 302 (1285) and 122 Selden Society 318 (1285).

sometimes list the witnesses they intend to bring before the jury.[113] While asserting a document did not conclusively bind a party, Bereford told a lawyer "You cannot use it except by way of evidence to the jury when it comes."[114] Lawyers' factual presentations became commonplace.

The theory that jurors had personal knowledge caused problems. Justice Saham tried an experiment that was not repeated.

12. (1285)[115]

[1] Claiming he had inherited his grandfather's farm, Adam sued[116] Bogo.

[2] Bogo: Your father's alive—he's your grandfather's heir, not you.[117]

[3] Jury: We don't know if the father's alive—he left to live in London.[118]

[4] Justice Saham: Is it more likely he's alive or dead?

---

[113] A father denying he agreed to give his son's widow a share in his land offered two witnesses "who were present at the espousals" in conjunction with his consent to go to a jury. 41 Selden Society 182, 184 (1315).

[114] 41 Selden Society 34, 35 (1315).

[115] 122 Selden Society 283.

[116] Writ of aiel. The writ claims the plaintiff is the heir of a grandparent who died in possession. Since Bogo doesn't claim Adam's father took possession, Adam would satisfy the writ's criteria if his father was dead.

[117] Interpreting "Through whom he is counting is alive and living in London…." Case at 283. *I.e.*, Adam has traced the descent through his dead father, but his father is alive.

[118] Interpreting "But they said he had gone to London and stayed there." Case at 283.

[5] Jury: Alive.

[6] Justice Saham: Since the jury thinks the father may be living in London,[119] Adam and Bogo should try to find him. They should tell Common Pleas or the Abbot of Westminster or some other reputable person if they succeed. We'll take this up again next year.

[7] *The Reporter*: Saham hasn't treated Bogo fairly. Saham forced the jurors to deliver a verdict, and they said Adam's father was alive. Saham should have dismissed Adam's case. He wasn't his grandfather's heir. His father was.[120]

Special Verdict

In challenging situations the court can test the jury to see if they have understood their instructions.[121] The

---

[119] In 122 Selden Society 302 (1285) the jury suggested an older brother was living outside of England, and the court disregarded their answer, probably on the theory their knowledge could not reach beyond the realm. But Saham was willing to ask the jury about events outside the realm. 122 Selden Society 270, 274 (1285). A merchant might render an account about a loan made outside the country. *See* 123 Selden Society 430, 431 (1289) (Norway).

[120] Interpreting "This is harassment from above: the jury {was} charged to say about his father whether they think it more likely that he was alive or dead and they said alive." Case at 283.The report is ambiguous as to the victim of the harassment. The text picks Bogo. The missing persons investigation hurts neither the jurors nor Adam (since entry of judgment against him is postponed). Bogo's the one that suffers. The jury took his side.

[121] When a jury's verdict contradicted itself on its face, the court might refuse to enter a judgment upon it. 4 31a Rolls Series 442 (1305) (Waste) (jury assesses equal damages against defendants who had held for different periods of time).

procedure is known today as a "special verdict," a jury response to a series of specific questions.[122]

13. (1293)[123]

[1] Claiming to be his father's heir Bogo sued[124] Cosmo to recover a farm.

[2] Cosmo: Your older brother Adam inherited the farm and sold it to me.[125]

[3] Bogo: He took possession but he wasn't my father's heir.[126]

[4] *The Reporter*: The court asked the jury if Adam was the heir.

[5] Jury: Yes.[127]

[6] Justice Roubury: That's not good enough. Why is he the heir?[128]

---

[122] *See, e.g., Federal Rules of Civil Procedure*, rule 49.
[123] 2 31a Rolls Series 268. Multiple defendants make different defenses. The text isolates the question to the defense "D" made: "{the father} had a son {Adam the first born} who after his death entered and alienated: judgment of the writ." The text assumes D himself bought from the father.
[124] Writ of mort d'ancestor.
[125] Interpreting "Entered as son and heir, and was seised and who alienated…" Case at 270.
[126] Interpreting "Whereas he says that Adam entered as son and heir, we say Not as son and heir." Case at 270.
[127] "And as to D … they said Adam entered as eldest son and heir of the father…" Case at 272.
[128] "How do you say that he was next heir?" Case at 272.

> [7] Jury: Adam and Bogo had the same parents and while their father was on his deathbed he acknowledged Adam as his heir.[129]
>
> [8] Justice Roubury: That's still not good enough. Try to do better. If you can't produce a satisfactory response to my question you can spend the night without food or drink.[130]
>
> [9] Jury: He's the heir because he was born after his parents formally agreed to marry. They had a church wedding later.
>
> [10] Justice Roubury: That's better. I'll take some time before I enter a judgment.[131]

Lawyers would say whether Adam qualifies as his father's heir presents a "mixed question of law and fact." The court decides the law, the jury the facts.[132] But some questions require knowledge of both law and fact. By questioning the jury Roubury learns their first verdict was based on a mistake about the law. They say the father's deathbed acknowledgment made Adam his heir. The law requires not only acknowledgment but also reputation.[133] The deathbed blessing came too late to create a reputation. The jury's second try satisfies Roubury. They

---

[129] Interpreting "For the reason that he was born and begotten of the same father and mother, and that his father on his death-bed acknowledged him to be his son and heir." Case at 272.

[130] Interpreting "Roubury. You shall tell us in another way how he was next heir, or you shall remain shut up without eating or drinking until tomorrow morning." Case at 272.

[131] Interpreting "Roubury. Await your judgment." Case at 272.

[132] A litigant asked Bereford to submit a question of law to the jury. He replied "I should never do that, nor would any competent justice do it." 31 Selden Society 72, 78 (1311).

[133] *See* 34 Selden Society 218 (1312–1313).

tell him all the relevant facts. Adam has two bases to be heir. His parents agreed formally to marry before his birth and they had a ceremonial marriage after his birth. The jury has told the court all the facts they observed. Now Roubury himself faces a difficult night. If Adam had kept possession he could have qualified as heir by using pleading techniques to get the church rules applied. Those rules would have made him the heir.[134] But Adam didn't keep possession—he sold the place to Cosmo. Roubury has to decide if Cosmo can step into Adam's shoes.

Roubury did the jury a favor by ensuring their verdict was valid.[135] They could have been punished if a second jury—an "attaint" jury—said their verdict was wrong.[136] Since jurors spoke about facts they had a duty to observe [137] an attaint jury in effect tried them for perjury.[138] Too much was at stake for a guess.

---

[134] *See* 33 Selden Society 161 (1312) describing how he could get the church court to make him legitimate.

[135] Perhaps the court might refuse to answer a request for guidance. 1 31a Rolls Series 8 (1292) (Entry) (The case is ambiguous. After the jury says to the court "we pray your direction" the report reads "And they were afterwards commanded to say if he had good seisin… and at last they said, on their oath, that he had." *Ibid* at 10. "Afterwards" might mean after they received judicial advice).

[136] *See* 2 Britton 231. If the attaint jury confirmed the first verdict, the complaining party might be imprisoned. 1 31a Rolls Series 108, 110 (1292).

[137] *See* Curia Regis Rolls, V 258.

[138] Brabazon said the first jury could not be convicted for failing to realize a party had acquired a theoretical possession. When a second jury disagreed with the first Brabazon said, "it would not exactly be an attaint, for the jurors could not be imprisoned and held to ransom, for they could not know what was contained in a judicial settlement." 19 Selden Society 155, 157 (1310). Bereford gave a presentment jury (the precursor to the modern grand jury) immunity from attaint. 31 Selden Society 114 (1311).

14. (1313–1314)[139]

[1] Adam had just a limited interest in Stone Farm.[140] When his daughter Anna married he gave her outright ownership.[141] Later Anna sued him for dispossession.[142] The court asked the jury if Adam had dispossessed her.

[2] Jury: As we understand the facts Adam purported to give the farm to Anna but a court said the gift was

---

[139] 29 Selden Society 136. The text is a hybrid presentation that combines reports I and II. The text ignores the identity of the actual claimant (the two reports are inconsistent) since his identity is irrelevant to the relevant legal principle.

[140] A fee tail.

[141] The text interprets the passage "the said fine was not permitted because the estate was in tail" (concluding line, paragraph two, page 136) to refer to Adam's interest—his own estate "was in tail" and therefore his gift in fee tail to Anna was invalid. The court that refused to enter the fine probably took the following approach. Adam's gift to Anna had the potential to interfere with his grantor's right to a reversion. Suppose Anna and her husband had a child who died shortly after birth—her husband would acquire a curtesy right to stay on the land for his lifetime. But if Adam, Anna, and her issue were all dead, Adam's grantor would have the right to take the farm back. Anna's husband's curtesy interest would interfere with the grantor's reversion. The court's reasoning is not free from doubt. If Adam never gave Anna the farm, but instead just died in possession, Anna would get the farm (as his surviving child), and her husband would have a valid curtesy right just as a widow would have a valid dower right to such land. *See* 33 Selden Society 81 (1312). The court therefore refused to enter the fine because Adam's gift provided Anna's husband an invalid curtesy interest even though the curtesy interest would have been valid if Anna had taken possession not by Adam's gift but rather by Adam's death.

[142] Writ of novel disseisin.

invalid.[143] Adam then moved onto the farm with Anna and her husband. After Anna's husband died she remarried, and Adam quarreled with the new family. He then threw them off the farm. We don't know if he dispossessed her.

[3] Justice Spigurnel: When Adam first went to live with Anna did he say he was moving in because the court said his gift was no good?[144]

[4] The Jury: No. He didn't talk about that. He just said he wanted to live with them.

[5] Justice Spigurnel: Although Adam's gift was invalid it still gave Anna possession. Since Adam didn't say he was moving in so that he could reclaim possession, Anna's possession continued. Even if Adam had a legal right to the farm he couldn't use self-help. He'll go to prison for what he's done.[145]

---

[143] While version 1 states the court refused to enter the fine (case at 136), version 2 says "disputes arose amongst them, with the result that the fine was not levied." Case at 137.

[144] "Justice Spigurnel: Did the father, when he entered the tenements after the forty days, claim them as his own right of his former estate…." Case at 137.

[145] Interpreting "Justice Spigurnel: Seeing that it has been found by the assize that Anna and her husband were enfeoffed by the enfeoffment of Adam and had undisturbed seisin during forty days; and further seeing that we have ruled that the entry of Adam subsequent to the seisin could not defeat it, as it was good in its nature, and that he entered in defiance of his own deed, this Court gives judgment that Anna recovers her seisin and that Adam go to prison because he entered in defiance of his own deed." Spigurnel's remarks are made in version 2 which takes the view that the judicial settlement was never completed because the parties argued and therefore failed to follow through. The outcome of the case, however, is identical to that of version 1 in which the fine is rejected because Adam had only a fee tail. A revision of Spigurnel's remarks to reflect

The jury didn't realize the actors' mental state was the key. If Adam entered the farm to re-take possession, he would then afterwards have been privileged to eject both Anna and her new husband. But he didn't think he was taking back possession. Jail time will help him realize that everyone should hire a lawyer before they do anything.

Another case also involved a determination of a person's state of mind, a subtle determination the jury failed to realize it needed to make.

15. (1302)[146]

[1] Claiming her father died in possession of a farm, Anna sues[147] Bogo to recover her inheritance.

[2]Bogo: Since I own and possess you as my serf, you can't sue here in royal court.

[3]Anna: You don't own me; the previous owner of the manor sold my grandfather the farm, and the sale

---

the scenario of version 1 would be as follows: "Justice Spigurnel: Even though the gift was subsequently disclosed to have been invalid, the gift and the parties' acts in reference to the gift show that Adam gave possession to Anna and her new husband. That possession was never invalidated because Adam's subsequent entry was in his capacity as a guest, not as an owner. When Adam physically ejected Anna and her new husband, he committed an act of dispossession. Any enforcement of the rights he retained because his gift was defective had to be done by a law suit, not by self-help."

[146] 3 31a Rolls Series 136. A person possessed as a serf cannot claim the land he resides upon. 122 Selden Society 24 (1268–1269). "Anna" stands for two sisters who sue together.

[147] Writ of mort d'ancestor.

necessarily proves my grandfather's descendants are free.[148]

[4] Bogo: I've had possession of both you and your father as my serfs.

[5] Anna: So what? Once a person has been freed, he and his descendants are forever free even though they voluntarily work as serfs. Only a formal confession of serf status in a court of record can reestablish serfdom.[149]

[6] *The Reporter*: At last the parties went to the jury. They said Anna's father had been Bogo's serf.

[7] Justice Berrewik: {Jurors, you not only have given a legally incorrect answer, but you've failed to answer the question I put to you.} Again, you must tell me whether Anna's father claimed a right to possess Stone Farm.[150]

[8] Jurors: Sir, he did not.

---

[148] Interpreting "One Robert Lord of C., whose estate William now has, enfeoffed our grandfather of these tenements by homage etc… ." As purchaser Bogo is bound by the deed of the earlier owner.

[149] Interpreting "Once enfranchised he shall be for ever free, if he be not afterwards enslaved by his own act in some Court of Record." Case at 138. Cf. "Justice Howard. Think you that even if you had brought him, and that your predecessors had brought his father, grandfather, or great-great-grandfather into servitude, and kept them in that condition by grievous distress while perchance their ancestors before them were free, he would be therefore a villein? (Reporter: intimating the negative.)" 5 31a Rolls Series 10, 12 (1305).

[150] Interpreting "Did he die seised in his demesne as of fee?" Case at 138. The modern common law of "adverse possession" embodies a similar approach. A long time possessor of land will only acquire title to that land if he entertains a "claim of right."

> [9] Justice Brumpton: {Although Anna is free,}[151] she has no right to inherit Stone Farm.

By selling the grandfather land, the previous owner of the farm acknowledged his and his descendants' freedom. Since a serf cannot own land, a sale to a man acknowledges his freedom. Anna's claim is not dismissed; she litigates as a free person, but she loses.[152]

Why then did the court ask the jury some question about her father Adam's status? And how did the jury misunderstand the question? The justices were not interested in whether Anna's father was a serf—he wasn't—but they were interested in whether Anna's father died in possession of the farm, the necessary requirement for the writ she brought.[153] Even though he was in fact free, he could not acquire "possession" unless he believed himself capable of acquiring possession. He did not since he erroneously believed he was a serf, a person without capacity to acquire possession. The jury answered the wrong question—"was the father a serf"—with the wrong answer—"he was a serf." After Berrewik forces the jurors to answer the correct question—did the father think he was a serf—Brumpton dismisses Anna's claim that she was the heir of a person who died in possession. Anna has proven her freedom but she hasn't proven her father died in possession. If she has enough money in the bank for some protracted litigation, litigation to prove she "owns" the farm, she might still wind up with the place.[154]

---

[151] Having litigated and suffered an amercement, Anna is necessarily free.
[152] She made a "false plaint," not a plaint that was dismissed.
[153] The writ of mort d'ancestor.
[154] In a writ of right she could prove she inherited the farm her grandfather owned.

Decorum

The court allowed litigants to challenge jurors for bias.[155] The following case shows the court set a low bar for decorum in some deliberations. Along the way the report portrays a memorable litigant.

16. (1294)[156]

> [1] Claiming his guardian gave his stepmother Babs too large a widow's portion, Adam got a reappraisal.[157] Babs and her new husband challenged the reappraisal. When the court convened Babs appeared alone.
>
> [2] Babs: Even though I've remarried I've got to be here by myself. Everyone's trying to cheat me.[158] The reevaluation was a farce. I've spent ten pounds every year fixing up my widow's portion but the jurors counted my improvements as part of my original

---

[155] *E.g.*, a defendant "offers to the king one mark of silver for a lawful inquest of the country, [to be made] by such as are not the Abbot of Peterborough's men, [to find] whether this is a true appeal or spite." Select Pleas of the Crown, no. 91. The objection had to be made during the litigation, not afterwards. 4 31a Rolls Series 356 (1305). *See also* 1 31a Rolls Series 42 (1292) (utrum). An intervener was allowed to challenge for bias. 1 31a Rolls Series 42, 44 (1292) (utrum). A challenge could be made to the knights of the grand assize. 27 Selden Society 82 (1313–1314) (Wyberd).

[156] 2 31a Rolls Series 460. The text simplifies the facts by making Adam rather than his wife the heir.

[157] By a writ of admeasurement.

[158] Interpreting: The new husband "made default and faintly defended the plea; wherefore Babs came before judgment given, and said that her husband intended by collusion to lose her rightful dower." Case at 460. Babs challenged the stepson's reappraisal as an attempt to cheat her, and therefore the text says "everyone's trying to cheat me."

portion. They even included a manor I bought with my own funds. Their calculations were irrational—they figured out my third without putting a value on what my stepson kept. How could they calculate a third of an unknown quantity?[159]

[3] Justice Mettingham: If I order the reevaluation I want your solemn oath that you won't complain about anything else.[160]

[4] Babs: Of course.[161]

[5] *The Reporter*: The Sheriff was ordered to investigate, a job he did even more fully than Mettingham ordered. The case resumed.

[6] Babs: Wait until you hear what happened. The Sheriff had the jurors make their decision in town's pub.[162]

[7] Justice Hertford: There's nothing wrong if the jury decides either on the land or in the village—it's just the same.

[8] Babs: Exactly. The final decision wasn't made in either place. My stepson took them to a tavern in Nottingham where he stood them to drinks while they deliberated.[163]

---

[159] Interpreting "Sir, when the third part is extended we think that the other two parts should be extended as well…." Case at 462.

[160] "Justice Mettingham: Will you challenge anything besides these two points?" Case at 462.

[161] Interpreting "No, Sir. —And he was avowed." Case at 462.

[162] Interpreting "the Sheriff went to the dower land and made those who were to make the extent swear, and then commanded them to go to the inn…" Case at 462.

[163] "They went with the other party to Nottingham to the tavern at the costs of the other party…" Case at 464.

[9] Justice Hertford: That would be wrong if they were making an initial decision in a contested case. But this was just to set a value. A tavern's fine for that.

[10] Babs: If you say so. But their reevaluation was no good. They ignored the ten pounds worth of rabbits my stepson's land produces every year. They said my tenants pay two pence a day, but they pay no more than a pence and a half, and nothing on fair days. They said…

[11] *The Reporter*: Babs harangued on but these two examples should be sufficient to provide a sense of her participation.[164]

[12] Justice Mettingham: If you're done now it's our turn. You promised to keep to your two specific complaints. Now you've got a new litany. We won't have it.

[13] Babs: Justice Mettingham, you need to remember that you sit in place of our lord the king. You've got to stop this outrage. The whole world gives widows a fair share. This reevaluation will live on in infamy.[165]

[14] Justice Mettingham: Madam, you asked for this reevaluation because you wanted more; you'll have to make do with less. The jurors have decided you got too much the first time. The peasants and their colleagues on the jury know more than we do about

---

[164] "(And he put forward many other challenges of which much notice need not be taken, because they only went to show how the thing was done.)" Case at 464.

[165] Interpreting "She would not have a third part for her dower; and that would be against the law the world over … one comes before judgment given before you who have power to make an amendment as being in the place of our Lord the King…" Case at 464.

these facts.[166] You agreed to live by their verdict and you will. If you want we'll put your objections down on the court records.

[15] Adam: I think Justice Mettingham you will regret giving her an opportunity to make further objections—she will keep this dispute alive until the end of time.[167]

---

166 "When you challenge such petty things, the peasants of the country and the others who made the extent know all about these petty things and how the extent ought to be made as well as we do and better…" Case at 466.

167 Interpreting "If they had been received to challenge the extent, it would have been wrong; for so they might have challenged the extent, after every return, ad infinitum." Case at 466.

CHAPTER 7
The Thing's Been Decided

A LOSER HAS EVERY REASON to keep on trying. But the court has every reason to object. As the Romans put it, "*res judicata*"—"the thing's been decided." Litigants get one, but only one, fair hearing.[1] In deciding whether a judgment barred a second hearing Bereford's court balanced the goals of efficiency and fairness much like American courts do. An efficient court allows a litigant one fair chance, but only one fair chance, to make her case.[2]

---

[1] A litigant received an adjournment (an essoin); his opponent later argued the adjournment was improperly granted. The litigant replied "seeing that that essoin was received and adjourned, it cannot be turned into a default … Chief Justice Bereford: If he cannot challenge the essoin now, when ought he to challenge it? When the essoin was cast there was no one present in Court on the other side to get it quashed… if he cannot challenge it now no essoin will ever be quashed in court …" 41 Selden Society 28, 29 (1315). The victor has to implement the judgment properly. "Justice Berewike: If I recover land by judgment … and I of mine own authority, without livery by the sheriff or bailiff, put myself in the tenements … the tenant {can recover against me} for that reason … I was not at once seised by virtue of the judgment etc., but that the tenant remained continually seised." (*The Reporter*: This is true)." 1 31a Rolls Series 48, 52 (1292). See also 41 Selden Society 144, 146 (1315).

[2] The court would reject a litigant's attempt to pursue two simultaneous court cases for the same wrong. "Justice Inge. Say whether he has {another proceeding pending} for you shall not have two cudgels…" 41 Selden Society 102, 103 (1315).

A VALID JUDGMENT

Notice

A court has no power to render a judgment against a defendant who has not received proper notice of the proceeding.

1. (1313)[3]

[1] Adam sued[4] Bogo in London to recover land in Norfolk. At a circuit court session in Norfolk the jurors rendered a verdict against Bogo. Adam asked Common Pleas to enter a judgment on their verdict.

[2] Bogo: The court can't do that. Although I defaulted once I was entitled to a second warning that the jurors were about to render a verdict. I didn't get it.[5]

[3] Chief Justice Bereford: Bogo's right. We can't enter a judgment on an invalid verdict.[6]

---

[3] 43 Selden Society 105. The text creates a location for the land.

[4] Writ of entry on novel disseisin.

[5] Bogo argues he is entitled to the same sequence of notice in Norfolk that he would have received in London. "If a jury were called up to the bar [here at Westminster] and the tenant did not appear the Justices [of the Bench] would not go on to take the inquest but would order the little *cape* to issue... ." Case at 106. "We ask judgment whether the claimant ought in these circumstances to have seisin of the land, seeing that the inquest was taken in the absence of the tenant." Case at 106. A second default caused the transfer of the claimed land; if a party asks to bring oath helpers to prove he hasn't been summoned, and then he fails to bring them, Justice Hengham instructed the court clerks to award possession at that time. 5 31a Rolls Series 16 (1305).

[6] Interpreting "Chief Justice Bereford ruled that Adam take out another writ of *venire facias* to have the same inquest summoned to be here...." Case at 106.

Jurisdiction

A court's authority reaches only a defined geographical location.[7] The boundaries can be litigated. An erroneous judgment about the boundaries binds the parties. The loser can appeal and have the judgment overturned.[8] But if he does not he cannot argue in a later case that the court overstepped its jurisdiction.[9] A person who has not received notice has not had a fair chance to make his case. But a person who has argued about the court's boundaries has had a fair chance to make his point. If he loses, the judgment—right or wrong—binds him.[10]

2. (1313)[11]

[1] In the Court of King's Bench Anna sued[12] Bogo for beating her.

---

[7] "{If} I were to send a writ issuing from the Rolls to Ireland to cause a {man} to come, and I were to say 'Teste J. de Berewike:' he would not know what it meant. Wherefore it seems to me that the {attempt to assert jurisdiction over a person in Ireland} is worthless." 2 31a Rolls Series 304, 308 (1294).

[8] American lawyers describe this as a "direct appeal."

[9] American lawyers describe this as a "collateral attack."

[10] Unless he has it overturned on appeal.

[11] 39 Selden Society 50. The text changes the sequence of arguments within the report. The Common Pleas reporter includes this judgment from King's Bench because it gives *res judicata* effect to a Common Pleas judgment. Elsewhere Bereford asserted Common Pleas would give *res judicata* effect to a judgment in King's Bench rendered in a plea brought without a writ. "Chief Justice Bereford: I do not think that this Court would have power to try this plea without the King's writ in which [that power] is witnessed. [But] why should not he himself in lieu of a writ warrant the holding of a plea? … Can we undo what was done before the King? Not so." 22 Selden Society 115, 122 (1310).

[12] Writ of trespass.

[2] Bogo: Since she's my wife the court should dismiss her case. A wife can't sue her husband.

[3] Anna: Previously I sued[13] you in Common Pleas.[14] You said I was your wife. The court asked the Bishop of Lincoln and he said we weren't married. The court entered a judgment based upon his conclusion. You're bound by that judgment.[15] We aren't married.

[4] Bogo: The court should ignore the judgment because the bishop had no power to make the decision. I told him we got married in Stone Village, a place outside his jurisdiction. He said he had jurisdiction over Stone Village. But he was wrong. The Abbot of St. Albans has exclusive jurisdiction over the place. The bishop's decision is void and so too is the Common Pleas judgment entered on his invalid finding.[16]

[5] Chief Justice Brabazon of King's Bench: Common Pleas says the Bishop of Lincoln conducted a proper proceeding in which you and Anna appeared and the bishop decided he had authority to rule upon the validity of the marriage. The Common Pleas judgment

---

[13] Writ of trespass.

[14] Interpreting "Katherine of Ravensden [at some earlier time] brought her writ of trespass against Philip of Hardwick…" Case at 50.

[15] Interpreting "The Court {of Common Pleas} hath been once certified {by the bishop} that she is not your wife, and therefore you ought not to be received" to argue she is. Case at 50.

[16] Interpreting "We were married in a village which is in the jurisdiction of the Abbot of St. Albans, and, consequently, the Bishop of Lincoln hath no power to certify the Court of aught done outside his jurisdiction. Judgment whether you can bar us from our answer by any record which was in deceit [of the court] and not rightly procured." Case at 50.

is entitled to *res judicata* respect. Anna isn't your wife. The question has been decided.[17]

The *res judicata* rule keeps the dispute within the first court that hears it. If Adam thought Common Pleas should have rejected the bishop's decision, Adam should have complained within the rules that related to Common Pleas' decision.[18] Instead he let it stand and tried to make his argument in a subsequent case.[19] Once he appeared he would be bound by the judgment unless he had it reversed on appeal.

Six hundred fifty years later the United States Supreme Court looked at a similar case. An island was located in a river that divided two states.[20] The litigants argued about the location in a Nebraska court that then ruled the island was in Nebraska. The loser brought a second suit in Missouri. He said the Nebraska judgment

---

[17] Interpreting "William of Bereford has sent us the certificate by which we find that the witnesses of the two parties were examined in the presence of the parties and that it was found {in the bishop's proceeding} that Anna was not Bogo's wife, and the King's Court is certified of that. And we shall not give effect to the suggestion that a writ should be sent to the Bishop of Hertford {who has authority over the Abbot of St. Albans} seeing that the parties appeared before the Bishop {of Lincoln} and produced their witnesses and proof was had in due form, and we will not, therefore, send to another Ordinary, for there is no need as judgment was given on the certificate." Case at 50–51.

[18] He should have asked for a rehearing or appealed to King's Bench, Parliament, or the king.

[19] The U. S. Supreme Court would have said Adam had the right to appeal his loss in Common Pleas to King's Bench. He took the wrong approach when he brought a new proceeding (rather than an appeal) in King's Bench. The doctrine would apply even if King's Bench could have refused to hear the appeal. Treines *v.* Sunshine Mining Co., 308 US 66 (1939) (denial of petition for certiorari).

[20] Durfee *v.* Duke, 375 U.S. 106 (1963). The text changes a dispute about avulsion and accretion into a dispute about an island's location.

was void because the island was outside Nebraska, the limit of the Nebraska court's jurisdiction. The Supreme Court took Brabazon's approach. Right or wrong the Nebraska judgment was *res judicata*—once the parties appeared in Nebraska they were bound. The loser could have appealed the judgment[21] but since he did not he could not have the location reconsidered.[22] *Res judicata* had greater power than the reality of geography.[23]

A Final Judgment

Some proceedings are dismissed before the court[24] reaches the merits of the controversy.[25] The plaintiff may have begun a proceeding and then failed to follow through.[26] The judgment has no *res judicata* conse-

---

[21] To the U.S. Supreme Court.

[22] The loser could have appealed the Nebraska judgment to the U.S. Supreme Court. In modern legal jargon, the loser could make a "direct attack" against the Nebraska judgment but not a "collateral attack."

[23] The Supreme Court said their case could bind only those who appeared. The Missouri tax authority would be free to argue the island was in Missouri.

[24] An *ex officio* inquest held by the king without a writ probably does not deserve res judicata treatment. See 123 Selden Society 436 (1289). A Sheriff's ruling does not qualify for *res judicata* treatment. 5 31a Rolls Series 92, 94 (1305). A litigant argues that because his writ was dismissed for the use of a mistaken name, the dismissal does not warrant res judicata treatment. 2 31a Rolls Series 370 (1294).

[25] Surprised by her opponent's appearance with a champion, a lady walks out of court. The reporter observes she took her lawyer's advice "for if she had awaited {her opponent's} formal denial [and wager of battle] she would have been barred from her action for ever. She was then non-suited by the Court." 43 Selden Society 134 (1313) (Anon).

[26] An early case says a party can withdraw from a proceeding even after it has been submitted to the jury and thereby deprive the case of res judicata consequence. The plaintiff asserts the litigant's grandfather did not die in possession; the defendant says the question

quences unless the court says it addressed the merits of the dispute.[27]

---

is *res judicata* because the plaintiff's father lost his claim to prove the defendant's grandfather died in possession. "{Plaintiff} I care not whether {a jury} passed or not; I am willing to aver it was never judicially decided. {Defendant} … judgment never passed on the verdict … for after the {jury} had passed … the {plaintiff} would not come into Court anymore … But it was found by the {jury} that {the grandfather} did not die {in possession} … judgment if {the plaintiff can here assert} he did. Justice Cave. Answer over {because the earlier proceeding has no res judicata effect}." 1 31a Rolls Series 398 (1293) (Ael). In another case a litigant withdraws after he learns the jury intends to render a verdict against him, and he is sanctioned by the court. 65 Selden Society 145 (1313). In an early case the defendant appeared but raised no defense, and a judgment was entered against him. A subsequent court per either Mettingham or Saham denied *res judicata* effect to the judgment because no jury verdict had been entered. 123 Selden Society 455 (undated report). Bereford's observation in the following case suggests such withdrawals would not necessarily deprive the proceeding of *res judicata* effect. In another case the defendant relies upon an earlier non-suit saying "the writ was crossed; and so we are puzzled to know how this writ issued, unless it be by the negligence of the clerks … Chief Justice Bereford: {The plaintiff} shall not have {a writ here} without our knowing {the circumstances behind the issuance of his writ} (as if to say, non-suit in such a case loses the action). *The Reporter*: This {Bereford's ruling} is doubtful, however. Therefore query." 63 Selden Society 270 (1311) (Anon).

[27] In a case in which the plaintiff takes a nonsuit because he had misconceived his claim by failing to base his claim to grazing rights upon his ownership of land the reporter observes "for if he had abided judgment … he would have lost his right of action to claim the common as appurtenant … seeing that he had claimed it as freehold by his own purchase {in the writ which he decided to end in a nonsuit}." 29 Selden Society 167, 167–168 (1313–1314).

3. (1311)[28]

[1] Adam gave his mother Anna her lifetime widow's portion in a farm and then sold Bogo the right he had retained to the farm after Anna died. Bogo sued[29] Anna to make her acknowledge the interest he would enjoy after her death.[30] Anna appeared and claimed Adam had given her the farm outright. Bogo dropped his suit.[31] Later he brought the same suit again.

[2] Anna: After Bogo dropped his first suit the court entered an order that I did not have to appear again.[32] Bogo can't take a second try at proving he has a right to the land after my death.

[3] Bogo: The court's judgment simply dismissed my case—the court didn't enter a judgment saying you owned the land outright.[33]

[4] Chief Justice Bereford: Sometimes a judgment dismissing a case simply interrupts the proceeding; sometimes such a judgment reaches the merits. Sometimes it is difficult to determine which doctrine a previous proceeding falls within.[34]

---

[28] 26 Selden Society 193. The text invents Adam's status as Anna's son. 111 Selden Society 162 (1284) suggests a litigant could escape the res judicata effect of a judgment by showing her lawyer had been inept.

[29] Writ of *quid juris clamat*.

[30] He sues to make her "attorn," that is, to acknowledge his rights.

[31] Interpreting "Therefore it was awarded that she go without day, and that Adam sue another *quid juris clamat*." Case at 193.

[32] Interpreting "It was awarded we should go without day." Case at 194.

[33] Interpreting "The award which was made was only 'that she go without day' and not that 'she go quit thereof." Case at 194.

[34] Interpreting "Sometimes it happens that the party goes without day; and this judgment is given on the principle matter. In such a case I do not think that the [other] party can again use a writ of the same nature. But in a case where a party is non-suited and the

[5] Anna: I will abide by whatever interpretation you put on the previous proceeding.[35]

[6] Chief Justice Bereford: I think we should ignore the previous proceeding.[36]

Judgments that Violate Res Judicata

The court extended the principle that an erroneous judgment binds the loser. If a loser does not appeal a judgment that denies *res judicata* respect to an earlier judgment, the second judgment—wrong though it was—deserves *res judicata* respect. A bad judgment preempts an earlier good judgment if the loser does not appeal.[37]

---

process fails through the negligence of the court or of the party himself, he can against use a writ issuing out of the same note." Case at 194. Elsewhere Bereford observed "If the demandant in his plea concedes something which is advantageous to the tenant and then perceives that he has pleaded foolishly and is nonsuited, do you not think that, if afterwards he brings a similar writ against the tenant, this confession of his will impede him? (Reporter: He implied that it would)." 19 Selden Society 11, 12–13 (1308–1309).

[35] Interpreting "If you award that we acknowledge again … we will acknowledge willingly." Case at 194.

[36] Interpreting the perhaps ambiguous "For myself, I am unwilling to annul the note through any award that may be made." Case at 194.

[37] American law concurs. See Treines *v.* Sunshine Mining Co., 308 US 66 (1939).

4. (1312–1313)[38]

[1] As sisters Anna and Babs jointly inherited the right to nominate a parson.[39] The older sister got the right to make the first nomination.[40] Anna sued[41] Babs to prove she was older. She lost—the court said Babs was older. Undaunted Anna brought a second suit by recycling her writ.[42] This time the court said Anna was older.[43] When Anna asked the court to tell the bishop its conclusion the court refused. The court realized its judgment had denied *res judicata* effect to the first

---

[38] 34 Selden Society 85 (1312–1313). The text simplifies a complicated report and an even more complicated record. The text's Anna and Babs replace the actual litigants who bought the sisters' rights. There were four sisters. If a decedent is survived only by daughters, the daughters inherit his land in equal shares. A right to nominate is considered land. The text ignores the original division among the heirs made by a writ of partition since the court itself ignores the possible res judicata consequences of that proceeding.

[39] The rule of primogeniture gives the decedent's land in its entirety to the oldest son. But if daughters alone survive they share the inheritance equally.

[40] "Willoughby: We have seen before Sir Ralph de Hengham that without the consent of the parceners the eldest could not begin her turn, and we understand that is still the law. Chief Justice Bereford: If they want to present in common, certainly they may; if not, the eldest will derive her turn necessarily despite etc. {the objections of her sister or sisters}. Reporter: And this he said as (a statement) of law." 34 Selden Society 59, 61–62 (1312–1313).

[41] Presumably Anna brought a quare impedit against Babs for interfering with her claimed right to nominate. As the joint heir to an advowson she had to prove her status as first born.

[42] Interpreting the implication of "Any judgment that was made upon a writ which was previously abated" and "whether he ought to (answer) to such a writ which was abated." Case at 86. The text identifies the judgment made on the abated writ as the second judgment.

[43] Babs ignored the case. Perhaps her guardian was lax in protecting her rights because she was nearly an adult.

case. Anna then told the bishop herself. Babs brought a third suit.[44] She said the first judgment ruled she was older. The second judgment was invalid because it denied *res judicata* respect to the first. Therefore, she said, the court had to recognize her status as the older sister was *res judicata* and that Anna had violated her rights by telling the bishop she was the first-born.

[2] Anna: This third case has to give *res judicata* respect to the second judgment, not the first.[45] The second judgment says I'm older. I acted properly when I told that to the bishop.

[3] Babs: If the second were valid you would be right. But you got the second "judgment" by recycling a writ and that you can't do. Therefore the second decision was an absolute nullity, something that in legal theory never happened.[46]

[4] Anna: So I take it you say the second judgment should be ignored because it wrongfully denied *res judicata* effect to the first.[47]

---

[44] Writ of *quare impedit.*

[45] "Scrope: We allege a judgment by which you were (put) out of possession, and that judgment is still in force." Case at 86.

[46] Interpreting "Judgment whether you can abate our writ by (pleading) any judgment that was made upon a writ which had previously been abated, so that those were only words of a judgment, and not a judgment, because they (the justices) had no warrant {to enter such a judgment.}" Case at 86.

[47] Interpreting "You do confess the judgment, but you say that they lacked a warrant to proceed to such a judgment. Do you mean to say, then, that there was an error." Case at 86. The Selden Society editors observe that Anna's question "is a trap, because the present proceedings are not in error, but upon a new writ of *quare impedit.*" Case at 86, footnote 5. The Selden Society editors mean the third proceeding is not an appeal from the second judgment; instead it is a new proceeding, and therefore the second judgment has not been reversed.

[5] Babs: No, I don't say that. Do you think I'm so lacking in legal sophistication that I would say an erroneous judgment is not entitled to *res judicata* respect?[48] What I say is the second "judgment" was an absolute nullity.[49] Because the writ was recycled the court had no authority to hear the case and therefore its words had no legal significance.[50]

[6] *The Reporter*: The court ruled for Anna. The court said that when Anna won her judgment by the recycled writ the judgment was wrong, but it was a judgment nonetheless.[51] The court's rejection of Anna's request to tell the bishop the outcome did not constitute a reversal of the judgment.[52] Therefore Anna's victory in the second proceeding preempted Babs' victory in the first. The third proceeding had to respect the second (rather than the first) judgment.[53]

---

[48] In 1292 Justice Mettingham refused to give an erroneous judgment *res judicata* respect. 1 31a Rolls Series 340 (1292) (entry).

[49] After a litigant argued a judgment of outlawry should have no res judicata effect Justice Howard said the justice had no power to render the outlawry and argued the judgment should be quashed. After a consultation among the justices Justice Stanton said "although there may be an error we cannot now upset it…" 5 31a Rolls Series 416 (1307).

[50] The paragraph interprets "That was not an error, because they had no warrant (as above)." Case at 86.

[51] Interpreting "The judgment stood, and albeit that it was mistaken. It could not be redressed in that way." Case at 86.

[52] Interpreting Justice Scrope: "Albeit that the execution of the judgment was suspended, the judgment was not thereby defeated. Therefore the judgment remains etc." Case at 86.

[53] The sisters settled before the court entered judgment. Case at 86.

Judgments Obtained by Fraud

Common Pleas gave *res judicata* respect to a judgment obtained by out-of-court fraud.[54]

5. (1312)[55]

> [1]Adam's writ[56] asked the court to award him a farm[57] despite a judgment Bogo had won giving him possession.[58]
>
> [2] Bogo: You admit I'm in possession because of the judgment. The court has to respect that judgment.[59]

---

[54] American lawyers would say this case concerned "extrinsic" rather than "intrinsic" fraud. The court's focus upon the out-of-court ("extrinsic") aspect of the fraud suggests the court would have treated in-court ("intrinsic") fraud differently.

[55]33 Selden Society 214. The actual dispute is probably described by Version I. The text instead adopts version II's simplification of the dispute into a simple claim for possession of land. The text makes explicit the implicit question in the report: Can Bogo repudiate Adam's claim for the land by arguing that he (Bogo) sits on the land pursuant to a court judgment, and therefore Adam cannot attack his possession, at least not until he brings a writ closer to ownership, a writ that would prevail over the res judicata consequences of a lower claim for possession.

[56] Writ of conspiracy.

[57] Adam's goal to acquire possession appears implicitly in Bogo's statement "If, then, the land be lost, it is lost by your own default, and you have your recovery by writ of right at the common law." Case at 215.

[58] As defendant to a writ of entry Bogo had vouched Adam. Case at 214.

[59] Interpreting "Conspiracy supposeth that false allegations and deceit were employed to the detriment of the other party contrary to the form of law. But you own words prove that we recovered the tenements against you by process of law and by judgment of the King's Court founded on right and reason." Case at 215.

[3] Adam: You told me at a tavern that you would drop the case if I agreed to arbitration. I did, and I didn't appear again in court.[60] By your out of court fraud you prevented me from making a valid defense.[61]

[4] Bogo: Here's an even more blatant fraud. Suppose I sue to get your land. Then we talk. I lie to you and say I made a mistake suing you. You've got every right to the land and I'm going to drop my suit. You're suspicious. I say I'll put it in writing. I give you a quitclaim that makes you the undoubted owner. You then ignore the case and I get a default judgment. The default judgment is valid even though it was procured by fraud. Nothing we did took away the court's jurisdiction. This case is the same.[62]

[5] Justice Spigurnel: Adam doesn't say the court proceeding was irregular. Therefore Adam's defense about the fraud is worthless. No out of court agreement can extinguish jurisdiction that the court has.[63]

[6] Chief Justice Brabazon and Justice Spigurnel of King's Bench, and Chief Justice Bereford of Common

---

[60] See case at 215. The text creates the tavern as the venue.

[61] Interpreting "You agreed, by your own deed, to arbitration, so that it was against your own deed that you recovered our tenements by deceit and conspiracy." Case at 215. For another case concerning arbitration, see 27 Selden Society 23 (1313–1314).

[62] The paragraph interprets "If I implead you in this Court … and I give you in the country a release and quitclaim, and yet, notwithstanding my deed, come on my day … {and} you knew very well that we had a day in the Bench, and that, that being so, no deed made in the country can, by the common law, make void the assignment of the day in Bench. If, then, the land be lost, it is lost by your own default…." Case at 215.

[63] Interpreting "No deed made in the country can extinguish in such case the jurisdiction of the King's Court…." Case at 215.

Pleas all agreed that Adam was bound by the judgment.[64]

In weighing the balance between fairness and finality for land judgments, this battery of the country's leading judges all choose finality. A judgment about the source of the country's wealth is money in the bank. The decision is not as toxic as it seems. Rather than claiming the land Adam should have just asked for money damages. He would have won.[65]

The Questions Decided

The plaintiff's writ shows the criteria she must prove.[66] If she wins the judgment should be *res judicata* regarding those criteria.[67] But sometimes the parties argue in court about different criteria. In order to save time a later court may say the judgment was *res judicata* regarding the criteria they volunteered to argue about.[68]

---

[64] Since the judgment was obtained in a possessory writ (a writ of entry) the court says Adam could overcome its *res judicata* consequence by bringing a higher writ, a writ of ownership. The advice provides cold comfort. Elsewhere Bereford derided the writ of ownership as a virtually illusory remedy. "Chief Justice Bereford: You will give a writ of right where a writ of possession would serve! (*as if to say,* No)." 42 Selden Society 85, 86 (1311).

[65] See 20 Selden Society 193 (1310).

[66] When a litigant (without his opponent's consent) asked to introduce proof about ownership—an ancestor's possession in the distant past—Bereford said "Will you teach us something new to take an issue on the right in a writ of possession colored with the right? By God's Sacrament! If you wish to undertake that, we will teach you something new." 63 Selden Society 268 (1311).

[67] A judgment about possession, for example, had no res judicata effect for litigation about ownership. 2 31a Rolls Series 428 (1294).

[68] Bereford's policy was not uniform about the question. In another case the defendant argued she committed no act of dispossession, and

6. (1311)[69]

[1] Adam sued[70] Babs to get possession of a farm.[71] He said he gave his brother a lifetime interest in the farm but that his brother wrongfully sold Babs outright ownership.

[2] Babs: You are bound by an earlier judgment that says I'm the outright owner. In that proceeding I sued[72] you for throwing me off the farm. You didn't want to argue about what you had done to me. You wanted to argue about the terms of the gift you made to your brother. You said you gave him only a lifetime interest so he had no right to sell me the farm outright. I agreed to make that the jury question. The jury then sided with me—they said you gave it to your brother outright. The court's judgment said your gift to your brother and his sale to me made me the outright owner

that she had bought the land. The jury found she had committed a dispossession and she had not bought the land. In later litigation the victor argued she could not again assert she had bought the land. Bereford said "what you found your case upon is that she did not {buy the land} and that matter lies outside the points of the {writ in the first litigation} and does not fall within the charge to the {jury}; for even without that [finding] it would have been enough had the {jury} found that she entered by {a dispossession}." 22 Selden Society 45, 46–47 (1310).

[69] 26 Selden Society 171. According to Adam he gave a fee tail; to simplify the text says the alleged gift was a life estate.

[70] Writ of formedon in the reverter. The brother is dead.

[71] In this context, Bereford says, the writ is a writ of possession. ("All writs of formedon are writs of possession until the tenements have come into the right blood either by descent or by reversion." Case at 176.) His description does not deny that formedon is closer to ownership than novel disseisin. Therefore Bereford's decision gives a judgment derived from a purely possessory writ—novel disseisin—res judicata effect upon a subsequent claim brought by a "higher" writ, a writ that is closer to ownership.

[72] Writ of novel disseisin.

of the farm.[73] You can't argue here I'm not the outright owner.[74]

[3] Adam: That earlier case was limited to the question your writ asked: did I throw you off the farm. You say the case decided what kind of gift I gave my brother. The case couldn't. The jurors had no right to talk about anything except the question your writ posed: did I improperly use self-help.[75]

[4] Chief Justice Bereford: Parties can tell the jury to decide something different from the limited questions the writ poses. {The parties can choose to litigate the question of ownership in a writ of possession}.[76] If Babs is right about what happened in the first case she wins.[77]

---

[73] Interpreting "Babs answered and said that Adam gave his brother in fee simple and not in fee tail, and was ready to aver it. The assize was charged upon this point and said that he gave the tenements in fee simple, whereupon Babs had her recovery." Case at 175.

[74] Interpreting "We ask judgment if you ought to be answered on any action founded upon the form limited to your brother which was annulled." Case at 172.

[75] Interpreting "Whatever was found then, the judgment rested solely on this, whether he was seised and disseised, without the right being tried." Case at 173. By conventional doctrine a judgment concerning dispossession had no *res judicata* effect in a subsequent suit for ownership. See 112 Selden Society 348 (undated).

[76] Whether a person with superior title committed a disseisin by ejecting another has inspired much modern scholarship. O.W. Holmes claimed a novel disseisin defendant could always rely upon superior title, O.W. Holmes, *The Common Law* 210 (1945), while Maitland, invoking Bracton to contradict Holmes, denied the defendant could. F.W. Maitland, *The Beatitude of Seisin, in 1 Collected Papers of Frederick William Maitland* 407, 426 (H. Fisher, ed. 1911). See also Sutherland 124, *supra*. Where the contest was between rival claims to inherit, Justices Bereford and Inge asserted title could be raised: "if the tenant in an assize of novel disseisin showeth a title in support of his tenancy he should not be forced to submit [his right to] his freehold to a jury unless the plaintiff supporteth his

Sometimes a plaintiff tries to limit the questions a case concerns. The court refuses and says she must litigate more questions. The court wants to save time by dealing with everything at once. A car crashes. The plaintiff sues for property damage. Later she wants to sue for personal injury. The court may say the first judgment resolved all her rights. Even though she just asked for damage to her car the judgment bars her from making a later claim for personal injury. The court rules forced her to combine all her claims, both property and personal injury, in the first proceeding.[78]

---

complaint by showing a title…" 37 Selden Society 24, 28 (1314). Where the parties were apparently unrelated and the defendant tried to raise a question of title, Bereford rejected the attempt saying "Will you teach us something new to take an issue on the right in a writ of possession colored with right? By God's sacrament! If you wish to undertake that, we will teach you something new." 63 Selden Society 268 (1311).

[77] Interpreting "There where you say that the judgment was obtained only upon this point whether he was seised and disseised, you speak irrelevantly … It was found that your brother had power to enfeoff Babs and to make a good and stable estate, and upon that they pleaded further upon her title and not upon the points of the writ {for dispossession} and the title was found good. And so you will not arrive at undoing that title now. Therefore be at one whether this was the case or not." Case at 173. If the court asks only the questions the writ properly poses but the jury renders a verdict that goes beyond those questions, the judgment will have *res judicata* consequences only for the questions posed by the writ. 22 Selden Society 45 (1310) (claim for disseisin in which the jury finds a disseisin, a binding finding, and then renders a verdict about the terms of a grant, a verdict the court ignores). Bereford says the jury verdict "does not fall within the charge of the {jury}." Case at 47.

[78] In the United States the federal rule of procedure 18 (a) addresses the problem.

7. (1294)[79]

Reporter's Note: If a tenant does not pay his rent his lord can take his cow. If the tenant sues[80] to get the cow back the lord needs to talk about more than the rent. He needs to list every duty the tenant has.[81] The judgment will be *res judicata* regarding them all.[82] He will lose the right to any service he does not mention.[83] {Suppose the tenant is supposed to pay rent and keep a bridge repaired. If the lord just mentions the rent he can say goodbye to the bridge repairs.}[84]

---

[79] 2 31a Rolls Series 360 (1294). The text changes the facts from a tenant who has bought land subject to an annual payment into a tenant who has bought a lease for a term of years. The text invents the bridge repair as a concrete example of the report's generalities.

[80] By a writ of replevin. He brings the replevin because he denies he owes the rent.

[81] Interpreting "The lord ought, in avowing the taking, to specify every kind of service by which his tenant holds of him…." Case at 360.

[82] Interpreting "Afterwards when other services were in arrear for which it was necessary to distrein, the tenant might boldly pray judgment of the avowry, for that at a certain time they pleaded in the same Court and he (the lord) avowing said he the tenant held of him by those services … (and of those services nothing is now in arrear…) Case at 360.

[83] A judgment gives a *res judicata* benefit to both parties. The "loser" has won a judgment setting a limit on the "victor's" claim.

[84] The text adds a concrete example of the general principle. The reporter then says some lawyers believe this res judicata doctrine applies only to the lord's defense of a replevin claim; not to the lord's suit for obligations the tenant has failed to perform. "But in the opinion of some, in a writ of Customs and Services it is necessary to mention in your count only what is arrear to you, without mentioning all whereof you are seised." Case at 360.

The Parties Bound

Court time is kept to a minimum if a judgment binds more people. But the court cannot let efficiency override fairness. Unless a person participates in a case the judgment cannot affect her rights.[85]

8. (1312–1313)[86]

[1] Adam sued[87] the prior for taking his cow. He said the prior violated a statute when he took his cow on a royal highway.[88]

[2] Prior: You can't sue to get this cow. You don't own it. I do. Bogo sued[89] me to get the cow. The court gave it to me. You're bound by that judgment.[90]

[3] Justice Stanton: The prior makes a pretty good point.[91]

---

[85] Directly or vicariously. Justice Saham speaks of a medieval proceeding that suggests a modern class action. "There we gave judgment as law that if {a majority of} the community agreed to a matter for the common good of the town ... and there are two or three who belong to the community who were overseas when they come home they cannot defeat what their companions have done..." 122 Selden Society 89, 91 (1281–1284).

[86] 34 Selden Society 134. The text focuses on the ban regarding the king's highway; the litigation gave more emphasis to the prohibition against a lord taking livestock outside his fee.

[87] Writ of trespass.

[88] Statute of Marlborough c. 15 (1267) (3 EHD 389). The common law also banned takings on the king's highway. 2 31a Rolls Series 54, 56 (1293). Even the grant of a franchise did not permit confiscations on the king's highway. 2 31a Rolls Series 54 (1293) (distress).

[89] Writ of replevin. Case at 136.

[90] The paragraph interprets the prior's argument about Bogo's default: "wherefore irreplevisable return was awarded. And thus we are seised of the beasts by virtue of such a judgment." Case at 134.

[4] Adam: That can't be—I've got nothing to do with a man called Bogo.[92]

[5] Chief Justice Bereford: Adam is right. The judgment against Bogo can't affect Adam's rights.[93]

Vicarious Representation

Even though someone does not appear in person her agent can bind her.[94] Equally a judgment against an ancestor will bind a person who sues as her ancestor's heir. Lawyers need to analyze the claim carefully.

9. (1310)[95]

[1] Adam sued[96] Bogo for throwing him off a farm.

[2] Bogo: You're my serf and serfs can't sue in royal court.[97]

[3] Adam: A judgment that has *res judicata* effect has established my freedom. I sued[98] your grandmother

---

[91] Interpreting "Stanton, J. He tells you etc. (as before) and thus he is seised by the sheriff's delivery and by virtue of that judgment." Case at 134.

[92] Interpreting "He alleges a judgment that was made against a stranger, and to which judgment we are not a party. Therefore that is no answer …" Case at 135.

[93] Interpreting "What is it to him or to the taking of which he complains, that a return was awarded to you {the prior} against a strange person (he implied that it had no importance)." Case at 135.

[94] Regarding agents see 104 Selden Society 96 (1320).

[95] 20 Selden Society 93. See also 1 31a Rolls Series 410 (1293). The text ignores the fact that Bogo's father survived his grandfather.

[96] Writ of novel disseisin.

[97] Interpreting "He ought not to be answered…" Case at 93. Claims for violence were an exception.

[98] Writ of mort d'ancestor.

Babs for throwing me off this very farm. She said I was her serf; the court said I was free.[99] As your grandmother's heir you're bound by that judgment.[100]

[4] Bogo: Babs had only a widow's lifetime interest in the farm. When she died her interest died too. I inherited the farm from my grandfather, not from her.[101] Although I inherited other land from her,[102] she's a stranger as regards the farm. The judgment you won doesn't bind me.

[5] Adam: Maybe your argument would hold water in another situation but you don't understand the king's law about serfs. In the beginning of the world every man was free and the law so favors freedom that any judgment proclaiming a person's freedom binds everyone whether they appear or not.[103]

---

[99] Interpreting "It was found by verdict of the assise that his father had died seised etc. and that he was next heir." Case at 93. A serf cannot have possession, and a serf cannot be an heir.
[100] Interpreting "To that {*i.e.*, your claim I am a serf} you shall not get … since in a court that bears record as a free man and of free estate {I} have recovered these same tenements against your grandmother." Case at 93.
[101] At Bab's death the grandfather's heir acquired the reversion after Babs' life estate.
[102] Bogo says he holds Babs "as a stranger in this respect" (case at 94), *i.e.*, as regards the farm. The text makes an implicit point explicit to show that *res judicata* would have bound Bogo regarding land he inherited from her.
[103] Interpreting "In the beginning every man in the world was free, and the law is so favorable to liberty that he who is once found free [and of free estate] in a court [that bears record] shall be holden free for ever, unless it be that some later act of his own makes him villein." Case at 94.

> [6] Bogo: Your so-called maxim is false. Cases can't bind a person who doesn't appear.[104] Suppose my grandmother decided to free all the serfs that lived on her widow's portion. She could free them for her lifetime but only for her lifetime.[105] That's all the freedom you got. If you think I've lost my rights because I didn't complain when Babs managed the litigation badly, you're wrong. I was in a cradle then.[106] Once I became a man I didn't sleep on my rights—my foreman taught you a lesson you won't forget.[107]

> [7] Chief Justice Bereford: If we said the Babs judgment bound Bogo we would bind Bogo by the representation of a person who was in the eyes of the law a stranger. We won't. Adam can't use the earlier judgment against Bogo.[108]

Adam's victory did not do him any good against Bogo. Bogo had not appeared. Bogo did not have a chance to make his case. But suppose Adam lost his suit against Bogo's grandmother. The court said he was a serf. After she dies Adam again tries to prove he is free. He sues Bogo. Adam could not use his victory against Bogo because Bogo did not participate. But can Adam's

---

[104] In the report Bogo says nothing to answer Adam's maxim. The text makes explicit the implications of his silence.

[105] Interpreting "{If Babs} had released and quitclaimed to him every kind of action of villeinage, and we had brought our writ of naifty, still we should not have been barred from demanding on the seisin of our grandfather ...." Case at 94.

[106] "But in her time Bogo ... was in the cradle." Case at 94.

[107] Interpreting "When he came of age, he saw that Adam would not submit to be 'justiced' as he ought. So he took him and held him as his villein..." Case at 94.

[108] Interpreting "If now he were answered, he would be enfranchised by a recovery against one through whom Adam claims nothing, for Babs is a total stranger." Case at 94.

hypothetical loss be used against Adam himself? Some would say Adam had a fair chance to prove he was free and he could not. The court should not waste its time letting him rehash the same losing arguments. The question was debated.

10. (1293)[109]

> *Reporter's Note*: A lawyer discussed a tough case. Suppose, he said, Adam sues some monks for dispossessing him from a farm. The monks say they have never taken possession—Bogo just lets them grow a few herbs there as a favor.[110] The monks also make a second defense: they say that since Adam has never possessed the farm, they could not have

---

[109] 2 31a Rolls Series 294. The text interprets the following note: Note that *Henry de Sutton* laid it down as a maxim (and said that he had seen many instances of it) that if Roger brings an assize of novel disseisin against the Abbat of Shrewsbury or some other person, who answers that he does not claim anything in the frank-tenement, but says that the frank-tenement belongs to one Richard Horsley (?), and says besides that Roger was not ever seised in such wise that he could be disseised, and prays the assize, and the demandant {Roger} also prays the assize, and the assize comes and says that Roger was not ever seised so that etc., whereby he (the demandant) takes nothing etc., and Richard enters, and Roger brings a writ against him and counts on his own seisin, —*Sutton* (I say) laid it down as a maxim that Roger will take nothing in this case by his writ; for the reason that his seisin whereof he counts was extinguished by the assize of Novel Disseisin, and that consequently he can not count of that seisin, albeit the assize did not pass between the same persons—This is strange, because of the rule "A transaction between different persons etc."

[110] The monks plead they are tenants at will, and therefore haven't acquired possession. Probably Bogo has given the land to the monks, but they are pretending he hasn't in order to avoid the Statute of Mortmain requirement that they buy a license for the sale. See 43 Selden Society 72 (1313).

> dispossessed him. The jury looks only at the second defense, and says the monks are right: Adam has never been in possession of the farm. They find for the monks. Afterwards the monks leave and Bogo keeps Adam off the farm. Adam now sues Bogo for dispossession. The lawyer said Bogo could reject Adam's claim by saying Adam's lack of possession is *res judicata*. It is true that Bogo did not appear in the earlier case. But Adam did. {Adam had a fair chance in court to prove he had acquired possession and he could not.}[111] His lack of possession is *res judicata*. I do not think the lawyer knows what he is talking about.[112] Everyone knows the Roman law maxim: a judgment has no *res judicata* consequences regarding a person who did not participate in the litigation.[113]

The lawyer thinks a stranger to a proceeding can use the judgment against a loser who participated. The reporter thinks not. The quarrel is still alive but the mass disasters of modern life make the lawyer's view that allows the judgment to be used less attractive.[114] A plane stops suddenly at the arrival gate. Two hundred passengers suffer bumps and bruises. Some say they saw the pilot kissing a flight attendant. He says he was not kissing her—the brakes malfunctioned and threw their faces together. Forty-nine passengers bring forty-nine cases and they all lose. There was no kiss. Passengers can keep on suing—since they did not participate in the earlier cases they cannot be bound. The fiftieth passenger

---

[111] The text adds the explanatory rationale.

[112] Interpreting "This is strange…" Case at 294.

[113] The reporter's Ango-Norman text includes his statement "*quod est mirum, propert illam regulam res inter alyos acta* &c." He refers to "*Res inter alios acta, aliis nec nocet nec prodest*" ("a thing done between others does not harm or benefit others.")

[114] The problem is now called the question of "mutuality of estoppel."

wins. The lawyer's view lets the next one hundred fifty passengers win automatically.[115]

Inconsistent Judgments Are Possible

Before the Bereford era court decisions about proof were consistent with a lesson from the gospels. Satan challenged Jesus to an experiment. After setting Jesus on top of the temple, he said "If thou be the Son of God, cast thyself down from hence."[116] Jesus refused to put God to the test.[117] Since earlier law relied upon divine intervention, the system took the gospel's counsel, and avoided putting God to a test, the test of consistency. As proof became mundane, a crisis in faith changed into a cost of doing business.

11. (1314)[118]

> [1] Anna sued[119] Bogo for her widow's share of a manor. She said since Bogo was in possession of the place as her son's guardian he had an obligation to provide her a third of the manor.[120]

---

[115] See Hart *v.* American Airlines, Inc. 304 N.Y.S. 2d 810 (1969).
[116] Luke 4:9.
[117] "And Jesus answering said unto him, It is said, Thou shalt not tempt the Lord thy God." Luke 4:12.
[118] 37 Selden Society 89. The report waffles between focusing upon whether Bogo or Cosmo sold the land and whether Bogo or Cosmo made the first feoffment. The text simplifies the controversy by focusing upon the sale because both present the same res judicata problem, and the sale is simpler to discuss.
[119] Writ of dower.
[120] "Guardian of the lands and of the heir…." Case at 89.

[2] Bogo: Since I'm your son's guardian you have to turn the boy over to me.[121] When you do you'll get your widow's share.

[3] Anna: First prove you're my son's guardian.[122] Cosmo says he's the guardian.

[4] Bogo: I don't have to prove that here. This case is not about a fight between Cosmo and me.[123]

[5] Chief Justice Bereford: She can make you prove your rights.[124]

[6] Justice Stanton: The chief's right. Suppose she sued you for abducting her son and you said you were the child's lawful guardian. She could say someone else was; and you would have to prove your rights.[125] A case for a widow's share should get the same treatment.

[7] Bogo: Suppose I win—I prove I'm the guardian.[126] Cosmo isn't here. The judgment won't bind him. Then he'll sue me claiming he's the guardian. We could wind up with this case saying I'm the guardian and the

---

[121] Since the lands are held in military tenure, the widow has an obligation to give her son to his lawful guardian.
[122] Interpreting "By reason of what tenements doth the wardship of the heir's body belong to you?" Case at 90.
[123] Interpreting "Even though we were willing to accept the averment which the plaintiff offereth, we do not think that the Court would receive us thereto." (Case at 91) and "We have no need to tell you that, for you cannot be a party to counterpleading etc." Case at 90.
[124] Interpreting "Reply to that, or give the woman dower." Case at 90.
[125] Interpreting "In a writ of ravishment of ward it is no answer … unless he {the defendant} can show that the wardship rightfully belongs to him.' Case at 92.
[126] Interpreting "If averment were now to be joined between us and should pass in our favor…." Case at 90.

> next case saying I'm not. The court can't let that happen.[127]
>
> [8] Chief Justice Bereford: Of course we can. Different cases can produce contradictory results.[128]

Different Rules for Land

Common Pleas created an exception to the rule that only participants in a case could be bound.[129] The court said that the sham lawsuits that transferred land bound virtually everyone.[130]

---

[127] "It might so happen that two inquests would pass upon a single right, one of which might be opposed to the other, which would be incompatible in law." Case at 92.

[128] Interpreting "Not incompatible with law, for different pleas between different parties have different results." Case at 92.

[129] Either in person or through their representatives.

[130] Statute of Fines Levied (1299) (3 EHD 491). The modern common law of in rem jurisdiction shows the statute's long shadow. A stranger to the fine, however, could avoid it in a voucher to warranty. See 81 Selden Society 96 (1319), 104 Selden Society 102 (1320).

12. (1317)[131]

[1] Adam sued[132] Cosmo. He said he had sold a farm to Bogo and since Bogo died without surviving relatives he had a right to take it back.[133]

[2] Cosmo: Bogo and I litigated a sham controversy about the farm.[134] The Common Pleas judgment approved our settlement that gave me the farm when Bogo died.[135] You can't contradict that judgment.

[3] Adam: I didn't appear. I can't be bound.[136]

---

131 61 Selden Society 182. The sale was in fact made by Adam's father. Case at 182. The case record includes the language of the fine that shows Bogo and Cosmo were father and son. Case record at page 188. Since the blood relationship of the parties is irrelevant to the validity of the fine, the case shows how a bastard father could provide a legacy to his bastard child. The fine let the father keep the land throughout his life, with his own bastard in effect "inheriting" the land when he died. "whereby this Bogo acknowledged the aforesaid tenements to be the right of Cosmo, as that which Cosmo had by his gift; and for this recognition Cosmo granted the same tenements in the same Court to Bogo for the term of his life, in such way that after Bogo's death the tenements were to revert to Cosmo and to his heirs." Case at 184.

132 Writ of escheat.

133 "Which ought to revert to Adam because Bogo was a bastard etc." Case at 182.

134 A writ of covenant to enforce an agreement about a supposed dispossession.

135 Interpreting "and for this recognition we granted the same tenements to Bogo, to hold for all his life; and after his death the tenements were to return to us and to our heirs." Case at 183. A "fine"—in the Anglo-Norman language an "end"—settles a dispute: "whereby this Bogo acknowledged the aforesaid tenements to be the right of Cosmo...." Case at 184.

136 Interpreting "We are quite strangers to the fine; and we do not think that we need to answer to any fine to which we are not a party.... ." Case at 183.

> [4] Cosmo: When the judgment was entered you were an adult, in the realm, in command of your mental faculties,[137] and not in prison.[138] You had a year and a day to complain about the judgment. You didn't. The judgment binds you.[139]
>
> [5] Adam: The court shouldn't approve such a doctrine.[140]
>
> [6] Chief Justice Bereford: But we do.[141]

Land with its perpetual existence created most of the realm's wealth. Landowners needed to be able to invest without worrying about some stranger bringing an unexpected claim.[142] Today countries have title registries that bind everyone. Common Pleas' exception to *res judicata* law achieved the same goal.

---

[137] A fine does not bind a non-party who was insane nor does it bind a party who was insane. This despite the argument "the court would not allow a fine to be levied … by a person of unsound mind." 2 31a Rolls Series 218 (1293). But see 2 31a Rolls Series 144 (1293) (fine conclusive regarding sanity, but voluntary entry of deed into the Roll is not).

[138] See 1 31a Rolls Series 430, 431 (1293) (Entry).

[139] "And when the fine was levied you were of full age, within the four seas, out of prison, and of sound memory; and no claim was entered by you within the year and the day. Judgment whether you can claim anything against this fine." Case at 183.

[140] Interpreting "If the Court thinks that we ought to answer to that, we shall answer certainly." Case at 185.

[141] Interpreting "Chief Justice Bereford: Answer." Case at 185.

[142] Perhaps when the settlement was done to sanitize an act of dispossession res judicata did not apply. "Reporter: And some were of the opinion that a non-claim does not bar in an entry sur disseisin, because it is no bar in the assize of novel disseisin etc. and this action is taken upon the same disseisin." 104 Selden Society 111, 113 (1320).

Chapter 8
Private Courts

THE CONQUEROR AND HIS SUCCESSORS let private courts supplement royal justice. The enterprise of creating a new court system that would supplant all the old courts was too burdensome. Furthermore the sale of private rights to conduct courts produced revenue for the crown.[1]

Private Peacekeeping Courts

The king might delegate the power to conduct a court that tried crimes, a court that could function only if the king gave the court holder the power to force jurors to swear to render a true verdict.

1. (1286)[2]

> [1] Adam sued to recover livestock Bogo had confiscated because he refused to take the oath necessary to serve on Bogo's court. Adam said Bogo couldn't force him to swear.[3]

---

[1] The profit stream a court provided made the power to conduct the court valuable.

[2] 112 Selden Society 258.

[3] "[W]hat the statute says is that no free man should be made to take an oath without special warrant from the king…" Case at 259. The statute is Statute of Marlborough, c. 22 (1267) (3 EHD 391) but the principle antedated the statute. *See* T.F. T. Plucknett, *Legislation of Edward I* 25–28 (1949).

[2] Justice Weyland: The king's delegation of the authority to conduct a criminal court necessarily includes the power to put men on oath to judge a man to death.

[3] Adam: You can't show that either you or your ancestors have ever made me take the oath.

[3] Bogo (by his lawyer William Bereford): Your obligation arises not out of your status as a landholder but rather from the king's command.[4] Bogo doesn't have to show you have served before.

[4] Justice Weyland: Bogo properly confiscated your livestock.

Common Pleas made sure court holders stayed within the limits of their jurisdiction.[5]

2. (1284)[6]

[1] Adam sued[7] Bogo because his court officials had leveled his embankment.[8]

---

[4] Interpreting "This is not a service issuing out of a free tenement but is something appurtenant to the crown." Case at 259. Cf. "Note that the presence of a man at a View of Frankpledge is not demanded by reason of tenure but as an obligation attaching on the person." 2 31a Rolls Series 398 (1294) (note).

[5] Common Pleas rejected a private court holder's claim his authority reached "concealments." 1 31a Rolls Series 338 (1292).

[6] 111 Selden Society 169. Version I includes a claim of a rival franchise; the text adopts the simplicity of version II. The two reports differ as to whether Bogo is the court holder or a member of the court, and whether Brompton is a judge or a lawyer. In trying to make sense of the dispute the text violates the integrity of the separate reports. The text omits argument about the geographical limits of Bogo's jurisdiction.

[7] Writ of trespass.

[2] Bogo: I've inherited a private peace-keeping court.[9] I can punish you for disrupting traffic on the king's highway. Although the embankment's footprint doesn't touch the highway its impact does. I've got jurisdiction over what you've done.[10]

[3] Adam: The embankment raises no interest of public concern even if it causes some people a bit of inconvenience.[11]

[4] The Justice: History puts Bogo's jurisdiction in context. After the Bastard [12] conquered England, violence was widespread. To pacify the countryside the king gave private courts the right to supervise small groups that insured their members kept the peace.[13] The courts exist only to investigate dangers to the peace.[14] The embankment just created a dispute

---

[8] "Leveled the bank by judgment of the court…" Case at 169.

[9] Interpreting "He and his ancestors have possessed view of frank-pledge … since time out of mind." Case at 171.

[10] Interpreting "If it was presented in a view that a sheepcote or embankment had been erected by a highway to the detriment of that highway, the presentment would authorize its demolition." Case at 171.

[11] Interpreting "The erection of an embankment or sheepcote to the detriment of a highway is a crown offence {but} here the embankment was … to the detriment of other individuals." Case at 171.

[12] *I.e.*, William the Conqueror.

[13] Interpreting "If anyone refused to be in a frankpledge then he was treated as a man who was against the peace" (case at 170) and "The only reason for these arrangements was the preservation of the peace." Case at 170. All men over fifteen had to join "except for knights and their eldest sons." Case at 169. Clerics were exempt. One had a letter from the Chancellor of the University of Cambridge proving his status as a student. 1 31a Rolls Series 296 (1292).

[14] Interpreting "They can only present things which are against the peace and by which the peace is less well kept." Case at 170.

> about the rights of landowners.[15] Chancery sells a writ for that.[16] Bogo's court has exceeded its jurisdiction.[17]

Common Pleas also defined the sanctions a private court could impose.

3. (1292)[18]

> [1] The king's lawyer sued[19] Anna because her court had executed criminals.[20]
>
> [2] Anna: Since I own Wisby Manor my right to hang felons has ancient roots. Before the Conquest my ancestor Hugh Longchamp defeated the Welsh and took Wisby as the spoils of war. As lord of the manor he continued the previous lords' policy of executing criminals. After the Conquest the Longchamps fought the king and Empress Maud confiscated the manor. She and her son Henry II followed the manor's custom of executing criminals. Subsequently King Richard returned Wisby to my ancestor Henry Longchamp.

---

[15] Interpreting "The wrongful erection of a bank and the wrongful planting of trees is a matter relating to a free tenement." Case at 170.
[16] "Of the nature of novel disseisin." Case at 170.
[17] Interpreting "If this trespass could be amended through a presentment of purpresture {in Bogo's court} then such writs {from Chancery} would serve no useful purpose: and that is false." Case at 170. The different versions have different outcomes. Version II says Bogo won because his court's customary authority exceeded the default jurisdiction of a leet.
[18] 1 31a Rolls Series 98.
[19] *Quo warranto.*
[20] Interpreting "The regality of taking ransom from and delivering those who are adjudged to death, which is a thing against the common law." Case at 98.

> Since then the lords of the manor have all imposed capital punishment and taken payment to grant mercy.[21]
>
> [3] The king's lawyer: The court can ignore your remarks about events before Richard's reign. Once the manor was annexed to the Crown all subsequent holders needed a new express grant to inflict the death penalty. Richard's grant of Wisby with "all its liberties" isn't good enough.[22]
>
> [4] Anna: If capital punishment on Wisby's criminals had been imposed by anyone else but the lords of Wisby you might be right.[23] But Wisby criminals have been executed only by the lord of Wisby Manor. That seamless history shows Richard confirmed all the manor's ancient franchises.[24]
>
> [5] Justice Berewike: You're wrong, Anna. Tear down your gallows.

Jurisdiction to arrest was easier to acquire than jurisdiction to conduct a trial.

---

[21] Interpreting "And there people were condemned to the gallows; and she took ransom etc…" Case at 100.

[22] Interpreting "The charter only contains the ordinary words, that is to say, 'with all liberties;' Case at 100.

[23] Interpreting "If that franchise had been, by the ancestors of our lord the King, once severed from the manor, then what he says would be perfectly correct; but inasmuch as the franchise was never severed…" Case at 102.

[24] "So that they were never annexed to the Crown except in right of the manor: and King Richard rendered etc., as before." Case at 102.

4. (1294)[25]

[1] Adam sued[26] Bogo for imprisoning him.

[2] Bogo: I'm a village official.[27] You were accused of wounding one of my villagers outside our town. When I found you inside the village I had a right to arrest you because you refused to post bond.[28]

[3] Adam: A village official can neither conduct a trial nor make an arrest for an event that occurs outside the village.[29]

[4] Bogo: The tests are different. A killer can be arrested anywhere even though he can be tried only where he dealt the blow.[30]

[5] Adam: Maybe you're right[31] but after you arrested me I offered to post bond. You refused to take it.

[6] Bogo: By that time the victim was almost dead. Bond was no longer an option—I had the right to lock you up.

---

[25] 2 31a Rolls Series 556 (1294). The text changes the report's sequence of arguments. *See also* 1 31a Rolls Series 122 (1292) (trespass).
[26] Writ of imprisonment.
[27] A bailiff.
[28] Interpreting "So he came to him and required him to find surety; but he would not, so he took him." Case at 556.
[29] Interpreting "The trespass was committed out of the liberty; and since the bailiff could not take cognizance of the trespass, neither could he attach him." Case at 556.
[30] Interpreting "For if I slay a man belonging to one vill, the bailiff of another vill may attach me; and yet he shall not have power to take cognizance of the matter by trying me." Case at 558.
[31] By presenting a new defense he concedes the bailiff's point.

Private Courts to Manage Monopolies

Just as modern governments claim monopoly rights to such unconventional property as radio frequency bandwidth, the king claimed to own such peculiar property [32] as wildlife, [33] wrecked ships, [34] and the authority to conduct fairs.[35] For a price he would sell the exclusive right;[36] sometimes, apparently, to two different buyers. Common Pleas had to intervene.

5. (1294)[37]

> [1] Adam sued[38] Bogo for tearing down the pillory Adam used to punish violators of his market and fair rules. Adam produced Henry III's charter giving his ancestor's descendants the exclusive right to conduct an annual fair and a twice weekly market[39] with all the standard attributes.[40]
>
> [2] Bogo: You never built a pillory. If you sleep on your rights you lose them.

---

[32] By charter the king apparently granted a right to sell cloth at wholesale despite contrary rules by the town of Gloucester. 1 31a Rolls Series 306 (1292).
[33] *See* 31 Selden Society 150 (1311).
[34] 29 Selden Society 183 (1313–1314).
[35] 26 Selden Society 93 (1310–1311).
[36] Despite his grant of a franchise, the king's rights could not be there determined. 31 Selden Society 57 (1311).
[37] 2 31a Rolls Series 482. The text changes the sequence of the arguments within the report.
[38] Writ of trespass.
[39] So stated in the writ, footnote page 482.
[40] Interpreting "We are to have a fair with all the franchises etc." Case at 482.

[3] Adam: Proof that I have conducted markets and fairs proves by implication that I have punished violators.[41]

[4] Bogo: Rather than debate the facts I'll just ask the court to focus on the sources of our conflicting monopolies. The fact that I've exercised my rights from before the time of legal memory {implies an ancient royal grant that has been lost.}[42] You rely on a later grant. Since the crown can't sell the same monopoly twice first in time wins.[43]

[5] Adam: The court should interpret the grants in a way that upholds them both. The court should uphold my monopoly for the times I'm conducting a fair. Your monopoly is valid at all other times.[44] Since my pillory was up during my market time you shouldn't have knocked it down.

[6] Bogo: {The "compromise" you suggest gives you everything, and me nothing.}[45] My ancestors have always used our pillory even when you were running a market or fair. If someone tried to get out of our jurisdiction by saying you had already fined him—say for selling bad bread—we ignored the defense and took our full penalty. We've never conceded your rival

---

[41] Interpreting "We have been seised of the main matter *i.e.* the fair etc.; and that is sufficient evidence of seisin of what is an appendant." Case at 482.
[42] An implicit argument.
[43] Interpreting "King Henry could not grant a franchise to our prejudice…" Case at 482.
[44] Interpreting "It may be that you ought to have amends … on days other than fair-days or market days, and we ought to have amends … in fair-time and market days…" Case at 484.
[45] Adam's "compromise" protects all the rights he claims from Bogo's conflicting authority.

> authority. The two grants can't be harmonized and since mine is older I win.
>
> [7] Justice Mettingham: The king can't sell the same monopoly twice but you both seem to say he has. We'll adjourn so that the king can tell us what to do.[46]

Mettingham respectfully defers to royal authority;[47] in contrast Bereford imposes his own view to resolve a comparable dispute:

6. (1310–1311)[48]

> [1] The Abbot of Shrewsbury sued[49] the Town of Shrewsbury for interfering with the fair {and the court} he had been conducting.[50] The abbot said the town's fair was diminishing his profits.[51]

---

[46] Interpreting "Toll and stallage are appendant to a fair and to a market, and the amends of bread and ale and a pillory belong to the Crown; and Bogo has the estate which the King had; and the King cannot grant anything to the prejudice of his fermor; and Adam claims a higher estate than what the King granted to him; therefore we will ascertain from the King what we are to do. Keep your days etc." Case at 484.

[47] Cf. "Justice Berewike. We cannot go on without knowing the King's pleasure in this case or in this plea. Reporter: And so they had a day to speak with the king." 2 31a Rolls Series 338, 342 (1294).

[48] 26 Selden Society 93. The two versions and the record do not clearly show which party won.

[49] Writ of nuisance.

[50] An implicit attribute of a fair that the text makes explicit in order to facilitate the transition between the text's cases.

[51] Interpreting "Whereby the merchants who were wont to come to the abbot's fair and to hire stalls and give toll, come to the fair of the said commonalty..." Case at 95.

[2] Town: Here's our charter;[52] you don't show yours. Apparently you think just because you've been running the fair that's enough. That's an argument a layperson could make but the common law holds monks to a higher standard.[53] Where's your charter?[54]

[3] {Chief Justice Bereford: I wouldn't insist monks have to behave better than laypeople.}[55]

[4] Town: Here's another reason. If the abbot wins he'll shut us down. The king takes part of our revenue. The abbot's argument he can keep the fair just because he has had the fair in the past isn't sufficient because his conduct reduces royal revenue.[56]

[5] Chief Justice Bereford: Sound reasoning. What have you got to say, abbot?

[6] Abbot: I didn't start the fair. My predecessor ran it too.

[7] Chief Justice Bereford: That's good enough unless the town has something else to say.

[8] Town: Twice in the last fifteen years the king's agents [57] have come to Shrewsbury to investigate

---

[52] Later in the case Bereford refers to the town's charter. Case at 94.The text assumes the town presented its charter at the outset.
[53] Interpreting "They are men of religion and cannot claim by conquest." Case at 93.
[54] Interpreting "Without showing specialty." Case at 95.
[55] The town's resort to another argument shows Bereford rejected the claimed higher standard for men of religion.
[56] Interpreting "Shrewsbury is the king's [borough] and answers for its issues at the Exchequer. We ask judgment if without specialty etc." Case at 93.
[57] The circuit court known as "the eyre" not only heard cases but also investigated claims to royal authority.

claims to royal authority. The abbot and his predecessors said nothing about the fair. Forfeiture is the penalty for concealment.

[9] Abbot: There's no forfeiture without a proceeding to enforce it.[58]

[10] Chief Justice Bereford: That quibble won't fly. You can't immunize your conduct with a boast that the king hasn't sued you.[59]

[11] Abbot: Perhaps our fair was on hiatus—isn't it possible we let the king run the fair then but later decided to take it back?

[12] Town: Can you prove your absurd hypothesis?

[13] Chief Justice Bereford: {The abbot's silence is deafening. We'll ignore his specious defense.}[60] Since the previous abbot ran a fair ordinarily the abbey would win. But the town's fair serves to profit the king.[61] Unless the abbot's has something more to offer the town wins.

[14] Abbot: We've run this fair from before the time of legal memory. {Even though we've lost the grant the king gave us the monopoly first.}[62]

---

[58] Interpreting "Unless the king brought his quo warranto." Case at 94.
[59] Interpreting "Chief Justice Bereford: If the king brought his *quo warranto* against you, it would not be a good answer." Case at 94.
[60] The hiatus theory disappears.
[61] Interpreting "But it would be otherwise if the town belonged to anyone but the king" (case at 94) in the context of the earlier argument that Bereford found persuasive.
[62] The rationale behind the time before memory argument. *E.g.*, "Justice Hengham. He alleges a prescription, and that is a sufficiently good specialty…" 4 31a Rolls Series 430 (1305) (Note, replevin).

Common Pleas nullified a prior's claim to taxing authority because he concealed his use of it.

7. (1313–1314)[63]

[1] The king sued[64] the Prior of Dover because he had no justification for taking tolls from passengers who disembarked at Dover.

[2] Prior: We've always done it.

[3] Justice Stanton: You didn't claim the right the last time the king's agents were in town.

[4] Prior: I made a mistake. Just like a child the church is entitled to reconsider its mistakes. I'm telling you about the toll now.[65]

[5] Justice Stanton: If your predecessor had committed the mistake your argument would have some force. But you were the one who kept quiet. As long as you lead the priory it can't collect.[66]

[6] Prior: Wait, I'm not done. The money is just paid for the damage done to the docks when cargo is off-loaded.[67] A toll is a royal right but a claim for compensation isn't.

---

[63] 29 Selden Society 183. The toll is described as a tariff at the vill of St. Margaret.

[64] Writ of *quo warranto*.

[65] The paragraph interprets "The church is within age." Case at 184.

[66] Interpreting "Justice Stanton: This Prior can never have it {*i.e.*, the church's opportunity to correct mistakes}, for he himself disclaimed." Case at 184.

[67] Interpreting "Damage done to our land by their disembarkation." Case at 184. He probably referred to cargo—a more plausible cause of damage than foot traffic.

> [7] Justice Spigurnel: Ingenious—perhaps your argument could have worked if the payment varied with the damage. But you just take two pence from each and every passenger. The king wins.[68]

Private Courts for Tenants' Disputes

At the Conquest the king took title to all England's land. He then gave away or sold large tracts. When the recipients subdivided they created private courts to resolve disputes involving their tenants.[69]

Due Process

Since the king guaranteed justice to all his subjects Common Pleas could review private court judgments.[70] A

---

[68] Interpreting "That which is certainly assessed, and you demand it as a fixed amount, cannot be assigned to trespass, but is more like a royal right." Case at 184.

[69] Serjeant Scrope observes "the law assumes that where one has a seignory and a tenant, the tenant is justiciable, according to the law, in the lord's court..." 104 Selden Society 25, 28 (1320). A reporter, however, said "in order that one may have a court he must have at least four free tenants ..." 2 31a Rolls Series 524, 525 (1294) (Replegiare).

[70] A private court allowed a woman to recover her widow's portion despite the tenant's claim she was living with another man when her husband died. Apparently because the court did not determine whether the husband died before the enactment of a statute that deprived such an adulterer of dower, Chief Justice Bereford repudiated the judgment and gave the land back to the tenant. 33 Selden Society 228 (1312). Bereford was willing to review a question of law. An earlier case refused to review a question of fact. The private court ruled a litigant had no obligations to a person who confiscated his livestock. On appeal to Common Pleas the claim was again made that he had an obligation. The court refused to review the private court's factual finding. "Justice Saham: Our understanding is

litigant attacked the system head on—the court, he said, had to provide due process of law. The court was necessarily biased in favor of claims the court holder brought.

8. (1287)[71]

> [1] In Common Pleas Adam sued[72] Bogo for taking his cows.
>
> [2] Bogo: When Adam refused to pay me what he owed I sued him in my court. He refused to appear, and my court properly told me to confiscate his cow to force him to appear.[73]

---

that false judgment can exist only in the process or execution of the judgment of a court; but we see no error in either of these." 122 Selden Society 78, 79 (1279–1281). In another case brought to Common Pleas by the writ of pone Bereford said "Neither in this writ nor in any other writ except the writ of false judgment can you deny the record of the county for the judgment will remain in force until it is reversed by the action of false judgment." 112 Selden Society 356, 357 (undated report). *See also* 111 Selden Society 74 (1277). Bereford was distinguishing cases brought to his court by the writs of pone or *recordari.* In bringing such a review proceeding the Sheriff was to certify the cause was true and then the parties would plead about defects other than the factual findings. If the Sheriff believed the findings in the private court were false, he was to retain the pone or recordari and certify to Common Pleas that the cause was false. 2 31a Rolls Series 14 (1293). A writ of false judgment could be brought to overturn the judgment, but a writ of false judgment could also be brought against the suitors, the decision makers, of the private or Sheriff's court. *See* 5 31a Rolls Series 116 (1306) (false judgment). According to Justice Hengham a writ of false judgment was proven by "one who heard and saw," not by a jury. 4 31a Rolls Series 376 (1305) (false judgment).

[71] 112 Selden Society 287.

[72] Writ of replevin.

[73] Interpreting Bogo "owed him two marks ... [so] he had him summoned to his court.... He defaulted ... we took one animal by the

[3] Adam: He can't bring his own claims in his own court. The court will be biased in his favor.[74]

[4] Bogo: I don't make the decisions; the community representatives do.[75]

[5] The Justice: Bogo's court can hear Bogo's claims.[76]

[6] Adam: I have another complaint. During the litigation Bogo took another cow because he claimed I had violated a court order. I asked to post bond so I could keep the cow until the court ruled on the alleged violation. The court said I couldn't.[77] The king guarantees local courts will provide fair procedures. A court has to provide a procedure so that a litigant can get his livestock back while the court takes time to decide a question.[78] The court's refusal to provide that procedure denied me due process of law.[79]

---

judgment of our court." Case at 287–288. This passage presents Adam's first avowry; he avows again pursuant to a court order when Bogo fails to make his law.

[74] Interpreting "If a tenant has wronged his lord or is indebted to him, he is not allowed to summon him to answer in his own court, because if he does he will be judge and party in the same plea." Case at 288.

[75] Interpreting "I am not the judge, but it is the suitors of the court who judge." Case at 288.

[76] Interpreting "It was adjudged that he answer over." Case at 288.

[77] Interpreting "Justice Brompton: ... you {Bogo} made distraint and refused to release the animals despite an offer of gage and sureties…." Case at 288.

[78] If the tenant refuses to appear, the livestock will remain impounded. 5 31a Rolls Series 248 (1306).

[79] Adam's contention appears in Brompton's judgment. To make the case more intelligible the text puts Brompton's remarks in Adam's mouth. Brompton says if Bogo's court "had released Adam's animals by plevin when he requested this in return for sureties to come to your court and do what he should do there he could have defeated the

> [7] Bogo: That's an argument you should have made in my court not here in Common Pleas.[80]

> [8] Justice Brompton: You're wrong. By posting bond a farmer has a right to get his livestock back until the court makes a decision.[81] Adam didn't have to waste any more time in your court. A judgment rendered by a court that doesn't provide due process of law is void.[82]

The decision lets private courts decide claims by the court owner. But Common Pleas imposes its own view of due process upon the procedures his court must observe.[83]

Bereford did not tolerate private court abuses.

---

summons by his reply; but you refused to release his animals, so he was unable to give an answer in your court." Case at 288.

[80] Interpreting "He should have alleged that in our court and could thereby have defeated the summons, and then we would not have made the distraint." Case at 288.

[81] Brompton rules in Adam's favor regarding defective procedures that the court applied to both the first and second confiscations. At common law a tenant replevying livestock did not even have to respond to the lord's justification until he received provisional return of the livestock. 2 31a Rolls Series 56 (1293) (unjust duress).

[82] Interpreting "To make us put his writ in suspense while your court decided the matter would mean this court would wait on the decision of your court, and that is not permissible." Case at 288. In effect the court rules the realm's unwritten constitution forces a court to provide the "delivery" procedure. Since Adam is making a "collateral" rather than "direct" attack on the judgment of Bogo's court (he brings a new replevin rather than making an appeal) American lawyers would say Bogo's court judgment was "void" rather than "voidable."

[83] So also the improper grant of an adjournment by a franchise court allows the royal courts to take jurisdiction. 38 Selden Society 41, 43 (1312–1313). A private court could not refuse to allow a continuance for service for the king. 52 Selden Society 37 (1316).

9. (1305)[84]

[1] Anna sued[85] the staff of Bogo's court for denying her justice. The sheriff told Common Pleas that the staff stood mute when he first demanded an explanation but that they had finally come to London to tell their story.

[2] Justice Bereford: Good people, what happened?

[3] Staff: Bogo's steward told us not to produce the record you wanted and he had one of us thrashed.[86]

[4] Justice Bereford: Who did it?

[4] Staff: Bogo gave the orders; his men did the deeds. Bogo's son was one of the thugs.

[5] Bogo's lawyer: Your honor, I can explain…

[6] Justice Bereford: Keep quiet. I'll hear from their own lips what these people were too terrified to record.[87]

[7] Staff: After Anna sued Bogo's son for throwing her off her land he asked for a postponement. When we refused he came up with a royal order granting a

---

[84] 4 31a Rolls Series 360.
[85] Writ of false judgment.
[86] "We made no record nor did we give any judgment; for the steward of Bogo's court would not suffer us … but threatened to beat and ill treat us; and he did beat and ill treat {one of us}." Case at 362. Although the report implies the steward did the beating Bereford's question suggests the suitors said something different.
[87] Interpreting "Bogo's lawyer: I will tell you all about the business. Justice Bereford: You shall not say a word about it; but they themselves out of their own mouths shall record it." Case at 362.

continuance.[88] We said we'd go ahead anyway. He flew into a rage and threatened to beat us. We were too frightened to do anything else.

[8] Justice Bereford: You were right about his claim for a postponement—I don't see how it could have been valid.[89] What happened next?

[9] Staff: Anna kept pressing her claim but we were too afraid to help. Then Bogo's son sued[90] us here for rejecting the postponement. Your court sent him away, saying until we entered a judgment the case wasn't "ripe for review."[91] Then we asked the steward to force Bogo's son to show up before us. The steward said he'd do nothing unless we produced an order from this court. Since Anna had received no satisfaction from us she sued here to force us to tell the story.[92] When the sheriff threatened to take our livestock unless we produced a record[93] we decided we had no choice. We had to travel to London. By staying together as a group we thought we'd be safe. You've got to help us.

---

[88] Bogo's son "on the same day put forward the King's letter of protection." Case at 364.

[89] Interpreting "As to the essoin and the Protection you did not do much amiss." Case at 364.

[90] Writ of false judgment.

[91] Interpreting "Because he did not by that judgment lose any tenancy." Case at 364. The text adopts American legal jargon about the timing of review. A case has to be "ripe" for review. "[I]ts basic rationale is to prevent courts, through the avoidance of premature adjudication, from entangling themselves in abstract disagreements…" Abbot Laboratories *v.* Gardner, 387 U.S. 136, 148–149 (1967).

[92] By the writ of false judgment.

[93] Interpreting "In order to save our property, we have come here…." Case at 364.

[10] Justice Bereford: Take a clerk with you and have him write down everything about the beatings and the abuse. Don't worry. Bogo and his steward will be brought to book.[94]

The Boundary between Royal and Private Jurisdiction

In cases where royal and private jurisdiction overlapped Common Pleas set the boundary.[95]

10. (1312)[96]

[1] Adam sued[97] his agent for embezzling receipts from wool sales in Comstock and Norwich.

[2] *The Reporter*: Bogo[98] intervened to tell the court to drop part of the case. He said the king had sold him exclusive jurisdiction over Norwich.[99]

---

[94] Interpreting "Bereford adjudged that the steward and Bogo should be distreined to compel them to appear…." Case at 366.

[95] Sometimes in favor of the non-royal court. A merchant sued his apprentice in royal court despite his agreement to resolve disputes in merchant court. He said royal jurisdiction was appropriate because his apprentice also acted as his receiver. Justice Mutford agreed. But Bereford for the majority said "if he were to render this account at common law, we should give him auditors by whom he would be judged, and this would be outside his covenant and against this deed…" 61 Selden Society 123, 125 (1317).

[96] 33 Selden Society 205. The American law of "pendent jurisdiction" addresses a similar problem. A franchise holder enjoyed no authority over the king. Despite the franchise a claim brought by the king would be heard in royal court. 31 Selden Society 57 (1311).

[97] Writ of account.

[98] Bogo is the Bishop of Norwich, but the text says nothing about his ecclesiastical status since he conducts a private rather than church court.

[99] Interpreting "Norwich is within the franchise … and in virtue of that franchise {he has} cognizance of this kind of plea." Case at 205.

> [3] Adam: My agent produced one single fraudulent accounting. My writ forced me to include all the damage the accounting caused and therefore royal jurisdiction reaches into Norwich.[100]
>
> [4] Chief Justice Bereford: Suppose this case involved a Comstock farmer's claim that his land while within royal jurisdiction had attached grazing rights in a meadow subject to Norwich jurisdiction. This royal court would decide questions about the grazing rights; Bogo's court wouldn't. In cases of conflict the king's jurisdiction prevails.[101]
>
> [5] Bogo: Your theory's too broad. Suppose Norwich land has attached grazing rights in Comstock. My Norwich court would decide a dispute about the grazing rights in the royal jurisdiction. The king's jurisdiction doesn't always trump mine.[102]

---

[100] Interpreting "You ought not to have your franchise in these circumstances, for the count is one whole and cannot be divided, though the receipt was in divers places…" (case at 205) and "The jurisdiction of this Court, which is higher, draweth to itself the jurisdiction of a franchise, which is lower and less authority." Case at 206.

[101] Interpreting "I put the case of a man having a freehold in a geldable vill, to which common is appendant, the said common being within a franchise. If he be disseised of this common, where will he plead? Not in the franchise, but in the King's Court. And, though the franchise be claimed, it would not be allowed, because it has no jurisdiction to try the fact of appendancy, to wit, whether the common be appurtenant or not." Case at 206.

[102] Interpreting "And what if the freehold to which the common is appurtenant be within a franchise? Where will he bring his action for disseisin?" Case at 206. Although the report attributes this remark to Denham, a serjeant whose only other remark is made on behalf of Adam, the question seems to have been posed by the Bogo. Since the identity of the lawyer who posed the question is unimportant—the important point is Bereford's answer—the text attributes the question

> [6] Chief Justice Bereford: No, you're wrong. Even then Common Pleas would decide the dispute.[103]

Royal courts can intrude into franchise jurisdiction but franchise courts can't intrude into royal jurisdiction.[104]

---

to Bogo. The Selden Society editor describes the passage as "apparently corrupt." Case at 206 footnote 2.

[103] He would "Certainly {sue} in the King's Court, because of the Franchise Court's lack of jurisdiction; and I have seen the Bishop of Ely claiming his franchise in like case, and it was not allowed, for the reason aforesaid." Case at 206. American law holds that even though a court has no direct jurisdiction over land outside its geographical competence its authority over litigants within its jurisdiction provides an indirect way to reach the land. *See* Massie *v.* Watts, 10 U.S. (6 Cranch) 148 (1810) (Chief Justice Marshall). A Year Book case suggests the same principle. Bereford ordered the summoning of owners of Welsh lands in the English counties nearest to Wales with the apparent threat that if they did not appear their personal rights in their English lands might be at risk. 70 Selden Society 62 (1319). The case suggests if they appeared the court might order them to take action regarding the Welsh land. But *see* 1 31a Rolls Series 146 (1292) (entry).

[104] The case is resolved not by theory but rather by Bereford's decision that Adam could have divided his claim. He could have bought a writ regarding just the Comstock fraud and then pursued separately in Norwich the fraud about the Norwich receipts. Case at 207.

CHAPTER 9
The Church

THE KING CONCEDED THE CHURCH had jurisdiction over marriage and death.[1] But Common Pleas took the same approach to the church courts that it did to private courts. The king's court resolved conflicts between royal and church jurisdiction.[2] The church courts did not.[3]

1. (1294)[4]

[1] Adam sued[5] the parson for violating the king's prohibition against claiming secular property in church court.

---

[1] *See* 122 Selden Society 125 (1284).
[2] Bereford rejected the argument that since land in Carlisle could be devised by will, the church courts should have jurisdiction to determine rights to the decedent's land. 20 Selden Society 198, 99 (1310).
[3] "Justice Bereford: Within these twenty years people have been accustomed to take bonds, binding debtors to submit to the decision of Holy Church in mercantile matters, and by those obligations they used to draw the Church into pleas of debt, to be pleaded before them; and it was seen that that was against the law … in like manner I tell you, in this case you cannot elect which kind of judgment you please; for if you were to plead here a matter which pertains to Court Christian, we would not admit you to do so; so in Court Christian, 'Christians themselves shall not there etc.," for you would be prevented by the prohibition." 3 31a Roll Series 486, 492 (1303).
[4] 2 31a Roll Series 588. The litigation probably concerns a disagreement about the local definition of heriot and mortuary, customary rights that vary from place to place. *See also* 3 31a Roll Series 440 (1303).

> [2] Parson: I sued in church court to enforce my ecclesiastical right to a dead parishioner's animal.[6] I didn't claim "secular" property.[7]
>
> [3] Adam: According to secular law the village lord gets to choose one of his dead villager's animals. As that lord I had already taken the cow. That means the parson claimed secular property in church court. The king prohibits the use of church courts to litigate secular rights.[8]
>
> [4] Parson: I wasn't litigating secular rights there. The church court will say the cow wasn't secular property —as the decedent's parson I have an ecclesiastical right to choose one of his animals.[9]
>
> [5] The Justice: If Adam had possession of the animal the king's court is the only place where this dispute can be decided. We'll ask the jury if Adam took possession of the cow. If he did the jury will resolve the question about whether Adam's or the parson's right to the cow is superior.[10]

The church can say whatever it wants about a parson's right to dead parishioners' livestock. But once a lord has taken a cow the parson can claim it only by

---

[5] Writ of attachment upon the prohibition.

[6] His right to a "mortuary."

[7] Interpreting "They did not plead about any lay chattel, but about a mortuary; ready etc." Case at 590.

[8] Interpreting "This was our heriot, and we were seised in the parson's time as of our lay chattel, we pray judgment." Case at 590. By "we pray judgment," Adam means that unless the parson agrees to have the secular jury define the lord's heriot the court should enter judgment that the parson violated the prohibition.

[9] Interpreting "We cannot be party to try the right to a mortuary in this court…." Case at 590.

[10] The paragraph interprets "The Justice: Answer if it was his heriot, and if he was seised." Case at 590.

bringing suit in secular court. Perhaps the jury will say the parson's ecclesiastical right prevails over the lord's secular right. But the secular court will decide the question.

Even if both litigants were religious institutions they had to litigate their disputes about secular property in royal court.[11]

2. (1313)[12]

> [1] The abbot sued[13] the prioress because the priory's workers had taken grain from the abbey's workers.
>
> [2] Prioress: My workers harvested the crop on my farm. As the landowner I keep ninety percent; the church gets a ten percent tithe. Since the farm falls within my priory's ecclesiastical jurisdiction my workers had a right to take all the grain. The abbot can't complain here. The secular courts have no authority to decide whether the abbey or the priory has the ecclesiastical right to the farm's tithes.[14]

---

[11] Two church entities resolved a dispute before the church court, and agreed controversies arising out of their settlement could be heard only in church court. Bereford refused to enforce their agreement "for [otherwise] the Ordinary could in that case enlarge his power entirely without warrant at his pleasure for no reason, and this does not take away from the king etc. {his authority to have the dispute heard in royal court.}" 52 Selden Society 121, 122 (1316).

[12] 36 Selden Society 16. The Prior of St. Bartholomew of Smithfield sues the Prioress of Clerkenwell. To avoid confusion, the text transforms the St. Bartholomew Priory into an abbey.

[13] Writ of trespass.

[14] Interpreting "If your {*i.e.*, the Abbot's} complaint is of your tithes carried away with our nine parts, then we ask judgment whether you ought to be answered in this Court." Case at 16.

> [3] Abbot: Your people put the grain in bundles and marked them as tithes. My people collected the bundles. At that point the grain had become secular property.[15] Anything your people did then would call for this court's application of the secular rules of self-help.[16]
>
> [4] Chief Justice Bereford: If the prioress hadn't separated the harvest this dispute wouldn't concern us. We won't decide whether the abbey or the priory has ecclesiastical jurisdiction over the farm. But the sheaves became secular property once they were separated and collected. Therefore this court decides whether the priory's people had the right to use self-help.[17]

The right to future offerings by the faithful[18] might be bought and sold, and the agreement would be enforced not in church court, but in secular court.[19]

---

[15] Interpreting "They were our tithes, separated and sent away out of your possession, ready etc." (Case at 16) in conjunction with the abbot's later comment "the corn was tithe, collected together apart from the nine parts, and we were seised of it until the demandants came…" (Case at 16).

[16] Interpreting "It was in our possession as a lay chattel until the defendants came with force and arms and carried it away, etc." Case at 16.

[17] The paragraph interprets Bereford's observation "Tithes separated from the nine parts and collected and put together become lay fee {*i.e.*, secular property"} (case at 16) in conjunction with the Prioress describing the issue as "we carried away the tithes as our chattels without doing any wrong." Case at 16.

[18] The "altarage": "The revenue arising from an altar in the form of oblations, offerings, etc.; the right to collect and retain this as income." *Oxford English Dictionary*.

[19] Expressing a dissenting view Justice Siddington said "In court Christian they only plead matters related to wills and marriages {that} touch man and God but tithes are connected with God alone.

3. (1302)[20]

[1] Adam sued[21] Bogo the chaplain. He said he had given Bogo the right to the offerings in Stone Church in return for a promise to pay ten pounds, a promise he had broken.[22]

[2] Bogo: This controversy can only be heard in church court.[23]

[3] Justice Berrewik: We have jurisdiction.[24]

[4] Bogo: I was supposed to get the offerings for a full year, but the parson died, and I got nothing for two weeks.[25] Since I got nothing for those two weeks I shouldn't be liable for the full ten pounds.

[5] Justice Berrewik. You're right about the two weeks, but otherwise you need to pay.

Another agreement between clerics involving a sale of future tithes was created by a church court settlement that expressly reserved ecclesiastical jurisdiction over

---

So it seems that tithes are something more spiritual that either wills or marriage." 122 Selden Society 125, 126 (1284).

[20] 3 31a Roll Series 158.

[21] Writ of Debt.

[22] Interpreting "Adam brought his writ of debt against Bogo, Chaplain, and counted that he tortiously withheld from him ten pounds etc. … whereas he had bound himself to the said Adam … for the altarage of the church of C." Case at 158.

[23] Interpreting "We do not understand that this court can take cognizance." Case at 158.

[24] Cf. "Rostone: This court has no cognizance etc.; for the fruit of a church is a thing purely spiritual … Justice Malore: By the buying and the selling would it be spiritual?" 5 31a Roll Series 510 (1307).

[25] Interpreting "The parson died, within the year, on which the bishop sequestrated the goods; and we lost the altarage for two weeks…" Case at 158.

future disputes. Bereford ignored the attempt. "[Otherwise] the {church official} could ... enlarge his power entirely without warrant for no reason..."[26]

Church courts judges bringing ecclesiastical claims[27] said the king's ban against suing for secular property in their courts did not apply to them.

4. (1310–1311)[28]

> [1] Adam sued[29] the bishop for violating the king's ban. The bishop had entered a church court judgment against him for two shillings of money and four pence worth of bread.[30]
>
> [2] Bishop: The king bans litigants from claiming secular property in church court. I've claimed the secular property in my capacity as a church court judge. I'm not a "litigant."[31]

---

[26] 52 Selden Society 121, 122 (1316). Elsewhere Bereford observed, "Within these twenty years people have been accustomed to take bonds, binding debtors to submit to the decision of Holy Church in mercantile matters, and by these obligations they used to draw to the Church pleas of debt, to be pleaded before them; and it was seen that that was against the law, and it was ordained that they should no longer intermeddle with those kinds of pleas..." 3 31a Roll Series 486,492 (1303).

[27] An ecclesiastical parallel to the eyre (the king's circuit court) enforcing royal claims to penalties.

[28] 26 Selden Society 97.

[29] Writ of attachment upon the prohibition.

[30] The bishop claimed the debt on the church's behalf. Bereford says "in matters enquired of your office." Case at 98. After Adam refused to pay, the bishop excommunicated him. Case record at 98.

[31] Interpreting "Their writ and their count suppose that we sued in Court Christian etc. and supposed this suit to be made before judges, whereas there were no other judges than ourselves. And we ask judgment etc." Case at 97.

> [3] Chief Justice Bereford: Your theory would let you oppress the poor at your whim.[32] The king has told us to keep the church in its place. You can't hide behind a technicality.[33]

Eternal Life

In dealing with the church Common Pleas had to create law for an institution that never died. The modern common law treats corporations as if they were people. The medieval common law dealt with hordes of artificial people—abbeys, hospitals, monasteries, priories, and more. Eternal life created problems.

Land

Today when a seller gets paid she has no further stake in the land. In contrast the medieval seller enjoyed rich rights when her buyer died. [34] Church ownership eliminated these benefits. The church never died. A lawyer came up with a theory to force the church to pay death duties.

---

[32] Interpreting "If this writ were abated a poor man in your court would never have his right at your suit in matters enquired of your office." Case at 98.

[33] The final two sentences interpret "And besides the king is a party in this writ, so say something else." Case at 98.

[34] Sales in military tenure gave the seller the right to "relief," a payment made when an adult heir took possession; "wardship," a stream of income while the heir was a minor; "marriage," the sale of the right to marry the minor heir; and "escheat," the right to take the land when a felony was committed or a person died without surviving relatives.

5. (1302)[35]

[1] The abbess sued[36] Bogo for taking a cow.

[2] Bogo: I sold her predecessor abbess[37] four hundred acres. When she died the abbey refused to make the payment[38] due when the buyer dies.[39] I took the cow to enforce my rights.

[3] Abbess: You're wrong to say a payment is due when a buyer dies. The payment is due when an heir takes possession.[40] I didn't take possession as an heir. I took possession because I was elected abbess.

[4] Justice Bereford: The abbess states settled doctrine. I'm not going to eliminate an exemption the church has always enjoyed.[41]

[5] Bogo: I certainly wouldn't want the court to break new ground. I'll agree the abbess has properly described the rule.[42]

Perhaps Bereford supported the church exemption. Or perhaps he did not want to stir up a hornet's nest by closing an ancient loophole. He declined the opportunity

---

[35] 3 31a Roll Series 60.

[36] Writ of replevin.

[37] Interpreting the predecessor "held of him." Case at 60. The sale could have been made to an earlier predecessor.

[38] "The relief."

[39] Or the buyer's descendants.

[40] Interpreting "Relief cannot be demanded except where one enters by succession after the death of another" Case at 62.

[41] Interpreting "He has said that you cannot avow upon him for the relief … wherefore reply you to their answer." Case at 62.

[42] Interpreting "In order to relieve the court, we tell you that {we can prove the past ecclesiastical tenants by voluntary payments created my customary right to a relief.} Case at 62–64.

to confirm a wholesale attack on a major church exemption.

The King's Tax on Gifts to the Church

Since no one sold or gave away more land than the king no one suffered more from the church exemption. By requiring the purchase of a royal license to sell or give land to the church "The Statute of Mortmain"[43] restricted the growth of the exemption.[44] Common Pleas shut down attempts at evasion.

6. (1313)[45]

> [1] Two years after Adam sold a farm to Bogo he saw some monks harvesting crops there. When he learned Bogo hadn't bought a license to give the church the farm he took the land back.[46] The Statute of Mortmain allowed a seller to reclaim land if the buyer transferred the land to the church without acquiring a royal license. Bogo sued[47] for dispossession. He said he hadn't given the church anything.
>
> [2] Adam: Yes, you did, but you didn't sign a deed so that you could avoid buying a license. Since the

---

[43] Statute of Mortmain (1285) (3EHD 419). The Anglo-Norman term "mortmain" means "dead hand."

[44] *See* 34 Selden Society 191 (1312–1313) for a transfer by fine with a Mortmain license.

[45] 43 Selden Society 72. The sale was to two men. The text invents Adam's observation of the monks. The text's monastery is "the Hospital of St. Mark of S." Case at 72.

[46] "Whereupon Adam entered as he was well entitled to do." Case at 72.

[47] Writ of novel disseisin.

> Statute of Mortmain lets me take back the land I didn't "wrongfully dispossess" you.[48]
>
> [3] Jury: Bogo gave the land to the monastery but he and the monks concealed the transaction.[49] The statute says Adam had a year to take back the land. He didn't meet the deadline. What should we do?
>
> [4] Adam: I acted as soon as I realized what they were up to.[50]
>
> [5] Justice Inge: Jurors, you can extend the time period if they hid their scheme.[51]
>
> [6] Jury: He acted quickly enough.[52]

Modern common law jurisdictions "toll" the statute of limitations—postpone the running of the statutes that bar claims because time has passed—until a reasonable

---

[48] Novel disseisin provides a remedy for a dispossession committed "unjustly and without a judgment." Early Registers of Writs, 87 Selden Society 358 (#645). Adam implies the privilege provided by the Statute of Mortmain makes his entry either "just" or pursuant to the statutory equivalent of a "judgment."
[49] Interpreting Bogo "permitted the Master to enter with his consent, and that by artfulness and collusion no deed of appropriation was executed; they said further that a year passed before Adam entered." Case at 72.
[50] Interpreting "As soon as I understood that the Master was claiming fee and freehold I entered; and that is sufficient in the circumstances, when the Master entered without a deed." Case at 72.
[51] Interpreting "Inge, J.: ... What is your opinion? Were they disseised or not?" Since Adam has just argued the concealment extended the one year period, the text says Inge adopted Adam's position and tolled the statute. The report is muddled, with conflicting statements about whether Adam entered within a year.
[52] Interpreting "We think that {Bogo was} not {dispossessed}." Case at 72.

person could have discovered the wrong. Inge adopts the same policy.

Inventive schemes to evade tax require careful thought—they can have unexpected consequences. In the following case the church colluded with a donor but by bad pleading they both lose their rights to a farm.

7. (pre–1290).[53]

> [1] When Anna's father died she sued[54] the abbot[55] to recover a farm. She claimed her father had possessed the place at his death even though she knew her father had in fact sold the place to Bogo.
>
> [2] Abbot: Anna can't sue us because her father sold the farm to Bogo, and Bogo just let us work the place as a favor. {She can't claim because he didn't die in possession of the farm.}
>
> [3] *The Reporter*: As everyone knew the abbot was lying— the abbey had bought the farm from Bogo {but no deed was executed in order to avoid the cost of a Mortmain license}.[56] The court, nonetheless, entered a judgment in favor of the abbey. By disclaiming any possessory interest, the abbot had acquired immunity from a claim for dispossession. However the court told Anna that the abbot's disclaimer meant he couldn't complain if she ousted him. Anna and her men then

---

[53] 123 Selden Society 532.
[54] Writ of mort d'ancestor.
[55] The text describes "the master of St. John of L." as the abbot. The final clause interprets "(*Note*: Now the Abbot was enfeoffed by Bogo and Anna kenw this well." Anna's mort d'ancestor claim requires a showing that her father was in possession at his death.
[56] Interpreting "Now he was enfeoffed by Bogo, and the woman knew this well." Case at 532.

just took possession. [57] Bogo then sued Anna for dispossession. The case went to the jury.

[4] Jury: Bogo gave the farm to the abbey. Bogo has no interest that supports his suit against Anna.

[5] *The Reporter*: By its too clever pleading the abbey lost forever any right to the farm.[58]

"Land" Defined

Common Pleas had to define the Statute of Mortmain's term "land." The owner of an "advowson" had the right to nominate a parson to a parsonage whose parson had died or left. The right to nominate his replacement could be sold, and the sales price would reflect the value of the land that had been given to the parsonage. Sometimes owners of advowsons gave them to religious institutions. Was the gift of an advowson a gift of land?

8. (1315)[59]

[1] Saying he had the right to nominate the Stone Church parson, the king sued[60] an abbot who claimed a competing right.

---

[57] Interpreting "The Justice adjudged that the woman should enter the land." Case at 532. More precisely the reporter should have said the Justice dismissed Anna's claim but observed that since the abbey asserted no interest Anna could enter the farm without violating the abbey's rights.

[58] Interpreting "The master by his own folly loses action for all time." Case at 532.

[59] 45 Selden Society 43. The Dean has been renamed "the Abbot" to make his clerical capacity more apparent to American readers.

[60] Writ of *quare impedit*.

[2] The king's lawyer: Some time ago the bishop gave the abbot the right to nominate the Stone Church parson.[61] The bishop violated the Statute of Mortmain because he didn't buy a license. Then he tried to get a court to record the gift.[62] The king complained and the court said no license had been bought. According to the Statute of Mortmain the king gets the advowson because he complained about the fraud. The abbot needs to stop interfering with the king's right to nominate.

[3] Abbot: I'm interfering because the court was wrong. Mortmain applies only to land transfers and an advowson isn't land.[63]

[4] The king's lawyer: The court needs to apply the spirit of the law. An advowson should count as land.[64]

[5] Abbot: {I've got a better argument.}[65] The king says the court should apply the spirit of the law. I agree. The statute requires a license because the king's tax base is diminished when the church acquires land.[66] Once the bishop owned the advowson no one

---

[61] The sham lawsuit was designed to transfer the bishop's right to the abbot. Since the sham lawsuit was dismissed, and since the abbot still claims the advowson, he must have said he got the advowson before the sham lawsuit. Since the dismissal deprived the sham lawsuit of res judicata consequences the king has to make his arguments again.

[62] They submitted their feigned controversy in order to get a fine.

[63] Interpreting "The king had no occasion for seizing this advowson nor for inquiring about the collusion." Case at 44.

[64] Interpreting "Even if the statute be so worded, and an advowson be neither land nor tenement, it savours of the nature of a tenement; and it is the same law in both cases." Case at 44.

[65] By presenting a new argument the abbot abandons his earlier argument.

[66] Interpreting "The reason why such purchases and recoveries were restrained was because by recoveries and purchases property which

> was going to derive any revenue because of an owner's death. The church never dies, and a transfer from one church entity to another had no relevance to the Statute of Mortmain policy.[67]

The rest of the manuscript has been lost. The argument an advowson doesn't count as land seems unconvincing, but an argument the advowson was already off the tax rolls seems persuasive. But tax claims have their own logic. Perhaps some royal justice might rule in favor of royal revenue despite a persuasive policy argument to the contrary.[68]

A Secular Court Will Enforce an Agreement Against Both the Church and the Pope

Once the church took land in return for creating an advowson, Common Pleas interpreted and enforced the agreement against the church.[69]

---

was previously in lay hands and chargeable with the maintenance of the estate of the realm was by the purchases and recoveries held in alms, and in abasement of the estate of the crown." Case at 44–45.

[67] Interpreting "So being in mortmain this advowson is only recovered from mortmain to mortmain; and the reason of the statute does not extend to this case." Case at 45.

[68] Cf. "Note, the Justices did this rather for the King's profit than in accordance with law…" 3 31a Roll Series 502,506 ((1302).

[69] Common law courts still enforce the terms of charitable gifts. The doctrine "cy pres" allows some modification.

9. (1294)[70]

[1] The parson discovered his predecessor had sold the land that enhanced the value of the parsonage. He sued[71] the buyer to recover the land.

[2] Buyer: Your predecessor got the donor's consent to sell.[72]

[3] Jury: The consent was provided by someone who didn't qualify as the donor.[73]

[4] Justice: The parson gets the land back.[74]

Common Pleas imposed its view of donor consent on everyone. Everyone. The pope himself couldn't violate English land law.[75]

---

[70] 2 31a Roll Series 620. Bogo argues the bishop authorized the sale in his dual capacities as bishop and as patron; the text avoids confusion by separating the bishop's two capacities, and by referring to him in his capacity as patron simply as the donor.
[71] Writ of Utrum.
[72] Interpreting "At the time the quit-claim was made … the then Bishop of the place was the patron… and consequently it was made with the assent of the patron…" Case at 622.
[73] Interpreting "The Inquest said that the Bishop was not at that time the patron." Case at 622.
[74] Interpreting "Inasmuch as {the bishop wasn't the patron}" the parson wins. Case at 622.
[75] Cf. "Note the King's Chapel is so sacred that no Archbishop or Bishop shall have anything to do with it…" 1 31a Roll Series 406–407 (1293).

10. (1320)[76]

[1] Claiming the right to nominate his candidate to the Stone Church parsonage,[77] King Edward II sued[78] the bishop for interfering with his rights.

[2] Bishop: Decades ago the pope told my predecessor to divide the extravagant Stone Church living into separate components. Since each component is occupied by a parson there is no vacancy.[79]

[3] The King: Although the pope may have ordered the division my father—the owner of the advowson—didn't consent.[80] Therefore the division was void and all the subsequent appointments are nullities. I've nominated my candidate to Stone Church and you can't say someone is the sitting parson there.[81]

---

[76] 104 Selden Society 105. The text simplifies violations by Popes Adrian and Clement (case at 107) into one Pope's violation.

[77] Interpreting "Upon [Percival's] death, the entire prebend became vacant and remained vacant until the temporalities of the aforesaid bishopric passed into the hands of our lord the king by the death of John de Dalderby, formerly bishop of Lincoln, after whose death our lord the king found this prebend, which was entire and of his right, parceled out into several parcels; and thus the presentation to the entirety of this prebend belongs to our lord the king…" Case at 106.

[78] Writ of *quare impedit.*

[79] Interpreting "Thus [Henry] found each parcel filled when he was consecrated bishop, but he had not suffered anything otherwise than as he found it. And we do not believe that our lord king will or can assign a disturbance in our person." Case at 106.

[80] Interpreting "You show nothing of the king's assent, nor that he or any of his forebears assented to this division…." Case at 106. Pope Adrian V made the first improper division (case at 107) in 1276 (the only year of his papacy) during Edward I's reign.

[81] Interpreting "The king presented … his clerk … for this entire prebend and you refused his presentation…." Case at 106.

> [4] Justice Mutford: Since the bishop doesn't say our late king agreed to the division all the appointments to the divided parsonages are void. No one sits in the Stone Church parsonage; the several parsons appointed pursuant to the pope's invalid division all sit in different churches. Therefore the Stone Church parsonage is vacant.[82] The king's right to nominate is clear.[83]

---

[82] The king has brought a possessory writ, the *quare impedit*. "The king to the sheriff, greeting. Command X that [he] permit us to present a suitable parson to the church of n., which is vacant..." Early Registers of Writs, 87 Selden Society 128 (#83). A parson who improperly sits in a church nonetheless occupies the parsonage. 37 Selden Society 12 (1314). The report gives three versions of Mutford's rationale regarding the vacancy: 1."certain persons were presented to this entirety ... and what was once entire ought also to be an entirety to be presented in time of vacancy as of the right of the king. ... But you show nothing with respect to the king or his ancestors to the effect that they assented to this division, etc., nor do you {the bishop} deny that our lord the king presented his clerk to the entire prebend and that you refused to receive him." Case at 106. 2."The parceled out prebend is voidable as regards the king..." Case at 107. 3. "Our lord the king has advised by his writ that the right of the crown is this, that if the prebend has been divided without leave, he will have etc." Case at 109. The last two rationales suggest the king's prerogative allows him to ignore the criterion of vacancy. (Regarding his prerogative *see* 41 Selden Society 73, 74 (1315) and 1 31a Roll Series 68 (1292)). The text adopts the first rationale, the rationale that Mutford considered the entire parsonage vacant because no parson occupied the parsonage in its entirety. The choice of the rationale facilitates the transition to the next case. The other two versions of the case suggest Mutford might have relied upon the king's prerogative to explain why the king prevails over the pope. The text's principle point is that ordinary English land law binds the pope. Mutford's prerogative theory would restrict the case holding to the proposition the king's prerogative trumps the pope's wishes.

[83] Interpreting: The bishop shows "nothing with respect to the king or his ancestors to the effect that they assented to this division etc.; nor do you deny that our lord the king presented his clerk to this entire

Scams

The cases suggest the managers of the church's secular affairs adopted secular business ethics. One bishop got paid to reduce a tenant's annual payment. When the tenant sold, the bishop extorted a bigger payment from the buyer, an abuse Parliament expressly condemned. The bishop got away with it. Bereford said

> The men of Holy Church have a wonderful way. If they get a foot onto a man's land they will have their whole body there. For the love of God this bishop is a shrewd fellow. He's done a dishonorable thing but there's nothing we can do about it. He's figured out how to exploit a loophole in the statute.[84]

Another bishop saw an opening that he thought would validate his overreaching.

11. (1314)[85]

> [1] Adam sued[86] the bishop for claiming a rival authority to nominate the Stone Church parson.
>
> [2] Bishop: Because I was your father's secular lord I became your guardian when he died. {My fellow

---

prebend and you refused to receive him. You are thus a disturber." Case at 106.

[84] Interpreting 22 Selden Society 64, 69 (1310) (Chief Justice Bereford).

[85] 37 Selden Society 12. The record says Bogo was Bishop of Bath and Wells, and Adam's father held a manor by knight service from the bishop to which "the advowson of the aforesaid church is appurtenant." Record at 13. From these facts the text infers that the bishop had ecclesiastical authority over the parsonage, and he himself influenced the church decision to deprive the parson (case at 13) or accept his resignation (case record at 14).

[86] Writ of *quare impedit*.

ecclesiastical authorities and I}[87] removed the parson before you turned twenty-one.[88] That gave me the advowson as your then guardian. {According to settled law once it was mine} I kept it even though you soon thereafter became an adult.[89]

[3] Adam: The court has to determine a temporal question—whether the parsonage became vacant while I was still a minor. The proper question for the jury is not when the church hierarchy concocted the parson's marching orders[90] The proper question is when he in fact left. The jurors will say I was already twenty-one then. I got the right to nominate; you didn't.[91]

---

[87] The text adds this statement from an interpretation of the record. The facts suggest the bishop manipulated the timing of the removal (or resignation) in order to acquire the advowson. The parson's reluctance to leave suggests he challenged the order. The additional facts demonstrate that Bereford took the right approach.

[88] The report refers to his "deprivation" (case at 13) while the record refers to his "resignation." Case record at 14. If the deprivation implemented an ecclesiastical scheme to get the advowson for the bishop the resignation could have been procured with the same goal. The bishop himself had chosen the parson who possibly resigned. Twenty-one is the age of male majority for lands held in military tenure.

[89] The paragraph interprets Toudeby's argument on page 12. The text's addition is supported elsewhere by Bereford. "If you disseise me of a manor to which an advowson is appendant, do you suppose that I have lost my right to present by the mere fact of this disseisin? —*inferring that he would not so lose it.* " 43 Selden Society 38, 43 (1313) (Chief Justice Bereford). The text adds "soon" on the assumption little time passed between the order and the actual departure.

[90] The text adds the pejorative term "concocted."

[91] Interpreting "The church was filled … when we became of full age … ready etc." Case at 12.

[4] Bishop: The court shouldn't ask the jury what they saw. That's the wrong question. The court should ask the jurors when we told the man to get out.[92]

[5] Chief Justice Bereford: We ask the jurors about the facts they've seen. If a man was there celebrating services the church wasn't vacant. Jurors don't investigate what the hierarchy said.[93]

[6] *The Reporter*: Bereford is wrong. The church authorities decide the parson's fate. The jury should have asked them when they told the parson to leave.[94]

---

[92] Interpreting "Scrope: We will aver that the church became rightfully vacant while we were seised." Case at 13. The two versions switch the serjeants' clients. Scrope represents Adam in I; the bishop in II. In version I Miggeley represents the bishop, and he says "ready etc. the church became void while the manor remained in our hand by reason of your nonage." Case at 12. By using the term "ready" rather than "ready to aver where we ought," both reports suggest the bishop wants to go to the jury, but he wants the jurors to investigate when the hierarchy told the parson to get out. Bereford's comment "We shall not inquire" (Case at 13) might refer either to a jury instruction or to a question submitted by the court to the hierarchy. In light of the bishop's pleading that the question is for the jury the text interprets his remark as a reference to a jury instruction.

[93] Interpreting "We shall not inquire whether the church was vacant rightfully or not because our law doth not permit it." Case at 13. In another case in which the defendant claimed he was married to the woman he was alleged to have ravished, Brabazon, C.J. refused to ask the Bishop about the alleged marriage, but instead submitted the question to the jury. In his headnote Maitland describes the case as an example of "*de facto*" marriage. 22 Selden Society 4 (1310).

[94] Interpreting "And the averment stood. And it was a strange thing that they did not send to the Bishop etc. because either cause of the vacancy alleged, to wit, resignation or deprivation, cometh within ecclesiastical jurisdiction." Case at 13. The text assumes the reporter's observation "they did not send" refers to the jurors rather than the court. Perhaps, however, the reporter means the judges.

Despite the reporter's misgivings Bereford has made the correct decision.[95] The right to nominate is a right to land and rights to land are secular rights. By timing their removal order the church authorities might try to manipulate who gets the advowson, a right to land.[96] Bereford says they can't.

Another devious scheme was implemented because a prior found himself between a rock and a hard place. The pope ordered him to make Bogo the parson of the next church in his gift. Unfortunately he had already agreed with Anna that he would nominate her chosen candidate to the next vacancy.[97] How could he serve two masters?

12. (1312)[98]

> [1] Anna sued [99] Bogo for claiming the right to nominate a parson.
>
> [2] Bogo: You are suing the wrong person. I don't claim a rival right to nominate. I'm just the sitting parson.

---

[95] The Selden Society editor takes the reporter's side. 37 Selden Society xxvi. *See also* 43 Selden Society 95, 96 (1313) (dispute about whether a living is occupied). "Defendant: Resignation is a matter of which a jury of the venue may have cognizance. Reporter: But this was denied; and so the Bishop of the place is to have a writ to inquire of the plenarty of the church." Id. at 96.
[96] The predominant view. *See, e.g.*, 43 Selden Society 117 (1313).
[97] The text interprets the reporter's comment "Anna is entitled to name a clerk to the Prior of Langwell and he presenteth this clerk to the Ordinary; and in this way Anna is patron of this church" (*i.e.*, she isn't really the patron; she just has an agreement with the patron). 33 Selden Society 170,171 (1312).
[98] 33 Selden Society 170. Perhaps the dispute also appears in 63 Selden Society 123 (1311).
[99] Writ of *quare impedit*.

> [3] Anna: My writ is good against anybody who disrupts my rights. The bishop was about to consider the nomination of my candidate but he stopped when you sued him in secular court.[100]
>
> [4] Chief Justice Bereford: We've got no jurisdiction over dispute unless Bogo claims the power to nominate.[101]
>
> [5] *The Reporter*: The facts behind this case are interesting. Anna had paid the prior to nominate her candidate to the next vacancy. Bogo had his eye on Stone Church.[102] As soon as he heard the sitting parson had died he paid the pope to tell the prior to appoint him to the next vacancy. Armed with the pope's order, Bogo just took over as parson of Stone Church even though the prior hadn't nominated him.[103]

The reporter's addendum suggests how the prior solved a difficult problem. He whispered to Bogo that he should celebrate services in Stone Church even though he hadn't nominated him. The pope would be happy—Bogo had become the parson. Given his friend in the highest

---

[100] Interpreting "When we presented to the Ordinary you sued out the *indicavit* … and so you are a disturber." Case at 170.

[101] Interpreting "If you cannot say that he claimeth aught in the advowson, you cannot say he is a disturber." Case at 170.

[102] Probably a particularly rich living.

[103] Interpreting "This is the case of Anna and others. She is entitled to name a clerk to the Prior of Langwell and he presenteth this clerk to the Ordinary; and in this way Anna is patron of this church. And, when this same church became void, Bogo came and brought a purchase from the Pope to the Prior of Langwell bidding him bestow upon Bogo the first church in his patronage that should be vacant. And when he came he found this church vacant and took possession of it in virtue of his purchase, and Anna brought her quare impedit against Bogo etc." Case at 171.

place no church authority would object to his continued presence as parson. Anna would fly into a rage but the prior could tell her his hands were tied. He was happy to put her candidate into the next vacancy, but there was no vacancy—Bogo was acting as the Stone Church parson, and the propriety of his actions was not for the prior to dispute.

Although Bereford insisted on his power to decide secular rights he refused to intrude into internal church affairs. When a prior complained the church hierarchy had been acting improperly, Bereford told him his court had no authority to control their conduct.

13. (1307)[104]

> [1] The prior sued[105] Bogo for making a rival claim to nominate a parson.
>
> [2] Bogo: I'm not a proper defendant. I don't claim the right to nominate. Anyway the parsonage isn't vacant—I'm celebrating services there.
>
> [3] Prior: Since Bogo waives any claim to nominate, the court should tell the church authorities to act on my nomination.[106]
>
> [4] Bogo: That wouldn't be proper. Your writ says there's no one in the pulpit. Unless you're willing to

---

[104] 5 31a Roll Series 432. The text simplifies the dispute by ignoring Bogo's claim the prior nominated him.

[105] Writ of *quare impedit*.

[106] Interpreting "He claims nothing etc.; we pray a writ to the bishop." Case at 432. Since the prior thinks the church authorities have "deprived" Bogo (case at 432) he wants a court order to make them take action on the nomination he makes.

ask a jury if the parsonage is vacant the court has to dismiss your case.[107]

[5] Justice Bereford: He's right. Unless you offer to prove the vacancy your claim will be dismissed. We will have no reason to contact the church authorities.[108]

[6] Prior: Let me tell you what this scoundrel's doing. Here he says he makes no claim to nominate. But when I ask the church authorities to appoint my nominee, Bogo tells them he's got some claim to nominate and he's going to tie them up in secular court if they consider my nomination. The authorities have no appetite for secular litigation so they simply do nothing.[109]

[7] Justice Bereford: They should just ignore his bluster and do what's right.[110]

---

[107] Interpreting "We are vicars & and were instituted etc. under your patronage; judgment of this writ etc." Case at 432.

[108] Interpreting "Prior: I will aver the vicarage is vacant. Justice Bereford: And he will say that he is vicar by your patronage, and is there alive. Adam: He is deprived. Justice Bereford: As to that, sue where you think you will best succeed; for this court has no cognizance thereof, and we will not send to the bishop to ascertain if he be deprived." Case at 432–434.

[109] Interpreting "In the court Christian he claims something in the right of patronage … whereof the bishop does not receive our presentee.… And besides, if we sue before the bishop he will bring the Indicavit, whereupon the bishop will not dare to go further etc. and so without right etc." Case at 434. The indicavit is a secular proceeding brought against a church official to correct threatened error. *See* Fitz-Herbert, *The New Natura Brevium* 101 (1718). The text interprets the passage to mean Bogo threatens to bring the indicavit if the authorities act on the prior's nomination.

[110] Interpreting "If the bishop decline to receive your presentee on such a claim without more, he is not acting rightly." Case at 434.

[8] Prior: I'm talking about what really happens. They won't take a stand.[111]

[9] Justice Bereford: We can't right every wrong—we've got nothing for you here.[112]

Excommunication

Common Pleas could stop the church from litigating secular questions;[113] the church could stop Common Pleas from hearing cases by its power to excommunicate.

14. (1292)[114]

[1] The prior sued[115] the bishop for making a rival claim to nominate a parson.

[2] Bishop: This prior can't use the king's courts—he's an excommunicate.[116]

---

[111] Interpreting "The bishops do it every day." Case at 434.
[112] Interpreting "For every wrong that an ordinary does to you, you shall not have a remedy in this court…." Case at 434.
[113] Through cases brought by the writ of attachment upon the prohibition.
[114] 1 31a Roll Series 204. Cf. "We tell you that we are not within the jurisdiction of this bishop {of Rochester} nor subject to him; neither do these letters disclose any reason wherefore this bishop should have excommunicated us; nor do they even assert that he had excommunicated us, but they certify only that he understands from the testimony of others that we are excommunicate…" 27 Selden Society 185,186 (1313–1314 (winning argument by the Abbot of the Monastery of Battle). In another case Bereford refused to let a litigant rely upon a bishop's letter testifying that his opponent had been excommunicated. 20 Selden Society 134 (1310).
[115] Writ of darrein presentment.
[116] "We do not think he is answerable either in this Court or in any other Court for we tell you that he is excommunicated." Case at 204.

[3] Prior: Prove it.

[4] Bishop: Here's my agent's written statement.[117]

[5] Prior: His testimony is worthless.[118] If the court bought it you could confiscate any advowson and then protect yourself from suit by having your agent make a false statement.[119]

[6] *The Reporter*: The bishop decided the prior hadn't been excommunicated.[120]

Proper proof would work.

15. (1312)[121]

[1] Adam and his wife Anna sued[122] Bogo for ousting them from a farm.

[2] Bogo: Dismiss this case. Adam can't bring a joint complaint with Anna. She's a nun.[123]

[3] Anna: Bogo can't stop our suit by injecting some spurious side issue. Suppose some defendant says a couple suing as husband and wife aren't really

---

[117] "See here the letter of the Bishop's officer, which testifies that, on such a day, the Prior was excommunicated…" Case at 204.
[118] Interpreting "We do not think that this letter can delay the Assize." Case at 204.
[119] Interpreting "It would follow that he could deforce a hundred patrons of their advowsons, and then, in order to bar them of their actions, testify by his own letter that they were excommunicated…." Case at 204.
[120] Interpreting "He answered over." Case at 204.
[121] 33 Selden Society 211.
[122] Assize of novel disseisin.
[123] Interpreting "Anna ought not to be received, for she is a professed nun… Judgment." Case at 211–212.

married. The court would say the question was irrelevant to the case before it.

[4] Chief Justice Bereford: A woman can have a valid individual claim even though her marriage is void. A nun, however, can't pursue a personal claim in secular court.[124]

[5] Anna: Bogo's waited too long to object to my supposed status. He had to say something before the court let me appoint an agent.[125]

[6] Chief Justice Bereford: Anyone can appoint an agent in order to inaugurate litigation. How would Bogo object? How would any defendant object? Your argument would allow any nun to adopt the same subterfuge and air her complaints here.[126]

[7] Anna: I'm not a nun. As the church officials will say Adam claimed me as his wife (based upon our formal agreement to marry, the equivalent of marriage) before I took formal vows to become a

---

[124] Interpreting "The cases are not similar. For in the one case the woman is, in virtue of her profession, as one that is dead, so that she cannot claim aught by any way of law. But in the other case the wife can claim along with her husband and otherwise." Case at 212.

[125] Interpreting "Since she was seen in Court as a secular person, the Court will consider her to be such" in the context of Bereford's answer "And know that if all the nuns had come in the same way we should have received their attorneys…" Case at 212. A medieval "attorney" is a party's agent, not her lawyer.

[126] Interpreting "And know that if all the nuns had come in the same way we should have received their attorneys; and therefore answer, or we shall enter what you have said [as being your answer.]" Case at 212.

nun.[127] He had every right to force me to return to the secular world.[128]

[8] Bogo: You say Adam could take you back until you took your vows. That's not true. Adam lost the right to take you back to the secular world as soon as you put on a nun's habit.[129]

[9] Chief Justice Bereford: Bogo's right. Once you put on the habit Adam couldn't get you out of the Order if you subsequently took your vows. He would have a nun for his wife.[130]

[10] Bogo: Actually I don't agree that we need to look into whether Anna took her vows. After a year of wearing a habit she would be a nun even if she hadn't taken her vows.

[11] Chief Justice Bereford: Correct. Indeed the Order could make her a nun the very first day she put on the habit. Anna has to say she got married before she put on the habit.

[12] Anna: I did.[131]

---

[127] Interpreting "Then we say that we proved that she was our wife by contract made before she was professed; ready etc. to aver it where we ought." Case at 212.

[128] Elsewhere Chief Justice Hengham observed that a married woman could "deraign her husband {a monk} and demand him if she pleased…" 19 Selden Society 193(1309?).

[129] Interpreting "Your exception is not complete unless you say that the contract was made before she took the habit." Case at 212.

[130] Interpreting "For know if you were affianced to her after that she took the habit, and if she were professed afterwards, and if you have now proved her to be your wife in virtue of that affiance, you have now a nun for your wife." Case at 212.

[131] "We proved our claim by a precontract made before she took the religious habit…." Case at 213.

[13] Chief Justice Bereford: We need to get some information from the Order.[132]

[14] The Case Record: The Bishop of Lincoln says Sister Anna has become an apostate by returning to the world as a secular person in secular dress. She is excommunicated. The case is postponed indefinitely.[133]

Bereford refused to let a litigant use excommunication as a ploy to give church courts jurisdiction over secular debts.

16. (1310).[134]

[1] Adam sued[135] Bogo for using the church courts to collect a secular debt.

[2] Bogo: Adam can't make that argument here. Here's the bishop's letter showing he is an excommunicate.

[3] Adam: I've been excommunicated as a sanction for failing to pay the debt. You can't rely upon that

---

[132] "[T]ake a writ to the Ordinary of the place where Adam claimed her as his wife." Case at 213.

[133] Interpreting "The Bishop of Lincoln sent here his letters patent witnessing that Sister Anna of Hedesoie, a professed nun of the House of Burnham within his diocese, is, by reason of apostasy in leaving her house and returning into the world as a secular person in secular dress, bound in the greater excommunication with the fullest canonical authority, and, by the aforesaid authority, she is publicly declared etc. to be excommunicate. ... So the aforesaid parties go hence without day until etc." Case record at 214.

[134] 20 Selden Society 134.

[135] Writ of attachment on the prohibition.

sanction to get around the prohibition against using the church courts to collect a secular debt.[136]

[4] Bogo: The bishop's letter says he has excommunicated you for disobedience to ecclesiastical authority.[137]

[5] Adam: A jury will find I was excommunicated because you said I didn't pay my debts.[138]

[6] *The Reporter*: Chief Justice Bereford rejected Bogo's reliance on the letter and forced him to plead about whether he had wrongfully invoked church jurisdiction.[139]

---

[136] Interpreting "To that you cannot get, for the excommunication is our cause of action. Judgment, whether you can rebut our person by that which gives us our action." Case at 134.
[137] Interpreting "The letter testifies that you are excommunicated, not at our suit, but for contumacy." Case at 134.
[138] Interpreting "Excommunicated at your suit. Ready etc." Case at 134.
[139] Interpreting "Notwithstanding this, Chief Justice Bereford made him plead over." Case at 134.

CHAPTER 10

Women

THE NEXT TWO CHAPTERS CONSIDER WOMEN and serfs. The United States Supreme Court says "prejudice against discrete and insular minorities may be a special condition, which tends seriously to curtail the operation of those political processes ordinarily to be relied upon to protect minorities, and which may call for a correspondingly more searching judicial inquiry."[1] The Supreme Court's suggestion that the judiciary should be a vigilant advocate for the disadvantaged has ancient roots. During the Bereford era women had little political power; serfs none. Common Pleas favored them both.

As regards Bereford era property rights single women enjoyed near parity with men.[2] Marriage was the catastrophe that put them in chains. By medieval doctrine the husband and wife were one[3] and the husband was that

---

[1] United States *v.* Carolene Products Company, 304 U.S. 144 (1936) footnote 4.

[2] "No text-writer, no statute, ever makes any general statement as to the position of women. This is treated as obvious, and we believe that it can be defined with some accuracy by one brief phrase: private law with few exceptions puts women on a par with men; public law gives a woman no rights and exacts from her no duties, save that of paying taxes and performing such services as can be performed by deputy." 1 P&M 482. Bracton, however, said "Women differ from men in many respects, for their position is inferior to that of men." 2 Bracton 31.

[3] A husband cannot lease to his wife because "they are but one person." 27 Selden Society 175, 175 (1313–1314).

one.[4] In construing this dismal axiom Bereford pushed for women's rights.

Pre-Marital Deals

In deciding whether to enforce a deal done in contemplation of marriage[5] the court had to choose either security of title or protection for women. Justices Spigurnel and Stanton chose security.[6] Bereford chose women.

1. (1313–1314)[7]

> [1] Anna gave Bogo a farm because he promised to marry her. He took the land but he did not go through with the wedding. He transferred the farm to his friends Mr. and Mrs. Cosmo.[8] Anna sued[9] them. Cosmo denied he had taken the farm and he asked the court to appoint a jury to see if he had.[10] After a while

---

[4] For example, "Justice Stanton: … we think that if she was coverte when you entered, anything she did in that case was not her own act, but the act of her husband…." 5 31a Rolls Series 330 (1306). *See also* 27 Selden Society 45 (1313–1314).

[5] Gifts in contemplation of marriage presented problems. *See* 33 Selden Society 69 (1312).

[6] They contradict an earlier case describing a grant unconditional on its face as in fact conditioned on the marriage occurring. The court denied the suitor acquired possession. 123 Selden Society 389 (1288); also reported in 1 31a Rolls Series 258 (1292).

[7] 27 Selden Society 126. With her new husband Anna sues the married couple to whom Bogo has transferred the land; they vouch Bogo to warranty. Version III eliminates the voucher by treating Bogo as the original defendant.

[8] "By the gift" case at 127. The text describes them as "friends" because their delaying tactics suggest they are Bogo's confederates.

[9] Writ of entry *causa matrimonii praelocuti*.

[10] "Alleged non-tenancy" case at 128.

the jury convened but Cosmo did not show up.[11] The court issued an order giving him a final warning.[12] More time passed. Cosmo's wife then appeared. She complained Cosmo was not defending her rights and she wanted time to prepare her defense. The court gave her a postponement.[13] She then sought and received more delay so that she could force Bogo to step into her shoes because he had guaranteed the gift.[14] After taking more time to prepare his defense, Bogo finally appeared.

[2] Bogo: She can't bring this case. She's married to someone else. Does she want two husbands?

[3] Justice Spigurnel: She's not trying to get married; she's just trying to get her land back.

[4] Bogo: I've got a better defense. The deed says nothing about the marriage—it just says that she sold me the land for twenty-five pounds. A jury can't contradict a deed's language.[15]

[5] Justice Stanton: Bogo's right. Look, if we take Anna's side then the people who got the land after Bogo—the Cosmos—could be taken by surprise and deprived of their rights. The security of title

---

[11] "Made default" case at 128.
[12] "The petty cape issued" case at 128. The little cape gave the defendant another extension of time.
[13] Interpreting she "prayed to be received to defend her right, and she was received." Case at 128.
[14] Interpreting "Mrs. Cosmo vouches to warranty in form aforesaid the aforesaid Bogo. And she is to have him here on the Tuesday next after the Feast of St. Faith the Virgin…" Case at 127.
[15] Interpreting "Judgment whether she ought to be received to aver other cause that that disclosed by her own deed…" Case at 129.

> throughout the realm will be unsettled. Any single woman who grants land can concoct the same tale.[16]
>
> [6] Justice Spigurnel: Agreed. The language of the deed controls.

Spigurnel and Stanton paint an illusory devil on the wall. Land sales to bring about a marriage that fails to happen do not often occur. And purchasers—even a fraudster's confederates like the Cosmos[17]—almost always get a guarantee of title. They will have a remedy they can use against their seller. But the damage caused to the duped women is dramatic. Unless they are rich like Anna,[18] they will probably live out a single life in sight of the land they had hoped would underwrite their marriages, children, and happiness.

Bereford and Mettingham show more sympathy for women.

2. (1306?)[19]

> [1] Anna sued[20] Bogo for her father's wedding gift of forty pounds worth of gold, silver, sheep, cows and oxen. Their "marriage" was annulled when Bogo got his actual wife to tell the church court that she and

---

[16] Interpreting "[T]here would be nothing to prevent any woman who has given or sold her land from recovering from the hands of the tenants the land she has sold by {alleging that the gift was made in contemplation of marriage}." Case at 130.

[17] Cf. the collusion to delay a claim discussed in 2 31a Rolls Series 288 (1293).

[18] She has found a new husband in a society which views marriage as an institution to serve economic goals.

[19] 19 Selden Society 194.

[20] Writ of detinue.

Bogo had previously been married by entering into a formal agreement to marry.[21]

[2] Bogo: Since the church courts have jurisdiction over marriage, the secular courts shouldn't get involved in this controversy.

[3] Justice Mettingham: The annulment ended church jurisdiction. This court hears post annulment claims for land; we can certainly hear claims for personal property.[22]

[4] Bogo: She says her father gave the gifts. If there's a claim he's the one to bring it.[23]

[5] Justice Bereford: Once he gave away the property he no longer had "standing to sue."[24]

[6] Bogo: Anna says the property was a wedding gift. She's entitled only to half.

[7] Justice Bereford: Then give her half now and we'll decide what happens to the rest.

[8] Bogo: You misunderstand my point. I'm saying she can't ask for more than twenty pounds. {You should dismiss her claim as defective on its face.}[25]

---

[21] Interpreting "Bogo procured {his wife} to demand him in Court Christian as her husband by precontract…." Case at 194.

[22] Interpreting "Besides, land is higher than chattels; but if a divorce be made between man and wife, she shall have an action for the higher [the land], and therefore for the lower." Case at 194.

[23] He "or his executors." Case at 194.

[24] American lawyers use the phrase "standing to sue" to describe the common law policy that only those who have been injured can complain about wrongful conduct.

> [9] Justice Bereford: Her father included you only because you were marrying his daughter. You had the marriage annulled. Anna can claim the entire amount.[26]
>
> [10] Bogo: His gift was not worth forty pounds.
>
> [11] Justice Bereford: If you think we will dismiss the case because you only got thirty-nine pounds of value, you are wrong. Here's what you should do: either prove you got nothing or else give Anna what you say you got. Then we'll ask the jury if you got more.[27]

Married Women as Litigants

The merger of the wife's existence into her husband's meant if he decided to waive her rights, she could not access the courts to complain. Parliament decided wives deserved better.[28] "If a husband refuses to defend his wife's right to land she can appear in court."[29] Then as

---

[25] Perhaps (in the context of Bereford's response) the meaning of "Hunt[ingdon]: We tell you that by this writ she can only have an action to demand a moiety." Case at 194.

[26] "The chattels were given to Anna and Bogo, but Anna is the cause of the gift; and by the procurement of Bogo and {his wife who went to church court} the annulment was made. So Anna has an action to demand the whole …." Case at 194.

[27] The paragraph interprets "You must add that 'never any penny,' or confess how much you received." Case at 195.

[28] Justice Hengham asserted married women had a common law right to intervene in some cases before the statute was enacted. 5 31a Rolls Series 298, 400 (1307).

[29]Interpreting if "A husband absent himself and refuse to defend his wife's right or wish to surrender it against his wife's will, if the wife come before judgment ready to answer the demandant and to defend her right, she is to be admitted." Statute of Westminster II, c.3 (1285) (3 EHD 430–431). Although the term "right" typically refers to "ownership," in the principle case the court extends the statute to include a lifetime interest.

now everything might depend on which judge decided the case. One wife had the bad luck to draw Stanton.[30]

3. (1307)[31]

> [1] Because she was entitled to take possession of a farm after Babs died, Anna sued[32] Babs and her husband Bogo for cutting down a grove of oaks. Since Babs enjoyed only a lifetime right to the farm she had no right to harvest the oaks. After Bogo put in a weak defense on Babs' behalf, Babs appeared in court.
>
> [2] Babs: The statute says I can show up if my husband just pretends to defend my rights.[33] He waived a good technicality that I could have used;[34] he only pretended to watch out for me.
>
> [3] Justice Stanton: I remember a case like this where a wife appeared. Let's hear what you have to say.
>
> [4] Babs: I didn't cut down those trees—Bogo did.[35]

---

[30] His lack of sympathy appears also in 27 Selden Society 126 (1313–1314), discussed supra.

[31] 5 31a Rolls Series 474. The text uses the harvest of old trees as a concrete example of waste. Bogo made the losing argument that Babs had fee simple. To simplify the presentation the text jumps to the point at which Babs' life estate has been established.

[32] Statutory writ of waste. Statute of Gloucester, c. 5 (1278) (3 EHD 417).

[33] Interpreting "Makes default, or faintly defends, or is desirous to surrender in the life of his wife." Case at 476.

[34] Interpreting "Anna is under coverture of a husband not named etc; judgment of the writ: thereby it appears well that Babs' husband, who for that reason might have abated the writ, pleaded faintly." Case at 476.

[35] Interpreting "She has not committed any waste ready etc." Case at 476.

> [5] Justice Stanton: You can't hide there. What he's done will fall on your neck too.[36] Your lifetime interest has been forfeited because the oaks were harvested.

Stanton nullifies the statute designed to protect married women. He gives lawyers a roadmap to help their clients sell off their wives' property. Do a deal with the person next entitled to the land. "Pay; and you can count on me to cut down the trees, run off the serfs, whatever you want. You can take possession long before my wife dies."[37] Stanton makes a mockery of a wife's right to intervene. She can appear but she'll lose.

Bereford undoes the mischief.

4. (1319)[38]

> [1] Adam sued[39] Babs. He asked the court to let him take back a manor, a place he sold to Babs and her husband for their lifetimes. He said she had cut down trees, demolished buildings, and then sold off the lumber and dressed stone.[40]

> [2] Babs: My husband sold the place to a tenant who ran amok.[41] After my husband died I sued[42] the tenant

---

[36] Interpreting "It will not do; for if waste be found, it will fall on her neck just as fully as if she were sole and as if she while sole had committed the waste." Case at 476.

[37] *See* 2 Britton 296.

[38] 81 Selden Society 86. *See* 39 Selden Society 147, 148 (1314) regarding the question whether a claim could be brought against a widow with a dower interest for her tenant's waste.

[39] Writ of waste. *See* Statute of Westminster II, c. 14 (1285) (3 EHD 440).

[40] "[Babs] has made waste etc." Case at 86. The specific allegations come from the case record at 89.

[41] Interpreting "our husband enfeoffed one T. of the same manor..." Case at 87.

> and recovered possession of the manor. Since then I've done nothing wrong. Adam can't sue me for things that happened before I took the manor back.[43]
>
> [3] Chief Justice Bereford: If you insist on your theory that you're not liable for anything that happened before you got the manor back you'll lose. If you are willing to take responsibility we'll listen to any argument you offer.[44]
>
> [4] Babs: I concede his complaint is legitimate. But I should be able to stay on if I repair the damage the tenant did.[45]
>
> [5] Chief Justice Bereford: Fair enough. We won't ask the jury to investigate what happened. Instead we'll ask them to look at the place now. Make it right and you can stay there.[46]

The statute talks about "waste committed in any way."[47] The statute provides no period for repentance and repair.

---

[42] Writ of *cui in vita*.

[43] Interpreting "And we tell you that since this recovery no waste has been made, and you ought not to be answered concerning anything that happened before then." Case at 88.

[44] Interpreting "Would you say that because [your] husband alienated etc. and you afterwards recovered etc. he ought to have no action for waste made before [your recovery]? If that is what you wish to say, you will have your judgment speedily for to say that he ought to have no action against you in respect of waste is a different matter from saying that he ought not to be received to this writ of waste." Case at 87.

[45] Interpreting "We tell you that when he to whom our husband alienated etc. was the tenant he allowed {the waste} and since our recovery we have {repaired it.} That we wish to aver." Case at 87.

[46] Interpreting "Chief Justice Bereford: Inquest will not be made of your repairs but of deterioration permitted by you, and if it be found that nothing has deteriorated and that no waste has been made, then you will be quit." Case at 87–88.

[47] Statute of Westminster II, c. 14 (1285) (3 EHD 440).

Bereford gives a widow an advantage no man gets.[48] Stanton would have told her to get out. Bereford lets her stay.[49] She could not control what her tenant did, and she should not lose her land because of his acts.[50]

Widows' Rights

At her husband's death a woman turned back into a juridical person. She could claim a widow's portion, a right called "dower."[51] If she could show her husband possessed land during their marriage she got a lifetime

---

[48] Perhaps the case "holding" applies only to widows. No reported case from the era gives anyone but a widow a defense for a tenant's waste.

[49] How Babs will put back the trees doesn't appear. Perhaps she can pay Adam what they were worth.

[50] Much modern scholarship has investigated whether medieval law applied a doctrine of strict liability (liability without fault) or negligence (liability only if fault can be established). *See, e.g.,* Arnold, Accident, Mistake, and Rules of Liability in the Fourteenth Century Law of Torts, 128 *U. Pa. L. Rev.* 361 (1979) and Gilles, Inevitable Accident in Classical English Tort Law, 43 *Emory. L. J.* 575 (1994). In keeping with the general view that the Bereford era reports are incomprehensible, neither scholar pays much attention to the Bereford era even though the reported cases provide germane information. In 1303 a lessee had to pay for the value of the rented mill the Scots had burned down. He may well have been obligated to continue to pay his rent. 3 31a Rolls Series 476 (1303). Bereford, however, said a flood (an act of God, as later judges would put it) would excuse a lessee from paying for timbers and posts that were washed away. Note, 3 31a Rolls Series 480 (1303). A case from 1293 explicitly adopts a rule of negligence as regards damage caused by a fire. "And if the Sheriff hold the inquest {and does} not say whether the conflagration was caused by the default of the tenant or not, the Sheriff will be again ordered to inquire whether the conflagration was caused by the default of the tenant or not; and if he return that it was the default of the tenant, {the owner} will recover his damages {against the lessee}." 2 31a Rolls Series 28, 30 (1293).

[51] "Dower" should not be confused with "dowry," a gift from the bride's family.

right to a third.[52] Her rights were valid even against those who had bought her husband's land.[53] Bereford said the common law favored a widow's claim to her portion.[54]

5. (1313)[55]

[1] Anna sued[56] Bogo for her widow's share.

[2] Bogo: Since you were nine when your "husband" died you couldn't have been his wife.

[3] Anna: Nine? I was eleven.

[4] The Jury: She was ten and a half—can the court tell us if she qualifies as a widow?

[5] Justice Inge: What should we do, Bogo?[57]

[6] Bogo: Don't answer the jury's question. Just enter judgment for me. She pled she was eleven; the jury says she wasn't. I win.

---

[52] A premarital deal could change her rights. *See, e.g.*, 36 Selden Society 235 (1313).
[53] *See* 2 Britton 238; Magna Carta, c.7 (1217) (3 EHD at 342).The common law no longer gives a widow "dower." But modern law provides a comparable interest. If a husband dies without a will, the modern widow takes part of his estate. If a husband attempts to disinherit his wife, common law jurisdictions allow a widow to "elect" against his will, and take a set fraction of his property (land as well as all his other assets) despite his stated intentions.
[54] 20 Selden Society 189 (1310). The court imprisoned a lawyer who delayed a widow's claim for no reason. 22 Selden Society 194 (1310).
[55] 39 Selden Society 26.
[56] Writ of dower.
[57] Interpreting "Consider whether you have aught to say to show that a wife of that age is not entitled to have dower." Case at 28.

[7] Chief Justice Bereford: Suppose she said twenty and the jury said fifteen? Would you stand by your argument?

[8] Bogo: I've got a better argument. The church says a girl who isn't pregnant can annul her marriage until she's twelve. Anna's not twelve; not pregnant; not a widow.[58]

[9] Chief Justice Bereford: The church has a black and white age cut-off. We don't. We'll examine Anna ourselves and if we think she could have consummated the marriage she'll get a widow's share.[59]

A few years later Bereford favored a child bride whose husband had died very soon after their marriage, a marriage that must have consisted of a formal agreement to marry.[60] "Afterwards the girl was seen by the justices,

---

[58] Interpreting "At any time before {the age of twelve} she could withdraw her consent {and if} we had said that she was never his wife ... you would then, consequently, have sued out a writ to the bishop. The bishop would have refused to certify this Court that she was her husband's wife unless he had found that she was of such age that she could consent etc." Case at 29. "If the Court could presume that she will acquire a right to dower for such a reason, say, as that she is great with child, that is one thing...." Case at 28.

[59] Interpreting "And so [here] the Court is able [by inspection] to judge whether she is able to be entitled to dower." Case at 27. The Selden Society editor interpolates the phrase "by inspection" into the passage. Whether "inspection" amounted to observation or interrogation or both does not appear. In another case the report says "And she was examined as to how she and her husband behaved in bed." 20 Selden Society 189 (1310). The case record adds "And for that it seems to the Court by the aspect of the body of Mirabella that at the time of her husband's death, since when so short a time has elapsed, she was of marriageable age..." Case record at 191.

[60] Seven was the earliest age for marriage. 2 P&M 390. Bolland, however, refers to a marriage between a three year old woman and a seven year old man. 39 Selden Society xxix.

and they ruled in her favor. Many were shocked—she seemed to be about seven."[61] Bereford joked "Unless the fellow was a giant, the marriage could have been consummated."[62]

In contrast Bereford seems to have no sympathy for a woman whose husband had run off to a monastery.

6. (1304)[63]

> [1] Anna sued[64] Bogo for her widow's share of land her husband had sold him.[65]
>
> [2] Bogo: Your husband's alive.
>
> [3] Anna: He's a monk—in legal theory he's dead. The courts have already said it. My brother-in-law took away our house[66] because the courts said he qualified as my husband's heir.[67] How can my husband be dead to his brother but alive to me?[68]

---

[61] 20 Selden Society 189, 190 (1310).

[62] Interpreting "If the husband were not a giant, she could deserve dower at the time he died." 20 Selden Society 189, 190 (1310). The Anglo-Norman reads "*Si le baroun ne fust geaunt, ele poet dowere deservir au temps qe son baroun morust.*" Perhaps Bereford's joke was a bit raunchier than Maitland's translation. "*Fust*" can mean a "piece of … wood…." J.H. Baker, *Manual of Law French* 121 (2d ed. 1990). Bereford might have used the medieval version of an American teen vulgarity, a "woodie." *See* http://www.urbandictionary.com/define.php?term=woodie).

[63] 4 31a Rolls Series 166.

[64] Writ of dower.

[65] Since her husband's brother has inherited his lands, and Anna doesn't refer to the brother as the defendant, she must be suing her husband's transferee.

[66] The brother's claim would have included such land—the text creates a focus on the marital residence to highlight the apparent miscarriage of justice.

[67] Interpreting "His brother recovered by the mort d'ancestor." Case at 166. The report says "*son frère recoveri par le mordancestre*," Justice Hengham said an heir wouldn't use the

> [4] Chief Justice Bereford: Anna's incompetent lawyer has wasted her time and money. Any decent lawyer knows she can't claim a widow's portion just because her husband's a monk.[69]

A shocking report.[70] The brother receives a double windfall. Since the monk has fathered no child, he is the heir. Then he does not lose the third he would have expected Anna to take as her widow's share. In contrast Anna loses the safety net guaranteed to widows. All this, and Bereford approves. Another case shows why.

7. (1309?)[71]

> [1] Anna sued[72] Bogo for her widow's share.
>
> [2] Bogo: Your claim isn't ripe yet. Your husband's living as a monk.
>
> [3] Anna: In the eyes of the law a monk is dead.[73] Since our son can recover his inheritance I can recover my widow's share.

---

conventional mort d'ancestor. Instead he would bring a variant focused on entry into religious life. 5 31a Rolls Series 130 (1306).

[68] Interpreting "He is dead as to the world; for he has become a monk at such a place, and professed; and his brother recovered by the Mordancestor; wherefore on that head you cannot etc." Case at 166. The text hypothesizes that the brother sued Anna because she probably insisted on retaining possession after her husband left.

[69] Interpreting "He who counseled the woman to bring this writ must have wished the woman to lose her labor." Case at 166.

[70] Bolland says "It is hard to see the reason for this or the equity of it." 33 Selden Society xxxvi (1916).

[71] 19 Selden Society 193.

[72] Writ of dower.

[73] Interpreting "Dead as regards the world." Case at 193. Hengham says a man "may be dead in two manners; naturally or to the world." Case at 193.

[4] Chief Justice Hengham: You don't get anything because you can force the abbot to eject your husband.[74] Your son can't and that's why he inherits when his father becomes a monk.[75]

Bereford's feminist attitude made him ignore some indiscreet behavior.

8. (1315)[76]

[1] Anna sued[77] her son's guardian[78] to get a widow's share of her late husband's land.

[2] Bogo: She left my ward's father to live with her boyfriend in Tasley. She never came back. She can't get a widow's portion.[79]

[3] Anna: My husband and I owned the Tasley place together. No court can investigate my behavior in such jointly owned land.

---

[74] Interpreting "And since her husband is alive, and no divorce has ever been made, so that the wife could deraign her husband and demand him if she pleased, this Court awards that Bogo go quit...." Case at 193.

[75] Interpreting "he cannot deraign his father out of the Order." Case at 192.

[76] 41 Selden Society 108. The defendant is one link in a chain of guardians. Anna was a famously quarrelsome and difficult woman. *See* 41 Selden Society xxxiii.

[77] Writ of dower.

[78] As Devereux's widow she sues the guardian of his heir. Case at 110. The text assumes that the underage heir is Anna's child. Perhaps he might not want to beggar his mother, but the guardian pursues his own—not his ward's—economic interests.

[79] Interpreting "She is not entitled to dower, for we tell you ....she left one of his manors … and went to Tasley … and there lived in adultery with one G., her paramour, and was never reconciled with her husband…" Case at 108.

[4] Chief Justice Bereford: She's right. We're not interested in your gossip. It's a husband's job, not ours, to keep an eye on his guests.[80]

Bereford's flip attitude makes sense. Maybe Anna's guilty but guardians and heirs have an incentive to tell tales about women who live apart from their husbands. They are the ones who pay for her portion. Bereford's prophylactic rule protects widows from gossip trumped up to delay their rights.

A Husband's Possession

The widow's share applied only to land her husband had actually possessed. During the Bereford era sham law suits became the best way to transfer land. A widow said that the sham law suit's phony assertion that her husband had possession could not be questioned. Bereford agreed, repudiating the historic standard of possession a jury had seen.

9. (1312–1313)[81]

[1]Anna sued[82] Babs for her widow's share of a farm.

[2] Babs: The jurors will say your husband never possessed the place.

[3] Anna: My husband used a sham lawsuit to sell you a lifetime interest in the farm. The case record says he

---

[80] "Your objection is not worth a half-penny, for when a wife is living in her husband's house she cannot be said to have left him etc., and it is the husband's business to keep an eye on his guests…." Case at 109.
[81] 34 Selden Society 8.
[82] Writ of dower.

sued[83] you for breaking a deal to sell him your farm. You admitted he was right and purported to put him in possession. In return he purported to put you back in possession for your lifetime.[84] {Perhaps my husband never actually had possession.[85] So what?} [86] A jury can't question a judgment – my husband's possession is res judicata.[87]

[4] Babs: The ancient common law rule says you get nothing unless a jury saw your husband in possession. That rule still applies.[88] You can't rely upon the judgment—you didn't even participate in the case.[89]

[5] Anna: A statute[90] says no jury can question a court settlement.[91]

---

[83] Writ of covenant. Case at 21.
[84] Interpreting "A fine was levied … as to (these) tenements between this same Babs and my husband, by which fine Babs made conusance that the tenements were the right of my husband, as those which my husband had by her gift, and for that conusance my husband granted and rendered the said tenements to Babs to hold etc. {for her lifetime.} And I tell you that at that time I was my husband's wife. Judgment whether you can get to such an averment in spite of the fine." Case at 8–9.
[85] "You will not be received to aver that he was not seised." Case at 9
[86] A fine could, for example, settle a dispute about whether the husband had had possession.
[87] Interpreting "Judgment whether you can get, against the fine, to any averment." Case at 19.
[88] Interpreting "The highest answer that one can give to oust a woman of dower at common law, is to say that her husband was never seised so that he could not have endowed her and such (an answer) we tender." Case at 15.
[89] "(She) that brings the writ is not (a party to the fine) but is a complete stranger." Case at 15.
[90] Statute of Fines Levied (*de finibus levatis)* c. 1 (3 EHD 492) ("exceptions or answers, or inquests of the country on such exceptions and answers, contrary to such recognizances and fines shall by no means be permitted henceforth").

> [6] Chief Justice Bereford: Settlements often include false statements about the transfer of possession. As a party to the settlement Babs is bound by what it says.[92]

Babs wanted the court to stick by the old rules requiring actual possession. Bereford treats law as an instrument of good policy and good policy has moved on.

"Land" Defined

Today a widow gets a share of all her late husband's assets.[93] Common Pleas gave the widow a right only to her late husband's "land."[94] What is "land?" Different rules do not necessarily define a single word in the same way.[95] American lawyers say courts have to engage in "characterization." In interpreting two separate statutes a court sometimes "characterizes" the same word differently in order to implement the statutes' different goals. A renter could not use Chancery's writs of possession. He did not "possess" the rented land. But if the lessor's widow claimed a share of the rented land, a court might say he "possessed" the land, and force him to

---

[91] "The statute orders that those averments which (go) to the avoidance of the fine be not received." Case at 10.

[92] Interpreting "Fines are (often) levied in this court without livery of seisin, (and they) may never be avoided by the parties or by their heirs, by an averment." Case at 18.

[93] If a husband tries to disinherit his wife common law jurisdictions typically allow her to "elect" against his will, and take a set percentage of his entire estate.

[94] The church courts had jurisdiction over a decedent's chattels.

[95] Speaking of the problem in another context an American scholar said "There is no doubt that what you might call the core of the concept … is the same in all these situations, but as you get out towards what I like to call the twilight zone of the subject, I don't believe the {definition} remains exactly the same for all purposes…" Walter Wheeler Cook, 3 *The American Law Institute Proceedings* 226 (1925).

give her a third: the renter didn't have enough possession to protect his rights, but he had enough possession to pay the lessor's widow. [96]

10. (1311)[97]

> [1] Anna sued[98] Bogo for her widow's share of grazing rights on his pasture.
>
> [2] Bogo: You can claim part of your husband's land but not part of his contractual rights.[99] Grazing rights are contractual rights, not land. Suppose I had kept your husband off my pasture. He wouldn't have sued to recover "land." He would have sued to enforce his contract.[100]
>
> [3] Anna: That's true today but only because a new statute creates a quick way to enforce grazing rights. Before then my husband would have used a writ to

---

[96] "Malberthorpe said that a writ of dower was quite maintainable against a renter…" 43 Selden Society 36 (1313). Another case takes a different view: the renter could vouch the husband's heir, and the voucher might change the late husband's guarantee of a term of years into a guarantee of a life estate, an expansion of the guarantee beyond its terms. The court dismissed the dower claim against the renter. 37 Selden Society 113 (1314). As a lawyer Bereford argued that a lessor's widow had no right to dower if the husband transferred possession before the marriage. Weyland, C. J., ruled she could claim anyway if her husband had retained the fee in the leased land. 112 Selden Society 360, 361 (1278?)
[97] 63 Selden Society 13.
[98] Writ of dower.
[99] Interpreting "We ask judgment of the writ, for her writ speaks of 'rightful dower which befalls her from the free tenement which belonged to her sometime husband etc.' The demand is for 'common of pasture' which is another matter." Case at 14.
[100] Interpreting "If the husband in his lifetime had been disseised of this common of pasture, he could not bring the assize *de libero tenemento* etc., but only the assise *de communa pasture*." Case at 14.

> recover land. By giving my husband a more efficient way to claim grazing rights Parliament {certainly didn't mean to take away my widow's interest in those rights.}[101] In any case this is the best writ I could find to enforce my widow's claim, and it's only fair I get my share.[102]
>
> [4] Chief Justice Bereford: Nothing in the world could make me dismiss Anna's case.[103]

The right to certain jobs was in a sense a right to land—a person who lost his job would sue with the writ a person who lost his land might use.

11. (1313)[104]

> [1] Anna sued[105] the prior for her widow's share of the bread and beer and other income her late husband received for managing the priory's farms.[106]

---

[101] The text assumes the widow's lawyer would have expressly added the imputation of Parliament's intention to the following reported argument. "At the common law if a man were in such a case disseised of his common of pasture [he would use] the assize *de libero tenemento*; but now it has been ordained by statute that he shall have a writ of novel disseisin *de communa pasture.* And this writ of dower is at the common law…." Case at 14.
[102] Interpreting "We can have no other writ in the chancery than this." Case at 14. Bogo suggests a quod permittat but Anna responds she could use the writ only if she had previously exercised the rights, and she hadn't because only her husband had put the livestock out to pasture: "Willoughby: She could have the *quod permittat* in this case. Denham: On whose seisin would he count? (*as if to say,* Of nobody's seisin). Case at 15. Bereford said the court implemented an exceptional doctrine regarding widows' claims to grazing rights. 65 Selden Society 73, 75 (1318).
[103] Interpreting "I certainly would not abate this writ for all the world." Case at 16.
[104] 43 Selden Society 117.
[105] Writ of dower.

[2] Prior: The only reason you say his job was "land" is because a statute gave some job holders the right to use the quick procedures created to sanction those who improperly took possession of land.[107] But at common law no one would consider this job "land."[108] If your husband had claimed his job in a writ to recover the ownership rather than possession of land his case would have been quickly dismissed.[109]

[3] Anna: I couldn't have made a better argument in my favor than you have. You admit my husband could have protected his job with a possessory writ. My widow's share attaches to property he "possessed;" not property he "owned." Your argument shows the court should just grant me judgment.[110]

[4] Chief Justice Bereford: We've let widows take a share of offices. I remember a case where the husband had been usher of the exchequer and ward of the gate of Westminster.[111]

---

[106] She "claimed the third part of the office of the Abbot's mower in the vill of St. Neots with the care of his crops, meadows and pastures, and to receive therefor every day bread and beer and much other profit…" Case at 117.

[107] Interpreting the defendant's argument that the widow claims "the third part of an office which is not a freehold, except by virtue of the statute …" Case at 117.

[108] Interpreting "this is not a freehold at the common law." Case at 117.

[109] Interpreting "her husband would not have been entitled to the *precipe quod reddat* …." Case at 117.

[110] The paragraph interprets "You are pleading in my favor, for you have shown that my husband could have had a writ of novel disseisin; and we are ready to aver that he was seised as of fee; and so he had fee and freehold, and of such estate his wife is entitled to have dower at the common law. Judgment etc." Case at 117.

[111] Cf. "Chief Justice Bereford: If your husband has a bailiwick in fee do you not think that his wife will have her dower therefrom?" 63 Selden Society 13, 14 (1311).

[5] Anna: There are other cases too such as claims for grazing rights and the rights to nominate parsons.[112]

[6] *The Reporter*: The parties asked for an adjournment {so that they could work out the terms of a settlement.}[113]

A long-lasting marriage meant a widow could get a share of the land her husband had sold decades before he died. A widow might try to profit from improvements the buyer had made. Here Bereford squelched a widow's overreaching.

12. (1311)[114]

[1] Anna sued[115] Bogo for a third of a farm.

[2] Bogo: You're asking for too much. Your husband sold me barren ground. I've put in new buildings. You can't take part of them.

[3] Chief Justice Bereford: Do you think, Madam, that if I built a castle on some wasteland you'd wind up chatelaine of a third?[116] Your share applies to the land as it was when your husband sold it.

---

[112] Another case concerning disseisin focuses upon whether the profits are variable or constant. 29 Selden Society 124, 125 (1313–1314) (Note).

[113] "And thereupon the parties took [an adjournment] *prece parcium*."Case at 118. Having heard Bereford's remarks, the prior will settle during the adjournment.

[114] 42 Selden Society 159 (1311). The text simplifies a claim in which the husband's heir was vouched to warranty.

[115] Writ of dower.

[116] The castle hypothetical was used elsewhere. 3 31a Rolls Series 298 (1303). *See* also Anon, 22 Selden Society 11 (1310). Even if the widow's share attached to the subsequently erected buildings, the buyer would still have some leverage to get compensation. "Rule. If

Bereford's *reductio ad absurdum* seems self-evident but the problem had been debated for decades. In the mid-1200's a law teacher asked

> Suppose a man buys some land and builds beautiful houses on it. Later the seller dies and his widow sues for her share. Will she get a third of the houses? Lawyers disagree. Those who say she has a claim on the houses compare it to a widow's claim against farmland. If the buyer has sown the fields the widow will get a third of the crops.[117] They say the houses are no different.[118]

The court also rejected the widows' claims for resources that could not be effectively divided. Although the court barred their claims to the resource itself, the court gave them compensation for their lost interest. Bereford understood what a twentieth century economist called "the tragedy of the commons."[119]

---

a man impleads another for a piece of land, and he has erected buildings on this piece of land, and he thinks that he will lose this land, it is lawful for him to tear down and take away the buildings...." 69 Selden Society 25 (dated in the mid-1200's—*see* introduction at xi). When the owner complained his tenant had destroyed buildings erected during the tenancy, Justice Berewike said "We put you back in possession; that's all you asked us to do. We can do no more. Owner: Issue a judicial writ that compensates me for the house. Berewike: No such writ has ever existed." 1 31a Rolls Series 218 (1292).

[117] In a later case Bereford said an heir who became an adult would be entitled to crops the guardian had planted during his minority. But the hypothetical guardian would have known when his ward would become an adult. In contrast the law teacher's farmer had no way to predict the husband's death. *See* 43 Selden Society 149 (1313).

[118] 69 Selden Society 15 (dated in the mid-1200's—*see* introduction at xi).

[119] *See* G. Hardin, The Tragedy of the Commons, 162 *Science* 1243–1248 (1968). If the widow and the heir each had an unlimited right to lumber, they would both have an incentive to take as much as possible even though together they might turn the woods into a wasteland. In one ruling (later repudiated by Bereford in 17 Selden Society 58 (1308–1309) the court allowed a custom to create the evil

13. (1308–1309).[120]

[1] Anna sued[121] Bogo for her widow's share of the privilege her husband had exercised when he took building materials from Bogo's woodlands.[122]

[2] Justice Bereford: A right that includes an almost unlimited access to lumber can't be divided.[123] The husband's heir gets it; he has to compensate the widow for the part she doesn't get. We do the same thing when daughters take equal shares of their father's estate.[124] The ladies don't each get a right to take wood; instead one gets the right, and the others take an enhanced share of the other assets. {When you negotiated you should have asked for more land to make up for the lumber you didn't get.}[125]

Defective Possession

A lucky widow got something she did not deserve—a share of land her husband wrongfully possessed.

Hardin feared. Sisters were given an unlimited right to lumber even though the defendant argued "this inconvenience would follow, viz. that if the manor descended to ten parceners {*i.e.*, ten sisters who became equal heirs because their parents had no son} and each one of them married some great lord, then, whereas we are bound to find housebote and heybote for one hearth only, we should be holden to find housebote and heybote for ten hearths; which would be a great hardship." 2 31a Rolls Series 418, 420 (1294).

[120] 17 Selden Society 58. *See also* 2 31a Rolls Series 506 (1294).

[121] Writ of dower.

[122] She "demanded the third part of a reasonable estover, to wit, housebote and haybote appendant to her free tenement which belonged to her husband in N." Case at 58.

[123] Interpreting "Such manner of profits cannot be partitioned…" Case at 58.

[124] The surviving eldest male child inherits all the land; but if only daughters survive, they divide the inheritance equally.

[125] The text adds a rationale.

14. (1306)[126]

[1] Anna sued[127] Bogo for her widow's share of a farm.

[2] Bogo's lawyer: A jury will say her husband never had possession.

[3] Jury: The husband bought the farm from Bogo's father but Bogo's father had no right to sell it.[128] Bogo got a court judgment invalidating the sale.[129] An invalid sale can't convey possession and therefore Anna shouldn't get a widow's share.[130]

[4] Justice Malore: The court must enter a different judgment than the jurors expected. They say a fraudulent sale can't transfer possession. They misunderstood the law. We decide the law, they don't. The possession was wrongful but the possession was possession nonetheless.[131] Anna gets a widow's share. Too bad Bogo's lawyer was incompetent.[132]

---

[126] 5 31a Rolls Series 348. The text changes the report's narrative into a dialogue, and eliminates as irrelevant a sale by Bogo.
[127] Writ of dower.
[128] Interpreting "The father held these same tenements by the law of England, which he sold to Anna's husband in fee." Case at 348. When Bogo was born, his father got a right to keep his mother's land for his lifetime. He violated the limitation on his interest by selling the place outright to Anna's husband.
[129] He brought a writ of entry saying that Anna's husband had entered by a transfer from someone who had acted wrongfully.
[130] Malore's says Anna's husband's estate "was other than what is found by this verdict…." Case at 348. The jury must have said that her husband's estate was void because he was the recipient of a fraudulent sale and therefore Anna got no widow's share. Malore then repudiates the jury's view of the law.
[131] Interpreting "He was seised in his demesne as of fee." Case at 348.
[132] Interpreting "Shame to him who pleaded this plea." Case at 348.

> [5] *The Reporter*: Here's what Malore meant. When Anna sued Bogo's lawyer should have shown the court the judgment Bogo won. The court would have dismissed Anna's case right then. That would have been the end of it—the court would not have asked the jury if Anna's husband had possession.[133] {Instead the lawyer asked for a jury verdict about possession. Of course the jury had seen her husband in possession. Even if he had no legal right to be there, he was there. The jury is supposed to say what they have seen, not what they think the law is.}[134]

Although Malore gives the widow something she does not deserve at least he says a competent lawyer could bar her. Twenty-five years earlier Justice Brompton said her case was unstoppable. Suppose, a lawyer said, a younger brother takes possession of land his older brother should inherit. Once the older brother gets the land back, the lawyer said, the younger son's wife would lose her potential right to a widow's share. You're wrong, Brompton said, she'll get a widow's share. "I've seen the case."[135]

---

[133] Interpreting "And this he said because if he had disclosed the case and prayed judgment, —inasmuch as he recovered these tenements as his right by judgment etc., and the estate which her husband had was fully defeated—if she ought to have dower of those tenements, thereby of a truth he might have barred her etc." Case at 348–350. "To pray judgment" is to ask the court to decide the dispute without a jury submission.

[134] The text elaborates the reporter's explanation.

[135] *See* 111 Selden Society 116, 117 (1282). The question continued to be debatable. A man was survived by two sons. After the older took possession and died leaving his son as heir, the younger son improperly took possession. Although he was subsequently ousted, his widow nonetheless claimed dower. "Justice Spigurnel: They have laid an estate in {the younger son, your late husband} which does not entitle you to dower … *The Reporter*: And it is to be noted that the claim was a wild one, for {the younger son} was never so seised as to {qualify his widow for dower}. And some were of opinion that

Widows and Heirs

Since a widow's right attached to land her husband possessed during their marriage two widows might have rights in a single piece of land. If a father gave his son land, both their wives had rights. Both their husbands had been in possession. However the man first in possession provided his widow the dominant interest. A father gave land to his son who died soon thereafter. The son's widow got a third. But the father's wife still had priority. When the father died she took a third of the younger woman's widow's share. Her husband had possessed the land first.[136] The son's widow asked the court to make her whole. She said that since the father had guaranteed her share,[137] his heir had to compensate her for what the older widow took.[138]

15. (1312–1313)[139]

> [1] Adam gave a farm to his son Bogo. When young Bogo died Adam as his heir took back the farm.[140] Adam gave Bogo's wife Babs a widow's share. He guaranteed on behalf of himself and his heir that Babs

---

whether his seisin had been found tortious or good yet {his widow would have a valid claim for dower}. But of this there is a question etc." 27 Selden Society 80 (1313–1314).

[136] In addition to her one third of the other two thirds non-dower land, The rule is an exception to the maxim "there is no dower out of dower."

[137] On behalf of himself and his heir.

[138] The heir was the father's surviving son.

[139] 34 Selden Society 46. The text ignores the fact that the gift was in frank marriage (a variant of a fee tail) because the capacity in which Adam takes back the land is irrelevant to the widows' dispute. A wife has a dower right to land her husband holds in fee tail even though he dies childless. *See* 33 Selden Society 81 (1312).

[140] A wife is not her husband's heir. When Bogo died childless his father became his heir.

could keep the entire share. Later Adam's widow sued [141] Babs for a third of the share Babs had received.[142]

[2] Babs: I agree that she gets a third of my share. Her husband owned the land first.[143] But when he gave me my share he guaranteed I could keep it.[144] His heir has to make me whole.[145]

[3] Heir: As the heir I'm supposed to inherit the lion's share. My father's widow has taken a third.[146] You say as my father's heir I have to compensate you so that you will wind up with a full one third of the farm. If the court agrees I'll inherit only a third,[147] a percentage of the farm that treats me as a widow rather than an heir.[148]

---

[141] Writ of dower.

[142] She also took one third of the two thirds of the farm that her husband kept after he gave Babs' her one third.

[143] Interpreting the father's heir's statement "The dower which {the father's widow} demands is by an endowment prior to the dower of {the son's widow}, and in such a case by common law {the father's widow} ought to have dower of the whole and {the son's widow} only of the two parts…" Case at 46.

[144] The basis for Babs vouching Adam's heir to warranty.

[145] Interpreting "Judgment whether you ought not to warrant since you claim the reversion." The "reversion" refers to the right Adam retained for his heir to get back Babs' share when she died. The phrase "warrant" refers to the guarantee—the warranty—that Adam made to Babs that he or his heir would compensate her if she lost any part of her third.

[146] Anna got one third from the interests enjoyed by both the heir and Babs.

[147] During the widows' lifetimes.

[148] Interpreting "If we were to warrant etc. then the father's widow would have a third part of the whole and you a third part of the whole, and thus the heir would not have his heritage according to what (he) ought (to have)." Case at 47.

[4] Justice Stanton: That is the law.[149]

The feminist court created a rule that preferred widows to heirs.

Another contest between widows shows a judge falling into the trap an American law teacher called "mechanical jurisprudence"[150] —the application of theory without attention to real life consequences.

16. (1313)[151]

[1] Bogo and his wife Babs had no children. When Bogo died his father Adam was his heir.[152] Babs had a widow's right to one third of the two properties the hard-working Bogo had bought, a house and a meadow. But Babs wanted the whole house. She and her father-in-law reached an accommodation of their interests. He let her keep the whole house because she let him keep the whole meadow.[153] After Adam died his widow Anna claimed[154] a widow's share of two thirds of Babs' house. She said Babs had a widow's right only to a third. The other two thirds, Anna said, her husband had sold to Babs when they did their deal. As a consequence, Anna said, she had a widow's right to one third of two-thirds of the house.

---

[149] The heir's liability was limited to the land he had inherited: "if you have anything of the heritage etc." Case at 47.

[150] *See* Roscoe Pound, *Mechanical Jurisprudence* (1908).

[151] 43 Selden Society 36. The two property description somewhat simplifies the facts. The text states Bogo had bought the two properties in order to inoculate the reader against the erroneous assumption Adam gave Bogo the properties, a gift that would provide Anna a dower interest even if there were no exchange.

[152] A wife does not inherit from her husband.

[153] They think her one third of the meadow is worth the same as his two thirds of the house.

[154] Writ of dower.

> [2] Babs: I gave your husband my share of the meadow so I could keep the whole house. {Your husband never took possession of the two thirds of the house. Since he never possessed the two thirds, you've got no right to a third of it.[155] Let's look at the equities here. You have already taken a widow's share of the entire meadow. If Adam and I hadn't done our deal you would have taken only a widow's share of two thirds of the meadow. By laying claim to both the meadow and the house you are trying to double the size of your widow's share. The court shouldn't penalize me because your husband and I took a sensible approach to defining my share.}[156]
>
> [3] *The Reporter*: The court said Anna got a third of two-thirds of Babs' house {in addition to her share of the meadow}. One lawyer quipped that Babs had learned something useful. The next time she became a widow she wouldn't make the same mistake.[157]

The deal served a desirable goal—a widow should be able to negotiate so that she can stay put in her house. This case discourages such arrangements. The bad decision turns on a technicality. According to medieval theory a person had to possess land to sell it.[158] Adam had

---

[155] Interpreting "we are ready to aver that she holds them as dower of Adam's endowment and not by way of purchase." Case at 37. The text adds the assertion Adam never took possession. The text after the case explains this denial of possession.
[156] The report omits this obvious argument.
[157] Interpreting "Herle said … that Babs was consequently in the case of *discas.*" Case at 37. "The meaning of this phrase is 'Be wise another time.' Babs ought to have taken more care to ascertain the legal consequences of accepting the messuage in lieu of land." Footnote 3, case at 37. The text describes Herle's statement as gallows humor because it gives Babs no comfort.
[158] *See* 36 Selden Society 123, 125 (1313), 4 31a Rolls Series 412 (1305). Fines were an exception. 34 Selden Society 8 (1312–1313).

to possess the two thirds of the house to give Babs her extra share. His possession was just theoretical. He would not have moved his furniture into his dead son's house. But the court decides that theory forces it to give Anna part of Babs' house.

A better judge would not have been a slave to theory. He would have facilitated a worthwhile accommodation of interests.

17. (1317)[159]

> [1] As his father's heir Bogo[160] had to assign a widow's portion to his mother Anna.[161] They disagreed about a farm. Bogo said his father had owned the place. Anna said he was wrong—she herself had inherited the place when her mother died.[162] If Bogo was right Anna would get a third for life. If Anna was right she would own the place outright. They compromised and put their deal into effect by sham litigation.[163] The judgment said Bogo had inherited the farm but Anna could keep the whole place for her lifetime.[164] When Bogo died his widow Babs[165] sued[166] Anna. Babs said the judgment showed

[159] 54 Selden Society 143 (1317). In conjunction with the case record the report suggests or perhaps establishes the text's facts. Some footnotes are intended to simplify a comparison of the text with the case record and report. The text assumes the widow Anna remarried William of Cambridge, and therefore Babs sues Anna and her second husband.
[160] *I.e.*, John Croxtone.
[161] *I.e.*, Amice.
[162] The text hypothesizes a basis for her ownership claim to help the reader see the dispute in concrete terms.
[163] The report says Anna "rendered" the land to Adam. Case at 143. The term implies sham litigation to create a fine.
[164] Interpreting Adam "leased them to her who is now tenant, for a term of life." Case at 143. Anna's widow's share would have applied only to one third. The compromise gave her a life estate in the entire farm.
[165] *I.e.*, Elizabeth.

> Bogo had inherited the farm. By the settlement Anna got two things. She got a widow's portion for one third and a gift from her son Bogo for two-thirds. Babs claimed her widow's share of the two thirds.[167]
>
> [2] Chief Justice Bereford: When her husband died Anna had a right to a widow's share of his land. Even though the sham litigation said Bogo had inherited the place the sham litigation was nothing but a step in defining Anna's widow's share. Babs can't take a widow's share from what Anna got.[168]

Bereford lets widows and heirs negotiate their rights without giving a stranger an extra portion.

Waiver of Widows' Rights

A married man had to sell his land at a discount because the buyer knew his widow might someday take a part of the land.[169] If he could get his wife to waive her widow's right he could get full price. But making her waive her rights was difficult. A person could sell only land she possessed.[170] Until a wife had a dead husband

---

[166] Writ of dower.

[167] Babs claimed by "an earlier endowment." Case at 143. She said Anna "holds of our husband's lease." Case at 143.

[168] Interpreting "Because you have acknowledged that that which Adam held was her dower, and how she rendered and took estate again etc., this does not defeat her dower. Therefore the court awards that you take nothing by your writ." Case at 143. Bereford says Anna's "render," the fine's acknowledgment that he had possession, did not give Adam the type of possession that would support his widow's share.

[169] Although the seller typically guaranteed his heir would make the buyer whole, the guarantee applied only to land the heir inherited. The buyer would get nothing from an heir who inherited nothing.

[170] An "heir apparent"—a person who necessarily inherits if he outlives his ancestor—can't sell his interest while the ancestor is alive. *See* 36 Selden Society 123, 125 (1313); 4 31a Rolls Series 412 (1305).

she did not have anything.[171] A lawyer came up with a plan. A wife who owned land jointly with her husband had no widow's claim—if she survived him she became solo owner.[172] Her modest claim to a lifetime right in a third was swallowed up by the greater rights as a survivor to outright ownership.[173] The husband could make his wife joint owner by having her join him in a sham litigation. To be efficient the same sham lawsuit could transfer the land to the husband's intended buyer. The court judgment would say the husband and wife had sold him their jointly owned land.[174] As to be expected, when the husband died, the widow reneged. The sham lawsuit, she said, was a farce. She never had joint ownership. She deserved a widow's share.

The common law relies upon the adversary system as the engine to create good rules. A lawyer is a hired gun. Her job is to make convincing arguments. If she rejects an argument that offends her personal sense of justice she is not doing her job. She is supposed to be an advocate for her client, not an impartial creator of desirable rules. That is the judge's job, not hers. As a lawyer Bereford argued passionately for things he did not believe.

---

[171] *See* 43 Selden Society 87 (1313).
[172] *See* 122 Selden Society 109 (1281–1284).
[173] The court would express this conclusion by saying the husband never had the kind of possession that gave his wife a widow's share. "A claimant of dower is met by a fine to which she was a party tending to show that she and her husband were joint tenants. This is tantamount to 'Never so seised etc.'"20 Selden Society 69 (1310).
[174] She had to surmount one modest difficulty—she had to convince the court that her intention to sell was not the result of her husband's duress.

18. (1278)[175]

[1] Bogo sued[176] Anna to enforce a guarantee she had made when she and her husband sold him their joint ownership of a farm.

[2] Anna: The judicial settlement said I was joint owner but I wasn't. The court should ignore it. I can't be bound by its terms.[177]

[3] Bogo: You can't say that. The judge supervising the settlement concluded you were voluntarily entering the settlement. That established, no jury can question its terms.[178]

[4] Anna: Regardless of what I then said my husband coerced me into participating.[179] If the court enforces the judgment then husbands will be able to force their wives to waive their widows' safety net.[180]

[5] Bogo's lawyer, William Bereford:[181] Suppose a man is afraid his wife won't be able to get by on the income

---

[175] 112 Selden Society 338. The text simplifies a case in which Bogo's defendant in a writ of mesne vouches to warranty Anna's heir.
[176] Writ of mesne.
[177] Anna "never had any estate … which would have enabled her to enfeoff" him. Case at 339.
[178] The paragraph interprets "That is not something you can say because after the enrollment Anna and her husband came into court and acknowledged the tenements to be our right, and she was examined on this, and the fine levied." Case at 338.
[179] Interpreting "Although Anna made the acknowledgment she had to do that while she was under her husband's control." Case at 338.
[180] Interpreting "If a woman claims dower … and her adversary says that she …with her husband {had joint ownership as established by a fine} she {should be} allowed to get to a jury {to repudiate the implications of the sham lawsuit}." Case at 339.
[181] The text interprets Bereford's argument in the paragraph beginning "I bring my mort d'ancestor …" Case at 339.

a third of his land produces. He decides to make her joint owner by using a sham lawsuit settlement.[182] After he dies his son says his mother has received more than the law allows. He sues[183] to invalidate his parents' plan. He says no wife can participate in a settlement that gives her joint ownership of her husband's land. The son shouldn't be allowed to overturn his parents' arrangement. If this court says Anna couldn't participate in the settlement no husband can act in a generous way towards his wife.[184]

[6] The Justice: I'm persuaded. The deal Anna and her husband made is valid.

Bereford blows smoke in the judge's eyes. Few sons cheat their mothers but cash-strapped husbands often beg for help. Too many wives will comply and later rue the day they did. Thirty-five years later Bereford addressed the same problem as a judge.

19. (1312–1313)[185]

[1] Anna sued[186] Bogo for her widow's share of a farm.

---

[182] Interpreting "My mother comes with others to whom she has granted the land and they produce a charter showing that she had as much right in the land as my father and had survived him." Case at 339. The reference to "had survived him" shows Bereford is talking not about a genuine sale to a third person, but rather about a sale to a straw man who immediately sells the land back to the couple in joint ownership.

[183] Interpreting "I bring a mort d'ancestor on the death of my father…." Case at 339.

[184] Interpreting "We ask for judgment if they can get to a jury against the evidence of the charter and the fine." Case at 339.

[185] 34 Selden Society 26. *See also* 20 Selden Society 69 (1310). The text simplifies a claim the widow brought against the widow of the buyer's heir. When she defaults, her son intervenes.

[186] Writ of dower.

> [2] Bogo: She and her husband sold me their joint interest in the farm. She can't attack a judicial settlement in which she participated.[187]
>
> [3] Anna: A woman can't waive her widow's right while she's married. Even if she tells the court she's willing the court can't let her do it.[188]
>
> [4] Chief Justice Bereford: Anna's right. I don't care what the settlement says. If a jury decides her husband owned the place before the sham litigation the settlement's worthless. She can recover her widow's share.[189]

Bereford won't let a wife sacrifice her future rights.

---

[187] Interpreting "Judgment whether against the fine which is her own deed she ought to have dower." Case at 28.

[188] Interpreting "Judgment whether by any fine levied while she was covert (she can be debarred) from this action (which) accrued to her by the death of her husband etc." Case at 27.

[189] Interpreting "Chief Justice Bereford: Did she have anything in the tenements at the time the conusance was made, yes or no? Bogo: She had a freehold at the time of the settlement.... {*i.e.*, she was already a joint owner when she and her husband engaged in the sham settlement.} Anna. I had {no interest} except as {my husband's} wife. *The Reporter*: Issue Joined." Case at 27. If the jury finds Anna was not the joint owner before she and her husband did the settlement Anna gets dower. In another case a litigant offers a hypothetical example in which a widow claims dower after executing a fine during her marriage conveying away her joint ownership. One party contends the widow would recover; the other replies "That is open to question." 36 Selden Society 123, 125 (1313).

CHAPTER 11
Serfs

COMMON PLEAS CREATED A NARROW SLICE of serf law. Local courts decided most controversies.[1] An owner who possessed an agricultural laborer tied to the place of birth, a serf, never asked Common Pleas for help. He just locked up a malingerer.[2] Most Common Pleas judgments were about fugitives. If a serf had actually escaped, the court could offer only the writ of "naifty," the writ to prove ownership.[3] As a complex and slow-moving claim the writ to prove ownership of land was undesirable. The writ to prove ownership of a serf was even worse. A landowner got something that stayed put; a serf owner did not.[4]

---

[1] The text does not address the administration of justice by local courts.

[2] In the Simon of Paris case discussed in the introduction, had Robert possessed Simon he would have been privileged to detain him. 17 Selden Society 11 (1308).

[3] The criteria to prove ownership is discussed in 122 Selden Society 24 (1268–1269). For serfs in the king's towns a short limitation of a year and a day applied. Outside the king's demesne the case suggests the ownership claim had to be brought within four years of the escape. Britton, however, describes the period of limitation as the "time of prescription limited in {the} writ of mort d'ancestor." 1 Britton 200.

[4] The owner could lock up a bad serf, but an imprisoned serf was a liability.

Proof of Ownership

1. (1268–1269?)[5]

[1] Adam sued[6] to prove he owned Bogo, a serf who had run off years earlier. He said he owned Bogo's grandfather, father, brothers and Bogo himself, and his escape did not make him free.[7] Adam offered to prove Bogo's status by showing he had taken arbitrary payments from Bogo and his relatives.[8]

[2] Bogo: That can't be proof. Any landlord can use duress to force a free man to pay him money. Maybe if he said I paid him to get my daughter married—

---

[5] 122 Selden Society 24. As the Selden Society editor notes, the attribution to 1268–1269 is questionable. Bereford became a judge in 1290. Sir William Bereford (entry by Alan Harding), *Oxford Dictionary of National Biography*. The Selden Society report includes five different versions each presenting somewhat different factual and legal statements. The text re-orders the materials and extracts the dominant themes.

[6] Writ of naifty. Another case from the same period also reflects the justices' generous attitude towards freedom. In discussing a single claim made to both a father and son as serfs, Chief Justice Weyland said "Because you have only enough suit to prove your right to one body and you are attempting to recover two, we adjudge that the son, against whom you have no suit, go quit from this court. Where this writ is quashed in part it will be quashed as a whole. So the court adjudges {the father is also free}." 112 Selden Society 329 (1278–1289).

[7] "He asks for judgment if, as a result of his own flight outside the possession of his lord, he can claim to be in a state of freedom." Case at 24.

[8] Interpreting "Tallage high and low at our will." Case at 32. Sometime he took two shillings; sometimes, four. Case at 25.

something only a serf would do—that would be enough. But naked extortion can't make a man a serf.[9]

[3] Justice Bereford: Bogo is right. If we allowed a coerced payment to make a man a serf no free person would ever feel safe. He would live under the sword that some jury could say he had made an arbitrary payment.[10]

[4] Bogo: He can't prove that I'm a serf until he shows up in court with serfs who are related by blood to me.[11]

[5] Adam: Suppose they're all dead.[12] Suppose they've all escaped en masse.[13] I have to be able to prove his status without marching some serf into court.

---

[9] The paragraph interprets "we do not think that on the basis of that tallage you can claim us ... unless he can show that we have made ransom of our flesh." Case at 32.

[10] Interpreting "Justice Bereford: {The claim of having collected tallage} is a proof that is too general to try your seisin. For this will become a general action for all men to say to the most free man of the area that he is the villein of every man and say that he is seised of him as of his villein and thus might every man be forced to put himself on a jury as to whether he is villein or free." Case at 33.

[11] Interpreting "We ask judgment since he had brought no proof of blood kinsmen to prove the blood which is being claimed whether he may have action to prove title to the blood or whether we are obliged to answer him." Case at 28.

[12] Interpreting "Nothing remains to us of that blood, neither brother nor uncle nor other kin from whom we could bring suit, for all are dead…." Case at 29. "We do not think that for lack of blood kin, who are dead, we ought to be barred…." Case at 32.

[13] Interpreting "That this might give rise to a great problem for, if someone had one hundred villeins and all fled from the land of their lord, so that none of their kin remained with the lord, when the lord wished to bring action against these fugitives his action would fail because he could not produce suit, as all had fled together. This

> [6] Justice Bereford: You must produce his relatives[14] —you're asking for a judgment that will condemn his blood forever.[15] You haven't, and therefore Bogo is forever free.[16]

Not only was ownership difficult to prove but by making the claim in court a lord lost the most important power over his workforce, the power of self-help.

2. (1302)[17]

> [1] After Babs took her cow Anna sued[18] to get it back. Anna argued that since Babs did not possess her

---

would be very unfair if he could not be allowed to prove his possession." case at 25.

[14] Even the production of serf relatives in some situations would be insufficient. A free man who chose to become a serf would not thereby make his blood relatives serfs. "{Supposed serf's lawyer:} Sir we tell you that his great-grandfather Ralph was a free man … and the {other descendants} would be so, had they not made their admission of villeinage… Justice Loveday: Even if his brothers and kinsmen who are free have acknowledged themselves villeins this does not prejudice one who is free to prevent him from having his freedom." 123 Selden Society 444, 444–445 (1278-88). Cf. 122 Selden Society 289 (1285).

[15] Perhaps Bereford is changing the law to make proof of ownership more difficult. An earlier law book asserted "In a writ of naifty there is no occasion to present anyone of the same blood when one counts of his own seisin. If it is of his ancestor's seisin, one must of necessity, or he loses his writ." Casus Placitorum, 69 Selden Society 101. The reference to "his own seisin" refers to a seisin the owner previously had, but lost. In the principle case the claimant makes such an assertion. 122 Selden Society 24, 24 (1268-69).

[16] Interpreting "This writ is the highest writ to try the blood, where one may have no other suit than proof of the same blood, which you do not have, therefore this court adjudges that Bogo go quit of villeinage from you in perpetuity…." Case at 33.

[17] 3 31a Rolls Series 164.

[18] Anna complains "by bill." Poverty probably gave her the privilege to proceed without a writ.

as a serf she could not use self-help. She could not take her cow.[19]

[2] Babs: I possess you as a serf and therefore you can't sue me in royal court.[20]

[3] Anna: You don't possess me.[21] Recently you brought an ownership claim against me in local court. I've appealed that case so this court can see the record.[22] An ownership claimant admits she doesn't possess her serf—if she did, she would have no reason to sue. She would just lock up the bad serf.[23] You've conceded in court you don't possess me.[24]

---

[19] The case ends with Babs conceding Anna's freedom, and denying she took Anna's livestock: "We did not commit any tort..." Case at 168. A person who does not possess a serf cannot confiscate her livestock. 4 31a Rolls Series 430 (1305).

[20] "We are seised of you as of our neyfe; judgment." Case at 164.

[21] "Judgment if you can now say that you are seised of us as of your veileine." Case at 164. *See also* 4 31a Rolls Series 430 (1305) discussed below.

[22] Interpreting "We appeared, and sued out a Monstravit ... and the writs are still pending here...." Case at 164.

[23] Interpreting "Inasmuch as by your own {ownership} proceeding you then supposed us to be out of your seisin, judgment whether you can now say that you are seised of us as of your vileine." Case at 164. A plaintiff in possession had the power to discipline her serf (20 Selden Society 93 (1310), and therefore Bereford said no one in possession sued to prove ownership. "[I]f while {an owner's writ of naifty} was pending, {the owner} found you in your nest, for what purpose should he sue out his writ?" 5 31a Rolls Series 202, 04 (1306). A lawyer said by bringing a writ of naifty the plaintiff "supposed that {he was} out of possession...." *Ibid.* Anna provides no explanation for her theory; the text adds Bereford's rationale. A waste case provides another theory. The defendant told the court to dismiss the plaintiff's waste claim because the writ provided possession as a remedy, and the plaintiff had conceded he already had possession when he brought his writ. 39 Selden Society 32 (1313). A successful writ of naifty created a judgment that not only

[4] Justice Berrewike: Sheriff, did Babs bring an ownership writ in the local court?[25]

[5] Sheriff: Although Anna has appealed, Babs herself didn't bring the case.[26]

[6] *The Reporter*: Since Babs did not sue below, the court rejected Anna's argument.[27]

If Babs did not sue, who did? Anna's lawyer.[28] He paid some vagrant to masquerade as Babs' agent.[29] Common Pleas had used fictions to reform the law.[30] The lawyer hoped the court would refuse to let Babs deny she had brought the case. If the plan had worked a few shillings of filing fees would prove a serf's escape. Since the ownership writ was a failed remedy legions of workers could follow the same charade in order to become de facto free. Common Pleas was not ready to drive a stake through an ancient institution.

---

established ownership but also awarded possession. Therefore the argument could be made that a person in possession could not sue for ownership.

[24] Interpreting "Inasmuch as by your own proceeding you then supposed us to be out of your seisin, judgment if you can now say that you are seised of us as of your vileine." Case at 164.

[25] "Is there any such writ here?" The phrase "such writ" might refer to the ownership writ, or the removal writ. The Sheriff responds regarding both.

[26] Interpreting "The Sheriff said, the Monstravit is here, but the lady did not bring any such writ against her in the county court." Case at 164.

[27] Interpreting "And so that exception was not allowed." Case at 164.

[28] For another bogus suit brought in an opponent's name, *see* 5 31a Rolls Series 132 (1306) (replevin).

[29] Strawmen were serviceable instruments to bring about desired results.

[30] The courts approved the fictional claim of deadly violence to turn the trespass writ into a vehicle for law reform. 4 31a Rolls Series 258 (1304).

The Presumption for Freedom

Bereford was quick to find freedom.

3. (1306)[31]

[1] Reporter: If a serf sues his owner for violence the owner's lawyer must be careful. A single mistake makes a peasant free.[32]

[2] Adam sued[33] Bogo for beating him, locking him up, and taking his horse.[34]

[3] Bogo: Since I possess Adam as my serf, I'm not going to plead with him. The king's courts don't hear cases brought by serfs. There's a single exception. The king's court helps victims of violence, even serf victims. I'm not guilty of using violence.[35]

---

[31] 5 31a Rolls Series 296. *See also* 1 31a Rolls Series 372 (1293) (By not raising the status question the moment the defendant vouched the serf to warranty, the lord recognized his freedom.) "If the lord asks for a continuance before he has pled otherwise, his serf gains no benefit; but perhaps the serf is freed if the lord requests a continuance thereafter." 31 Selden Society 113 (Note VII). "It is said that if I make my serf my attorney to sue for me in a court which bears record he is enfranchised thereby, for I put him in the place of a free man. But I {the reporter} question this." 26 Selden Society 130 (1310–1311).

[32] Interpreting the medieval reporter's headnote: "How a lord is to defend himself against his naif." Case at 296.

[33] Writ of trespass.

[34] Interpreting "Took him and imprisoned him etc. and assaulted, beat etc., and his goods etc. took and carried away." Case at 296.

[35] Interpreting "We tell you that Adam ought not to be answered, for he is our vilein, and we were seised of him on the day of which he complains; and as to any thing done against the peace etc., we say Not guilty etc." Case at 296. Cf. Bereford as a lawyer representing a serf complaining about violence: "Bereford: Whereas you say that

[4] Adam: Will you go on record with your defense?[36]

[5] Bogo: Certainly.

[6] Adam: Good. When you said you didn't use violence you denied using violence against me and you denied using violence to take my horse. In this court you argued with me about a horse. By pleading with your supposed serf in royal court you conceded my free status.[37]

[7] Bogo: No. I was just denying I had assaulted you. I know enough not to plead about property with a serf.[38]

[8] *The Reporter*: Bogo pled badly. He should have denied nothing except the beating. He had to deny that. But as for the horse he should not have said anything about the way he took it. A serf does not own a horse; his master does.[39] Justice Stanton decided to excuse Bogo's mistake as a mere technicality.[40] He said he would

---

you imposed discipline through the stocks we say that you put us in fetters, and this type of imprisonment is allowable only to the king…" 123 Selden Society 564, 565 ((pre-1290, uncertain court).

[36] Interpreting "Be avowed."

[37] Interpreting "You entirely negative our plaint, for you said Not guilty." Case at 296.

[38] Interpreting "As to the chattels you ought not to be answered." Case at 296.

[39] Interpreting "Here Bogo pleaded badly, at least in answering after his defense, because he ought rather to have distinguished his second exception, and to have avowed the goods carried away, because it is lawful for a lord etc." Case at 296.

[40] The report does not identify the judge, but Bereford and Howard come to court on a following day, and Stanton tries to convince Bereford to ignore Bogo's mistake. Even if Stanton was not the judge, he adopted the judge's position. Serf law included many technicalities that were unclear. But the serf's way as a litigant was not easy. By pleading the plaintiff was a serf an abbot avoided

interpret his pleading as just a denial he had assaulted Adam.[41]

[9] Adam: Make a record of your ruling. I'm going to have the full court overturn it.[42]

[10] *The Reporter*: At a later day Bereford took a seat.

[11] Justice Bereford: Bogo said he wouldn't answer and then he answered. By prattling on about the horse he put his earlier defense that Adam was a serf back into his purse. Adam is now free.[43]

[12] *The Reporter*: Speaking privately Stanton tried to make Bereford reconsider. He said Bogo had denied only the beating.[44]

[13] Justice Bereford: I can't agree. Bogo should have said: I'm in possession of Adam as my serf. I'm not going to talk about the horse or the detention. There's only one thing I need to answer. Adam says I beat him. I didn't.[45]

---

litigating whether he had broken into the plaintiff's house in order to destroy the charter that made him free. 36 Selden Society 201 (1313).

[41] Interpreting "Nevertheless at length {his exception that he would not plead about the horse} was so enrolled etc." Case at 296.

[42] Interpreting "We make protestation that we do not admit their exception of vileinage {*i.e.*, Bogo's refusal to plead about the horse and the detention}, but oppose it, and we pray that it may be so entered." Case at 296.

[43] Interpreting "When you at first took an exception to his person, and afterwards answered him, your first exception was worth no more than if you had kept it in your purse, and only amounts to saying You ought not to be answered, and then answering." Case at 298.

[44] Interpreting "Staunton (privately, between him and Bereford). He charges him with a trespass which is not avowable on a vilein, wherefore etc." Case at 298.

[45] The paragraph interprets "As to the carrying off the chattels nor as to what he says of the imprisonment, ought he to be answered,

[14] *The Reporter*: At Adam's request Bereford told the court staff to purge the record of any allegation that he was a serf.[46]

Freedom By Marriage

Marriage to a free man provided a path to freedom. If a serf's owner allowed her to marry a free man she became free at least during her husband's lifetime, perhaps forever.

4. (1302)[47]

[1] Born a serf on a manor, Anna married a free man and lived with him outside the manor until he died. She then returned to the manor with three oxen and two heifers. When she refused to behave as a serf, Babs, the manor's new owner, confiscated the livestock. Claiming her freedom, Anna sued [48] to recover the livestock.

[2] Babs: Once you returned to the manor your status as a serf reattached. You can't litigate here.

[3] Anna: At the time of my marriage the then owner of the manor gave me permission to marry. You bought the manor after I left, and since I have lived as

---

because he is our vilein and we were seised etc., and because he wished to flee from us, or did some other thing against our will, we put him in stocks and took his chattels as our etc: and as to the beating and wounding we did it not, ready etc." Case at 298.

[46] Interpreting Adam "Prayed the exception of vileinage might be ousted—and so it was; and the roll was amended by Bereford." Case at 298.

[47] 3 31a Rolls Series 164. The text changes the order of the arguments presented within the report.

[48] She does not bring the conventional replevin but rather sues by bill. The justices probably let her do so because of her poverty.

a free woman for thirty years, you can't have my case dismissed. You don't possess me as a serf.

[4] Babs: Servile blood courses through your veins, and while your body may have been free, your blood was always the blood of a serf belonging to the manor. I concede that if a lord marries his own serf, she is forever free. But when you married some stranger all you got was freedom for his lifetime.

[5] Justice Brumpton: If you were the original owner of the manor your argument might have some force. But when you bought the manor Anna was long gone. Since you never possessed her as a serf, you can't claim your possession has been reestablished by her return.

[6] *The Reporter*: Brumpton now seemed to drift off point as he rambled on about his memories of irrelevant serf litigation from long ago.[49]

[7] Babs: May I make a point? The manor is in Cornwall so the court should look at Cornwall customs. In Cornwall a serf can marry outside the manor only if she can find responsible people who will guarantee her return as a serf if her free husband dies. In any case by the common law a woman who becomes free through marriage loses that status when her husband dies.[50]

[8] Justice Brumpton: Your doctrine is false.

---

[49] Interpreting "Brumpton. I recollect {various cases.} *The Reporter*: This is nothing to the purpose." Case at 168.

[50] "Mutford: Sir, we understand this, that where a neyfe is married to a freeman, she, after the death of her husband, returns to her former condition." Case at 166. Mutford does not appear to be referring to exceptional Cornwall customs and therefore the text identifies his assertion as a claim about the common law.

> [9] Justice Hervey: False is too mild: I'd call it heresy.
>
> [10] Justice Brumpton: Babs, you have had the temerity to try to make this old widow work as your drudge even though she has been free for most of her life. I'll give you just what you've asked for. You say thirty years ago she produced some people to guarantee her return upon her husband's death. Here's your remedy: sue them if you can find them outside the graveyard.[51]
>
> [11] Justice Berrewik: As for Anna herself, she has a right to litigate as a free person, and if you took her livestock, you'll pay.[52]

The common law's progress towards freedom appears by a comparison of this case with a riddle a medieval law teacher posed at about the time Anna married her man. "When can a son ignore his mother's request for a widow's portion? Suppose his father was free and his mother was a serf. The son should give his mother nothing because she is no better than a serf once his father dies. If she manages, however, to marry another free man, she can then make him turn over her share of the land he has inherited."[53]

---

[51] Interpreting and expanding "Proceed against your pledges." Case at 166.
[52] Interpreting "Answer to the trespass." Case at 168.
[53] 69 Selden Society 33 (1272-1278).

POSSESSION

Escape

Common Pleas said a fugitive did not have to go far to escape from his owner's possession.

5. (1304)[54]

[1] Adam sued[55] because Bogo's men took him in Stone Village and locked him up.

[2] Bogo: I'm not answering a serf in royal court.[56]

[3] Adam's lawyer: You have to answer for what your men did unless you can show Adam was in your possession when they arrested him. He wasn't—he had escaped.[57]

[4] Bogo: You're not going to trick me into pleading here.[58]

---

[54] 4 31a Rolls Series 54.

[55] Writ of imprisonment.

[56] Interpreting "He ought not to be answered, for he is our villein, and we are seised of him as of our vilein, ready etc." Bogo's assertion of both ownership ("our villein") and possession ("seised") lets Adam choose possession as the issue. Only possessors could use self-help.

[57] Interpreting Stone Village "Where he took him, is of the fee of the Earl of Gloucester ... and is no part of Bogo's fee, or of his seignory; and he does not answer to the imprisoning; judgment etc. as undefended." Case at 56. The case does not focus on whether Adam escaped because he left Bogo's land, or because he reached Stone Village. On balance the report seems to imply the magic moment took place when Adam left Bogo's land. Perhaps the seignories were contiguous.

[58] Interpreting "First show yourself to be answerable, and then we will answer as to the place of taking." Case at 56.

> [5] Justice Howard: If he escaped you have to answer here for what your men did. A serf you don't possess has a right to sue you here.[59] {Once he has escaped you can't use self-help—you can't enforce your rights except by bringing a court case against him.}[60]
>
> [6] Justice Hengham: I'm not going to quarrel with the theory that escape provides immunity from arrest. But I don't like the sweeping language. Serfs leave their masters' lands to go on errands all the time. A trip to the market doesn't constitute escape.[61] What's more Adam isn't even in court. If he were his claim would be more plausible. But as things stand his lawyer has the burden of proving escape.[62]
>
> [7] Adam's lawyer: Adam wasn't on an errand. Bogo's serf catchers had no rights once Adam left his land.[63]
>
> [8] *The Reporter*: The question was put to the jury.

Hengham seems to think Bogo would set his captured serf free while the litigation was underway. His unrealistic assumption does not change the case rule. Unless he is on an errand a serf cannot be captured

---

[59] Interpreting "Although he be your vilein, do you think that you can take him wherever you find him?" Case at 56.
[60] The text's addition explains the rule more explicitly.
[61] Interpreting: If the serf "goes to market or elsewhere out of the limits of his fee, can he not take him wherever he finds him? (intimating the affirmative)." Case at 56.
[62] Interpreting "If he were here in proper person that would be something, for thereby there would be a greater presumption that he is not seised of him as of his vilein; and therefore answer." Case at 56.
[63] Interpreting the lawyer's assertion that Bogo "is not seised of Adam as of his vilein; ready etc." in the context of the comments by Justices Howard and Hengham. Case at 56.

once he is outside the area where his owner's authority runs.[64] The master can reclaim his rights only by going to court.[65]

Escape in Place

Escape suggests flight but Common Pleas said a serf who stopped working could become a fugitive—could escape an owner's possession—without even leaving the farm where he was born.[66]

6. (1314)[67]

[1] Adam sued[68] Bogo for taking his horse by force and arms and against the peace.

[2] Bogo: {As far as I can tell, you're not really complaining about violence. You're just saying that

---

[64] Adam says Stone Village is no part of Bogo's "seignory." Case at 56. The comment about "seignory" suggests Adam's escape occurred when he left lands Bogo controlled rather than when he reached Stone Village.

[65] If some free person has given the serf refuge (probably as a farm laborer) the lord can use the writ de nativis against the free person. Early Registers of Writs, 87 Selden Society 168 (#245).

[66] "[T]he lord's right of action to recover his fugitive commences when the naïf ceases to perform {serf} services and to acknowledge him for his lord." 1 Britton 201 (1865) (reprint Lawbook Exchange 2003). Britton says virtually any servile action constitutes a service: "if the lords are in possession of their services… a penny a year for chevage and one day's work in harvest, or other service, small or great, according to their ability." 1 Britton 201.

[67] 39 Selden Society 211. The text describes the defendant as "Bogo" rather than "the prior" because he bases his claim to ownership upon his ancestors' rather than his predecessors' rights.

[68] Writ of trespass.

> since I don't possess you I can't take back my own horse.}[69] My family has always owned your family and I possess you. You can't sue here.[70]
>
> [3] Adam: The past has no relevance to my present status. You can't show you possessed me when I bought my writ. {I may have been living on land you owned but the jury will find I wasn't working for you.}[71]
>
> [4] *The Reporter*: The court asked the jury if Bogo had in fact been in possession of Adam. It shouldn't have. Trespass is all about violence—the jury should have been asked about that.[72]

The reporter does not see that the court wants to implement the rule that an owner who does not supervise his serfs loses possession of them. As the case record

---

[69] Although omitted from the report, Bogo's rationale is implicit in his defense that Adam is a serf. Had Adam in fact claimed Bogo used violence, he could not have defended by referring to Adam's servile status. The royal courts protected serfs against violence.

[70] Interpreting "We are seised of him as of our villein, and our father was seised of his grandfather … and similarly of other generations." Case at 211.

[71] The paragraph interprets "your exception is not sufficiently taken by your merely saying that he is your villein, and we plead to it; and we tell you that you are not seised of him as of your villein; and … we ought not to be forced to answer a plea as to an earlier ancestor or that [simply] he is your villein." (Case at 211). The text's addition puts the statement in the context of the record as the subsequent commentary explains.

[72] The paragraph interprets "And afterwards they were at issue on the seisin; but it is strange that the issue was not taken as upon something done against the peace etc., seeing that the plaintiff counted that the defendant came with force and arms and against the peace." Case at 212.

shows Bogo bought land with its attached serfs.[73] Later he put Adam's livestock into a paddock and let the animals starve to death.[74] He was not paying attention to his land, his chattels, or his serfs. The court deprives negligent owners of the right to use self-help against serfs. "Use it or lose it" becomes the rule.[75]

In another case a serf does not use the trespass writ, the ultimate royal guarantee of his safety. Instead he just brings the free person's writ to recover livestock.[76]

7. (1305)[77]

[1] Adam sued[78] Bogo to recover a horse.

[2] Bogo: I own and possess Adam as my serf—he can't sue me in royal court.[79]

[3] Justice Hengham: Jurors, ignore the claim of ownership. Just tell me if Bogo was still exacting serf services from Adam when he took the horse.[80]

---

73 "A certain Bennnet of Breckles did some long time ago grant … a certain John Elom, then being his neif, with all his tenements and all his sequela, to hold to the same Prior and his successors forever…" Case record at 212. By its use of the term "successors" the record indicates the priory bought the land; the report instead refers to the defendant's ancestors, his grandfather etc. The text takes the report's approach.

74 "Did impark and did keep them so long imparked without food etc. that the aforesaid horse and one of the aforesaid cows died of hunger…." Case record at 212.

75 *See* 1 Britton 201.

76 Writ of replevin.

77 4 31a Rolls Series 430. The note has been recast into dialogue format.

78 Writ of replevin.

79 Interpreting "Vileinage was alleged…" in the context of Hengham's remarks. Case at 430.

> [4] *The Reporter*: After the jurors said he was not, Adam won.[81] Many lawyers said Bogo could still prove he owned Adam.[82]

The thinking of the "many" lawyers shows that the ownership writ was de facto dead. Open questions are questions no one litigates. Very few serf owners who could not use the right to self-help would bother engaging in litigation to prove their ownership.

A prior realized he had a problem. The priory owned a serf but the priory had never made him do serf work. The cases said the prior could not use self-help to discipline the man. The prior's lawyer gave him a good idea. The prior released his cattle upon the land the serf claimed while the crops were ready for harvest.[83] The prior then waited for the suit he knew the laborer would bring.[84]

---

[80] Interpreting "Justice Hengham: Good people, whether he is rightfully a vilein or rightfully a free man, of that we do not charge you; but only of what condition he was on the day of the taking." Case at 430.

[81] The report says "The Inquest said that he was a free man and of free estate." Despite this language, the reporter's comment and Hengham's instruction show their verdict meant not that Adam was free but rather that Bogo did not possess him as a serf.

[82] "And in the opinion of many this will not be a bar to the lord's having his writ of Neyf." Case at 432. A naifty plaintiff asks the court for a judgment that vindicates his ownership by providing him possession of the serf.

[83] The text assumes the prior took the best strategy to get rid of the peasant while protecting himself against a trespass claim for personal violence which a serf could bring. Physically ejecting the peasant would present that danger. Intentionally releasing livestock upon land with mature crops constitutes dispossession. 122 Selden Society 306 (1285). Another strategy to get rid of a serf: wait for him to leave the land temporarily and then peacefully bar his re-entry The report says nothing about what the prior actually did.

[84] Cf. "Justice Berrewik: ... if the distress be denied you, bring an assize, and you shall have right done you." 3 31a Rolls Series 156, 58 (1302).

8. (pre–1278)[85]

[1] Adam sued[86] the prior for dispossessing him of his farm.

[2] Prior: I know I can't stop you from suing me in royal court. I don't possess you as my serf. So I'm not going to ask the court to dismiss your case.[87] But even a free person can't complain about dispossession unless he can show he has had possession.[88] A jury will say you're a serf. A serf can't possess land. Since you never had possession, you can't sue me for dispossession.[89]

[3] Adam: No safeguards are more important than those the courts have put in the writ of naifty, the writ to claim ownership and condemn a man's blood forever. The court can't let you nullify those safeguards by changing my claim for dispossession into a forum to prove my blood is servile. You can't justify a dispossession by saying you own me.[90]

[4] Justice: Adam's right. Prior, if you think you own him bring an ownership writ. But we're not going to

---

[85] 123 Selden Society 489. The case is also reported in Casus Placitorum, 69 Selden Society 56 (1278).
[86] Writ of novel disseisin.
[87] Interpreting "The Justice. Were you ever seised of him as of your villein? The Prior. No." Case at 491.
[88] Cf. 29 Selden Society 90 (1313–1314).
[89] Interpreting "He could not have any free tenement…" Case at 489.
[90] The paragraph interprets "Since the writ of naifty is the most high writ which can be acquired in the king's court and novel disseisin the most tender, we ask for judgment whether something of the nature of that determined by the writ of naifty can be determined by the assize of novel disseisin." Case at 490.

> let you raise the ownership question in this case. He can sue you for dispossession.[91]

Each of these cases prevents a lord from using self-help when a serf has stopped behaving like a serf for a long enough time.[92] Unless he was willing to go to court, the lord seemed to have contracted an incurable parasite.

A Free Man

Another common law doctrine let the lord salvage something. The case will be presented first in its original translation. Then a narrative will explain what the case means. And finally the text will present a lay language version derived from the original translation. In this final case the reader will be able to track the process by which the text has created the modern language versions of the published translations of the medieval Year Book cases.

9. (1293)[93]

> A. made his plaint "de vetito namio" in the County Court for a horse taken; and deliverance was made; and the Prior purchased the Recordari into the Bench; and on the day given, A. counted against him. And the Prior answered that (A.) was his vilein.
>
> *Mutford:* He cannot get to that; for John is in a free state, and that by your own suit; for that you have

---

[91] Interpreting "The Justice says that the assize should not be stayed unless he were seised of him as of his villein or has a writ of naifty pending against him, because of which the assize ought not to be stayed." Case at 489.

[92] The Bereford era cases do not define the time period. Britton speaks about a year and a day. 1 Britton 200.

[93] 2 31a Rolls Series 106.

removed the plea here by the Recordari of your own purchase; so we pray judgment inasmuch as you have made yourself a party with us by the Recordari, if you can now get to say we are a vilein.

Hyham: It does not follow you are free, although you be a party with us; you are a party [only] pending the plea.

Sutton: That you cannot get to say we are a vilein, I will prove to you; for this writ is given between lord and tenant; and whereas your writ states that you have distreined for customs and services which are in arrear to you, you thereby suppose we are your tenant and not a vilein; wherefore we pray judgment.

Hertham: Sir, why did you allow deliverance of the beasts to be made? Why did not you avow the ownership?

Hyham: If we had avowed the ownership, he would have sued an appeal against us.

HERTFORD: Waive the body.

Hyham: We avow the taking; for the reason that he holds of us in villeinage; and it was presented by our vileins that he ought to be our bailiff: and because all the holders of that tenement have held of us in vileinage, doing therefor vilein service, such as being our bailiff; and thus we avow the taking.

Mutford: Then they waive the person.

HERTFORD: Not in this writ. Now answer to the allegation that the holders of the tenement held in vileinage; for he ought not to have the benefit of both.

Mutford: We hold freely, by escuage and by the services of ten shillings and suit to your court of C.

> every three weeks, &c.; and we have been often essoined in your court; ready to aver it.
>
> And the other side said the contrary.

In narrative form here is what the case is all about: Adam sued[94] the prior in local court to recover his horse. The prior removed[95] the case to royal court, and after Adam restated his complaint[96] the prior said he did not have to answer Adam's claim. He was a serf. Adam replied that the prior's removal proceeding showed he had already conceded he was free.[97]

If the prior thought he was a serf, Adam says, he would have asked the local court to dismiss his claim, a claim only a free person could make.[98] In addition, Adam says, the prior claimed he had not done some specific duties.[99] That also recognized his freedom. A serf owes no specific duties; a serf does whatever his master tells him to do.[100] Finally Adam says the prior said he had

---

[94] By the *de vetito namio.*

[95] By the writ of *recordari.*

[96] In his "count."

[97] Adam refers to the content of the prior's *recordari.* A medieval commentator says in a *recordari* that "there will always be a *causa.*" Early Registers of Writs 61 (#216). The "*causa"* will read the horse was taken "for customs and services owed to … B." *Ibid.* 156 (#191).

[98] That the *de vetito namio* is a free person's claim is implicit in the report; explicit in 2 P&M 524. *See also* 2 31a Rolls Series 84 (1293); 3 31a Rolls Series 222 (1302). Although the case refers to the *de vetito namio* as a "writ," the claim was not a Chancery writ. Elsewhere Bereford said "I would have you know that the Sheriff has no more authority to try causes by writ than I have to sing a mass." 31 Selden Society 96, 98 (1311).

[99] "Customs and services." They are defined and limited duties. *See* 122 Selden Society 143 (1284) (seven pence); 22 Selden Society 101 (1310).

[100] He can "tallage him high and low." *See* 1 P&M 368.

taken Adam's horse.[101] That also recognized his freedom. A serf does not own a horse—a serf's master owns what he appears to possess.

The prior answers that he did not want Adam to accuse him of theft and challenge him to battle.[102] His pleading avoided that danger. Justice Hertford accepts the prior's excuse. He tells Adam to waive the right to battle.[103] Adam agrees.[104]

The prior now changes his defense completely. He says he took Adam's horse because Adam violated his obligations as a tenant.[105] By this pleading the prior twice concedes Adam is free. He admits Adam owns the horse[106] and he pleads with him in royal court.[107] The prior then says that Adam chose to take possession of lands historically occupied by serfs, and therefore he had to perform some of the duties the serfs did.[108] Adam, the prior says, breached

---

[101] By "distraining" Adams' horse, the prior acknowledges Adam owns the animal. *See* 1 P&M 353. By "suffering the delivery," the prior returns Adam's horse because Adam posts bond to insure he will litigate. *See* 2 P&M 524.

[102] Adam would bring a criminal accusation against him, an "appeal" *See* 2 P&M 605; 4 31a Rolls Series 316, 318–320 (1304).

[103] When Hertford says "waive the body" he is referring to "proof by the body," a synonym for battle. *See* 4 31a Rolls Series 316, 318–320 (1304).

[104] The case continues so he must have agreed.

[105] "I avow the taking." By the distraint process a lord forces a free tenant to litigate the content of his obligations.

[106] The prior's justification does not say that he owns the horse; the prior's justification says he was privileged to take the horse because Adam refused to perform the duties he owed as a free tenant (a free tenant who occupies land previously occupied by serfs).

[107] A recognition of his freedom.

[108] "He holds of us in vileinage." Case at 106. A man who "holds in vileinage" is free—a serf does not "hold" land. In the context of the prior's previous statement he claims that Adam as a free occupant of lands historically worked by serfs has to do some serf work.

his obligation to undertake the management of the serfs.[109] By breaching his obligations as a free tenant Adam gave the prior the right to take his horse.

Adam answers the prior's new theory by stating the obvious—the prior has admitted he is free. [110] The reporter assumes his expert readers know what Adam said next. Adam asked Justice Hertford to enter judgment in his favor. The prior bet his case on Adam's servile status. Since he lost the bet Adam has won.[111] The reporter does not waste time writing down this critical point.

Although a serf does many different duties, the doctrine that a free person who lives on serf lands has to do serf duties probably excludes those duties that only a serf would perform. Both serf and free tenants work on land that belongs to the manor's owner, but only a serf conventionally pays to have his daughter marry. Denying a claim he has done uniquely servile duties, a litigant argued, "We do not think that on the basis of {my making payments to you} you can claim us ... unless {you} can show that we have made ransom of our flesh." 122 Selden Society 24, 32 (1268-69). "Ransom of flesh" is the marriage payment. *See* 1 Britton 196. However some free men did deals for land that obligated them to pay to have their daughters married: a free man "gives services ... including merchet for marriage of daughters outside manor and that unable to sell any horse or ox of their own breeding without license..." 123 Selden Society 499, 500 (pre–1290) (additional note). Sometimes merchet is described as a payment for either a daughter or son's marriage. *E.g.*, 122 Selden Society 289, 290 (case record). A born serf who acted as serf manager on the land of his birth would give his owner possession of him as a serf. 17 Selden Society 11 (1308) (the Simon of Paris case). The doctrine would not apply to Adam since the prior has conceded he was born free.

[109] They presented him as their bailiff, and he refused to serve. The prior's pleading shows his theory a free person who takes possession of land "in villeinage" may have to supervise the serfs.

[110] "He waives the person." Adam means he has dropped his objection to my status as a serf, and admits I am free. "By the exception {that you are a serf} he makes you to be not answerable, and it is wholly to the person." 5 31a Rolls Series 10, 14 (1305).

[111] Hertford's subsequent remarks support the text's analysis.

Hertford refuses to enter judgment in Adam's favor. He implies[112] he would have given Adam judgment if he had brought a writ to prove his freedom.[113] But Adam's writ[114] asked the court to define his duties as a free tenant. The writ did not directly address the question of his status. Therefore Hertford says he will not enter judgment against the prior. He will let the case continue. Hertford has given the prior something—he has refused to enter judgment against him.[115]

---

[112] He says "not in this writ."

[113] The writ of "*ne vexes*." The *ne vexes* sanctions the defendant for harassing the plaintiff by trying to make him act as a serf. In deciding a ne vexes case Justice Hengham said if the jury decided the plaintiff was free, the court would enter a judgment awarding him the land rent free. "Hengham: By the exception he makes you to be not answerable, and it is wholly to the person. Let the inquest run, and understand that it is ...equal risk {for both litigants}, for if it pass against the {defendant} the tenements will be discharged forever {that is, the plaintiff will keep the land without having to do any duties whatever}; but if it pass against {the plaintiff} then {he} ... is a vilein {forever} etc. ..." 5 31a Rolls Series 10, 14 (1305). For another context in which the court threatens to enter final judgment if an intermediate defense fails, *see* 20 Selden Society 190 (1310): "You say that if we see that she could deserve dower you will answer her. But if at this point we were to award that she was able {to get dower}, that would be for wine and candle. {We will just enter judgment in her favor; you will not be able to present any other defense to her claim.}" *See also* 5 31a Rolls Series 332,334 (1306) ("If we give judgment we shall give it with the benefit attaching.")

[114] Although a replevin (or a de vetito namio) claims confiscated livestock, its real purpose is to produce a judgment about a tenant's duties. Along with his livestock a victorious replevin plaintiff gets a judgment that says he can keep the land on the terms his replevin said the deal embodied.

[115] He has given the prior one "benefit."

Hertford now penalizes the prior for changing his story.[116] The prior now says Adam enjoys only "a tenancy in villeinage,"[117] a tenancy at will that obligates Adam to do some serf work.[118] Hertford says he will not ask the jury if Adam took a tenancy in villeinage.[119] Adam's duties will not be defined by the doctrines that apply to a free person who occupies serf lands as a favor from their owner, a tenant at will.[120] Adam's duties will be defined by his agreement with the prior.

Adam then describes the agreement. He got the land because he agreed to pay ten shillings a year and serve every third week on the prior's court. Adam preempts an

---

[116] By sanctioning the prior, Hertford denies him the second "benefit."

[117] The prior's doctrine has a long history. *See* 123 Selden Society 489 (pre–1278); also reported in *Casus Placitorum*, 69 Selden Society 56 (1278).

[118] Sued for wrongful possession of land, a free tenant pleads he "has nothing and claims nothing, but says that he holds the tenements in villeinage at the will of the Archbishop of Canterbury, in whose person the freehold is … we received it from the bailiff to hold by villein services; and so we are tenant at the will of the Archbishop and not in freehold."" 17 Selden Society 61, 61-62 (1308-09).

[119] He lets Adam answer the prior's claim that "all the holders to the tenement held in vileinage" by saying he has a defined deal with the prior that does not include serf work. When Adam sued he said the deal was for a payment and court service exclusively. The prior had his choice of defenses. He could argue the terms of the deal. He could argue Adam's tenancy in villeinage obligated him to do some serf work. He could argue a serf he possessed could not sue in royal court. He took the serf cannot sue route. Having abandoned that defense, the prior wants to choose the theory Adam took a tenancy in villeinage that obligated him to do some serf work. Hertford will not let him. He chose one defense and then abandoned it. Therefore Hertford says that Adam can choose the theory, the theory the purchase agreement did not force him to do serf work.

[120] *See* 1 31a Rolls Series 40 (1292). *I.e.*, the landlord can end the tenancy at any time and for any reason.

argument the prior might make—the argument that the deal's "court service" constituted a specific example of the many serf services Adam agreed to do.[121] His court service, Adam says, has been postponed for set causes.[122] Serfs do not get set postponements. They do what their masters tell them to do.[123] The agreement referred to a free person's court service.

This interpretation creates a modern version of the report.

10. (1293)[124]

[1] Adam sued[125] in local court to get back a horse the prior took. After having the case transferred to Common Pleas,[126] the prior asked the court to dismiss the serf Adam's claim.

[2] Adam: The record shows you've admitted I'm free. I brought my claim below as a free tenant[127] and you didn't ask to have my claim dismissed. You conceded my freedom. Then you said I hadn't done some limited duty.[128] A serf doesn't do limited duties. A serf does

---

121 Serfs can serve on courts. *See* 111 Selden Society 13 (pre 12173).

122 Essoins.

123 "[T]he {serf} tenant knows not in the evening whether in the morning he will be kept working in the fields or sent a long journey with a cart." [sic] 1 P&M 374. In contrast sokemen, the serf-like inhabitants of the king's original landholdings, the "ancient demesne," had set obligations. 2 31a Rolls Series 498 (1294) (writ of attachment).

124 2 31a Rolls Series 106.

125 *De vetito namio*, a county court version of the royal replevin.

126 By a writ of *recordari*.

127 Interpreting the writ of *de vetito namio* "is given between lord and tenant" Case at 106.

128 Interpreting "You have distrained for customs and services." A medieval commentator on recordari says that "there will always be a

what his master tells him to do. You conceded my freedom. Finally when I asked to get my horse back until the case was decided, you gave it back.[129] A serf owner would have kept it—he would have said the horse belonged to him.[130] You conceded my freedom.

[3] Prior: If I said I owned the horse you would have said I had stolen it and then challenged me to battle.[131] {I pled the way I did to avoid battle.}[132]

[4] Justice Hertford: A sensible decision by the prior. I'll dismiss Adam's case unless he waives his right to battle.[133]

[5] {Adam: Agreed.}[134]

[6] Prior: {I've decided to drop my defense that I possess Adam as a serf.}[135] Instead I say he refused to do his duties as a free tenant.[136] In the past his land

---

causa." Early Registers of Writs, 87 Selden Society 61 (#216). The "*causa*" will read the horse was taken "for customs and services owed to … B." *Ibid.* 156 (#191). A claim for customs and services identifies a limited obligation. *See, e.g.*, 122 Selden Society 143 (1284) (seven pence); 22 Selden Society 101 (1310).

[129] Interpreting "Why did you allow deliverance of the beasts to be made." Case at 106.

[130] Interpreting "Why did you not avow the ownership?" Case at 106.

[131] Interpreting "If we had avowed the ownership, he would have sued an appeal against us." Case at 106.

[132] The text makes explicit the prior's implicit argument.

[133] Interpreting "Waive the body." Case at 106.

[134] Implicit because the case continues.

[135] Implicit in the prior's avowry. An avowry in royal court concedes an opponent is free. In addition the prior pleads with Adam in royal court, another recognition of his freedom.

[136] Interpreting "We avow the taking." Case at 106.

was held by serfs.[137] A free person who takes possession of serf lands has to do many serf jobs.[138] When the serfs chose Adam as their manager he refused to serve. I had a right to take his horse.

[7] Adam: He has now admitted I'm free.[139] {Since he has abandoned the defense of serfdom upon which he relied the court should grant me judgment.}[140]

[8] Justice Hertford: I won't enter judgment for you {because you've brought a writ to set the size of your rent[141] rather than to prove your freedom.}[142] But the prior will pay a penalty for abandoning his defense. The prior says you took possession as a free tenant at will who must do some serf work.[143] While he might

---

[137] Interpreting "He holds of us in vileinage" Case at 106. Cf. "According to Master Roger of Seaton. If a free man holds land which owes villein service …" 123 Selden Society 489 (pre–1278).
[138] *E.g.*, service in the lord's fields, but not payment to have his daughter married.
[139] Interpreting "They waive the person" Case at 106.
[140] Justice Hertford's reply shows Adam made this demand.
[141] The true goal of the replevin-like de vitito namio. Although a replevin writ claims a chattel, the claim is used to get a judgment setting the terms by which a tenant holds land.
[142] The text interprets Hertford's statement "not in this writ." When a peasant brought a "ne vexes writ" to prove his freedom in royal court, Justice Hengham said if the defendant lost a pleaded defense that the plaintiff was a serf, the court would enter a judgment that the plaintiff could keep the land and never pay the defendant anything again. 5 31a Rolls Series 10 (1305). The text assumes Hertford's comment "not in this writ" contrasted the rules applied to Adam's replevin with the rules applied to a ne vexes.
[143] The true tenant in villeinage has no enforceable right to stay on his lord's land—he is simply a tenant at will, and his lord can either take his chattels if he neglects his duties, or eject him for no reason at all. *See* 1 31a Rolls Series 40 (1292) ("For it is no more to say, I hold the tenements in vileinage of the Dean etc. (not saying he is the

have pled that at the outset he didn't.[144] I'll just ask the jury about the content of your agreement with the prior.[145]

[9] Adam: Here's what it said. I would pay ten shillings a year and serve as a free man on the prior's court every third week. The jury will find I've postponed my service for set causes. A serf doesn't get those postponements.[146]

[10] *The Reporter*: The court asked the jury if Adam had correctly described the agreement.[147]

This case shows a way out for a lord who has lost possession of a serf living on his land. He needs to swallow a bitter pill. He wants to punish the serf. Instead his lawyer tells him to give the serf his freedom.

If the lord calls the man a serf he has already in trouble. He used self-help because his man has not been doing serf work. If the jury finds he has not worked as a serf for over a year[148] the man can stay put. He just has to do what the jury says he agreed to do when he took

---

vilein of the Dean etc.) than to say—I hold the tenements demanded against me at the will of the Dean etc.)" Case at 40.

[144] Interpreting "He ought not to have the benefit of both." Case at 106.

[145] The text interprets "Now answer to the {prior's) allegation that the holders of that tenement held in vileinage…" (Case at 106) in the context of the answer Hertford allows Adam to make, the answer that the terms of Adam's deal with the prior prevail regardless of the rules applicable to other tenants.

[146] Interpreting "We have been often essoined in your court." An essoin is a postponement of service granted for a set cause; a serf can serve on courts, but a serf cannot get an essoin. 5 31a Rolls Series 294 (1306) (challenge to an essoin). His owner tells him what he must do. Bereford rejected a litigant's claim he was a serf by observing he had previously been granted an essoin. 4 31a Rolls Series 240 (1304) (entry).

[147] Interpreting "And the other side said the contrary." Case at 106.

[148] Britton's time period. 1 Britton 201.

possession. The jurors will extrapolate the terms of the deal from what they have seen.[149] They have not recently seen the man working as a serf. If they say his deal did not include serf work the lord gets stuck with a parasite.

The better call is to say the man is a free person living as a favor on serf lands, a man who has taken up "a tenancy in villeinage." The proof is easy. The jury should say the land has historically been farmed by serfs. A free man living on serf lands has to help at planting and harvest. Maybe that is what the lord really wants. The lord has lost something. "A free man who holds land which owes serf service can walk away if he wants."[150] So what? Serfs could walk too—they just had to walk at night. Neither free tenants nor serfs were likely to walk. If a man did not want to live in the city[151] there was no place to go. Farm work was farm work

Hertford's decision implements the common law's preference for freedom.

Few cases involving serfs reached Common Pleas. Bereford's court did not have much to do with serfs. The court's rare decisions did what the United States Supreme Court later recommended.[152] The court shaded doctrine to favor the disadvantaged.

Unanticipated events can turn trivial cases into landmarks. Common Pleas divested a lord of possession

---

[149] A typical deal with an illiterate peasant farmer probably was not in writing. But see "the writing produced … was the deed … by which deed William of Newnham acknowledged holding the tenements in villeinage … by villein services as contained in the writing…" 123 Selden Society 499, 500 (pre–1290).

[150] 123 Selden Society 489 (pre–1278). The case is also reported in Casus Placitorum, 69 Selden Society 56 (1278).

[151] Where the king's statute of limitations would make him free.

[152] United States *v.* Carolene Products Company, 304 U.S. 144 (1936) footnote 4.

after a year of neglect. Few lords neglected their workforce for that long.

1348 changed everything. The plague came to England. The chaos meant many serf owners lost possession. Serfs became *de facto* free—they could not be detained. Then they became legally free. Proof of ownership required proof the claimant's ancestor had died in possession.[153] Because of the plague many lords died out of possession of their serfs. These sometime serfs and their descendants became free laborers.[154]

The plague made freedom worth having. The devastation forced landowners to offer better terms for work. In 1351 Parliament tried to put the genie back in the bottle. The Statute of Laborers called for the imprisonment of those "who were idle, and not willing to serve after the pestilence, without excessive wages…."[155]

---

[153] *See, e.g.*, 122 Selden Society 24 (1268–1269?) After an ownership claimant fails to prove possession of the serf's father Justice Mettingham decides the serf is free. Case at 30.

[154] Even more became free when their lords died from other causes before they reestablished possession.

[155] The Statute of Laborers (1351) (4 EHD 993).

CHAPTER 12
Conclusion

MAITLAND'S NINETEENTH CENTURY *History of English Law* continues to be the canonical description of medieval English law.[1] In over a thousand pages he paints a compelling picture. But he did not portray all of medieval English law. The complete title of his work is *The History of English Law before the Time of Edward I.* Maitland focuses upon the period before Edward became king in 1272 but his book stands as the definitive account of the entire medieval period.[2]

Maitland probably had two reasons to focus on the time before Edward took the throne.

During Edward's reign legislation transformed many doctrines. Maitland wanted to investigate theory;[3] he did

---

[1] "Though it has proved possible, and indeed necessary, to correct Maitland here and there, the main part of his work remains alive, and no question arises of interring or even embalming him." G. R. Elton, *F. W. Maitland* 97 (1985).

[2] Elton discusses the question. *Ibid.*, 50. Even J. H. Baker, one of Maitland's successors as Downing Professor of the Laws of England, misstates the scope of Maitland's work. Maitland "stopped his own *History of English Law* in 1307..." J. H. Baker, *Why the History of English Law Has Not Been Finished* 4 (1999). The year 1307 was the end, not the beginning, of Edward's reign.

[3] *E.g.*, "I believe that in some respects Maitland, working as it were backwards from Bracton, supposes too great a degree of general sophistication; and in particular, despite all his care, that he sometimes places highly abstract notions of property too early." 1 P&M lxxiii. (introduction by S.F.C. Milsom).

not want to parse legislative minutia.[4] Rather than making Edward the legislator his hero, Maitland glorified Bracton the scholar. Bracton's great thirteenth century treatise put English law into a theoretical framework. Maitland shared his goal.[5]

Maitland's assessment of the reports from the reigns of Edward and his successors gave him another reason to stop.

> The fourteenth century produced no great text writer, and we have therefore to rely upon the Year Books {the case reports of the era.} It may be well therefore to observe that the Year Books are not for this or any other purpose very satisfactory material, because they are chiefly concerned with points of pleading, and by the middle of the fourteenth century pleadings had become very unreal things. ... Often the whole object of the defendant's pleader is ... to puzzle the court and his adversary, and so no wonder if he puzzles us.[6]

In contrast to the firm footing Bracton's treatise provided the Year Books were a bog of thousands and thousands of pages.[7] In contrast to Bracton's elegant theories, theories that could be analyzed in the context of

---

[4] Plucknett did. T. F. T. Plucknett, *Statutes and Their Interpretation in the First Half of the Fourteenth Century* (1922).

[5] "The two things which struck one most in Maitland were, in the first place, the union of fondness and capacity for large generalization with scrupulous thoroughness in tracking a subject into minute details, a rare combination; and in the second place, his power of historical imagination." John Gray, In Memoriam: Frederic William Maitland, *The Law Quarterly Review*, April, 1907 at 138.

[6] Maitland, 407, 434, *supra*.

[7] Maitland "concluded that it was futile trying to write the early history of the common law without new editions of the medieval law reports—'the hopeless mass of corruption that passes as a text of the year books'..." Baker, 4, *supra*.

Roman law,[8] the Year Books were a jumble of fact-specific rulings. Maitland had no taste for the "mindlessness of the common law, with its concentration on particulars."[9] He set his cut-off date just short of the swamp.[10]

Maitland's successors also denigrate the Bereford era reports.

T. F. T. Plucknett said

> The new sort of law students ... seem to have been thoroughly philistine, deliberately cut-off from the universities and from the Roman and clerical tradition which the universities fostered. They chose instead to immerse themselves in ... graceless tracts, written in the vulgar tongue, so as to prepare themselves for a rude profession where wits rather than scholarship were in demand.... No one who reads only the Year Books would ever suspect that Bracton had lived or written.[11]

---

[8] "If Maitland set his watch by any one source, it was by Bracton." 1 P&M lxxii. (Introduction by S.F.C. Milsom).

[9] "Philosophy had ... its attractions {that} enabled {Maitland} to overcome the mindlessness of the common law, with its concentration on particulars. Maitland was always to display an inclination towards jurisprudence, an inclination which has never yet made for success at the bar." Elton, 7, *supra*.

[10] "With the arrival of the Year Books and the proliferation of plea rolls the writing of legal history assumes a very different dimension, quite unmanageable by one man." Elton, 50, *supra*.

[11] T. F. T. Plucknett, *Early English Legal Literature* 93–94 (1958). Milsom agrees with Plucknett's condemnation of the Bereford era lawyers. "When, in the half century after Bracton's death, his kind ceased to play any part in the common law and the bench came to be filled from below by counters {i.e., practitioners such as Bereford}, two qualities were lost. One was the administrative habit of seeing problems as a whole and making solutions work ... The other was a more specific quality. The ecclesiastical background of the clerical judges ensured that they had ... read what there was to read about Roman law ... But it was no part of the counters' world. What

S. F. C. Milsom said "Upon the infinite details of this problem {of pleading the lawyers} concentrated their great abilities; and they never looked up to consider as a whole the substantive system they were making."[12] By "substantive system" Milsom means the laws that govern behavior within society. He continues

> The modern reader can hear real arguments by lawyers who would shine in any age; but often he finds the point of the argument elusive. The difficulty is in his own mind. The terms into which he is trying to translate the argument, {his search for the medieval laws that governed everyday life},[13] were not much in the minds of those arguing. ... To hindsight, the important result ... was the creation of substantive law. But this was not a focus of attention at the time. The year books astonishingly preserve the true infancy of a modern legal system; but they will not often answer legal questions asked in modern terms.[14]

These scholars glorified Bracton as the acme of medieval legal thought. In Maitland's phrase Bracton was "the crown and flower of English medieval jurisprudence."[15]

Maitland was right but for the wrong reason. Bracton brought medieval law to its close. Bereford took English law into the renaissance. He ignored academic theory and

---

centuries of development had made so clear centuries earlier was to them alien learning in closed books; and they were starting again from the beginning." S. F.C. Milsom, *Historical Foundations of the Common Law* 41–42 (2d. Edition, 1981).

[12] *Ibid.*, 44.

[13] Interpreting Milsom's phrase "the terms of substantive law."

[14] Milsom, 48, *supra.*

[15] 1 P&M 206. Plucknett concurred. "Two generations after Glanvill's book we come to 'the flower and crown of English jurisprudence' —Bracton." T. F. T. Plucknett, *A Concise History of the Common Law* 258 (5th Ed. 1956).

focused instead on doing justice. He saw things as they were, not as they were supposed to be.

After he published his classic history Maitland reappraised Bereford. He devoted his last years to editing Bereford's reports.[16] He created the Selden Society to institutionalize his commitment to the Year Books. Aware of his failing health, Maitland issued a challenge.

> The Selden Society, which was founded 'to encourage the study and advancement of the knowledge of the history of English law,' {should endeavor} to redeem the Year Books from that kingdom of darkness in which they are captives, and hasten the day when they will once again be readable, intelligible and—we do not fear to say it—enjoyable books.[17]

Instead of describing the reports as "unsatisfactory material,"[18] he wrote "if to the whole mass of materials for the history of law England had nothing to contribute but these Year Books, England's contribution would still be of inestimable value."[19] Instead of saying "Often the whole object of the defendant's pleader is ... to puzzle the court and his adversary, and so no wonder if he puzzles us,"[20] he wrote "Our {writ system} as it stood and worked in the fourteenth century might be known so thoroughly that a modern lawyer who had studied {the

---

[16] By editing Selden Society volumes 17, 19, 20, and 22.

[17] 17 Selden Society ix (introduction by F.W. Maitland).

[18] F. W. Maitland, The Beatitude of Seisin, *Law Quarterly Review* 1888 (1 *Collected Papers of Frederick William Maitland* 407, 434. H. Fisher, ed. 1911).

[19] 17 Selden Society xvii (introduction by F.W. Maitland).

[20] Maitland, 407, 434, *supra*.

Year Books} might give sound advice, even upon points of practice, to a hypothetical client."[21]

During subsequent years Maitland's Selden Society has produced an astonishing body of primary sources—over thirty volumes of redacted medieval manuscripts and faithful English translations.[22] The work provides a springboard to satisfy another of Maitland's goals. He said the Year Books' conventions could be plumbed only through the mastery of many cases.[23] The reports adhere to rules but when Maitland wrote, many rules were buried inside inaccessible manuscripts. The manuscripts have now been brought to light. This book starts the process of deciphering them.[24]

As the first English judge appointed from the ranks of the practicing bar[25] Bereford set the pragmatic tone that the common law glorifies.[26] He believed a judge who

---

[21] 17 Selden Society xvii (introduction by F. W. Maitland).

[22] The figure includes four volumes of the Earliest English Law Reports.

[23] "Our commendation of the Year Books will not really be qualified by the remark, perhaps needless, that reports must be read in considerable quantities if they are to be appreciated. They cannot be tasted in sips….." 17 Selden Society xx (introduction by F.W. Maitland).

[24] "Once the fear of technicality can be overcome, few other fields apart from archaeology can offer as much opportunity to delve into unbroken ground and recover lost worlds." Baker, 32, *supra.*

[25] T.F.T. Plucknett, *Studies in English Legal History* IXX, at 332 (1983) ("the English method of appointing outstanding members of the bar to sit on the bench of the superior Courts is, in fact, typically medieval…").

[26] This book's demonstration of Bereford's pragmatism contradicts Maitland's early observation that "we may never safely refer to great changes in the common law directly and immediately to opinions as to what is politic or expedient, least of all changes which took place in the period of the Year Books. Judges and counsel talk little of public policy; '*Fiat justitia, ruat coelum*' is their maxim; the social

renders retail justice has something important to say. No general rule can comprehend life's variety. Through application of an innate sense of morality—a sense he called "reason"—Bereford constantly redefined the law.[27] Today common law judges speak with the same authority. The frank recognition that judges create law is the hallmark of a common law system.

History provides perspective and that perspective vindicates Bereford's philosophy. Many of his society's fundamental institutions are abhorrent to modern thought. The judiciary cannot reject the basic framework of society. The test should be whether Bereford's decisions improved his society. Fourteenth century critics may have thought he took too much liberty. Seven centuries later there can be no debate. Bereford made his legal system more efficient and more just. Bereford provides a shining example his successors should follow. A judge is not just a conduit between a rule and its application. A great judge adds wisdom.

---

fabric may fall in with a crash, but their legal logic must have its way." Maitland, 407, 445, *supra*.

[27] "{T]he law is founded on reason…." 20 Selden Society 78, 80 (1310) (Chief Justice Bereford). The view that the weak should be protected against the strong embodies morality rather than logic.

INDEX

www.ingramcontent.com/pod-product-compliance
Ingram Content Group UK Ltd.
Pitfield, Milton Keynes, MK11 3LW, UK
UKHW041131071026
15587UKWH00009B/429

9 781616 195045